Rival Conceptions of Freedom in Modern Iran

Rival Conceptions of Freedom in Modern Iran is an original historiographic examination of the idea of freedom in early modern Iran within a larger context of the formation of modern Muslim thought. The study develops an appropriate method for the historiography of ideas by taking into consideration cultural, linguistic, and sociopolitical limitations and obstacles to free thinking in closed societies.

The research shows how most locutions about freedom, uttered during early modern Iran, were formed within the horizon of the question of Iran's decline and were somehow related to remedying such situations. It challenges previous studies which employed Isaiah Berlin's distinction between positive and negative freedom as two fundamentally different concepts of freedom. It replaces Berlin's dichotomy of positive and negative liberties with MacCallum's triadic concept of freedom and argue that thinkers in early modern Iran could noticeably present rival interpretations of three variables of the concept of freedom, namely the agent, the constraint, and the purpose of freedom.

Rival Conceptions of Freedom in Modern Iran is a unique contribution to the histories of the 1905–11 Constitutional Revolution in Iran and comparative political thinking between Iran and Europe. It is an essential resource for scholars interested in Constitutionalism, History, Political Theory, and Sociology within Middle Eastern Studies.

Ahmad Hashemi obtained his doctoral degree in Oriental Studies (Intellectual History) from the University of Oxford in 2015. He is an Assistant Professor at the Encyclopaedia Islamica Foundation, Department of Contemporary Islam. His research interests include the intellectual history of Iran and Islam, Political Philosophy, Persian Literature, and Digital Humanities.

Iranian Studies
Edited by:
Homa Katouzian
University of Oxford
and Mohamad Tavakoli
University of Toronto

Since 1967 the International Society for Iranian Studies (ISIS) has been a leading learned society for the advancement of new approaches in the study of Iranian society, history, culture, and literature. The new ISIS Iranian Studies series published by Routledge will provide a venue for the publication of original and innovative scholarly works in all areas of Iranian and Persianate Studies.

Gender and Dance in Iran
Biopolitics on the twentieth-century stage
Ida Meftahi

Persian Authorship and Canonicity in Late Mughal Delhi
Building an Ark
Prashant Keshavmurthy

Iran and the Nuclear Question
History and the Evolutionary Trajectory
Mohammad Homayounvash

The True Dream
An English Translation with Facing Persian Text
Ali-Ashgar Seyed-Gohrab and Senn McGlinn

Popular Iranian Cinema before the Revolution
Family and Nation in Filmfarsi
Pedram Partovi

Persian Literature and Modernity
Production and Reception
Edited by Hamid Rezaei Yazdi and Arshavez Mozafari

Rival Conceptions of Freedom in Modern Iran
An Intellectual History of the Constitutional Revolution
Ahmad Hashemi

For more information about this series, please visit: www.routledge.com/middleeast studies/series/IRST

Rival Conceptions of Freedom in Modern Iran

An Intellectual History of the Constitutional Revolution

Ahmad Hashemi

Routledge
Taylor & Francis Group
LONDON AND NEW YORK

First published 2019
by Routledge
2 Park Square, Milton Park, Abingdon, Oxon OX14 4RN

and by Routledge
52 Vanderbilt Avenue, New York, NY 10017

First issued in paperback 2020

Routledge is an imprint of the Taylor & Francis Group, an informa business

British Library Cataloguing-in-Publication Data
A catalogue record for this book is available from the British Library

Library of Congress Cataloging-in-Publication Data
Names: Hashemi, Ahmad, author.
Title: Rival conceptions of freedom in modern Iran : an intellectual history of the constitutional revolution / Ahmad Hashemi.
Description: Milton Park, Abingdon, Oxon ; New York, NY : Routledge, 2019. | Series: Iranian studies ; 38 | Includes bibliographical references and index.
Identifiers: LCCN 2018043010 (print) | LCCN 2018044597 (ebook) | ISBN 9780429427121 (master) | ISBN 9780429763045 (Adobe Reader) | ISBN 9780429763038 (Epub) | ISBN 9780429763021 (Mobipocket) | ISBN 9781138385399 (hardback)
Subjects: LCSH: Liberty. | Constitutional history—Iran. | Political science—Iran—Philosophy.
Classification: LCC KMH2110 (ebook) | LCC KMH2110 .A46 2019 (print) | DDC 342.5502/9—dc23
LC record available at https://lccn.loc.gov/2018043010

ISBN 13: 978-0-367-66309-4 (pbk)
ISBN 13: 978-1-138-38539-9 (hbk)

Typeset in Times New Roman
by Apex CoVantage, LLC

Contents

Tables

Preface

Since the early nineteenth century, the idea of freedom has become ingrained in the Iranian political worldview and has played a major role in mobilizing sociopolitical movements. Prior to Iran's encounters with European modernity, the idea of justice was central to Iranian political thought. Throughout the pre-modern intellectual history of Iran, justice has often been considered the common shared value to which no one has expressed opposition. Even tyrants had to claim possession of the attribute of justice, for it was commonly believed that only a just ruler would possess *farr* (Divine Grace). Justice, in this tradition, was defined as an overarching concept covering all virtues. However, freedom, which was often understood as license, had been traditionally thought of as a less important value that would often come into conflict with other social and moral values.

Why has freedom acquired new significance in Iranian political thought over the past two centuries, gradually becoming, like justice, a comprehensive concept encompassing many social values, to the extent that in the Constitutional Movement it was sometimes presented as the equivalent of justice, equality, constitutionalism, or law? Which events provided the historical situation and horizon of meaning in which the question of freedom would be required to arise? How was the idea of freedom applied in the sociopolitical life of early modern Iran? After almost two centuries of reflection on the idea of freedom in Iran, why are many important questions regarding freedom still deeply controversial?

This book aims to answer these and similar questions. It attempts first to develop an appropriate method for the historiography of ideas by taking into consideration cultural, linguistic, and sociopolitical limitations and obstacles to free thinking in a predominantly closed society like Qajar Iran (1785–1925). By applying such a method, the study then investigates the history of the idea of freedom in Iran during one of the most important periods in the evolution of this concept and explores the thought and the unthought concerning freedom.

Acknowledgments

An earlier incarnation of this book was my DPhil dissertation at the University of Oxford. I would like to express my deep appreciation to all those who have contributed either directly or indirectly to this study and made it possible for me to conduct the research. First and foremost, my warm thanks go to my supervisor, Homa Katouzian, for all his support, insight, guidance, and advice during the course of writing the dissertation. He provided valuable and extensive comments on all the drafts of the text. I am also grateful to Stephanie Cronin, who was an assessor of Transfer and Confirmation of Status, and then my supportive co-supervisor, for her thoughtful remarks. Likewise, I express my gratitude to Edmund Herzig and Vanesa Martin, who examined the dissertation and proposed valuable comments and constructive criticism which significantly improved the work.

Special thanks to the staff and directors of the libraries at the University of Oxford, the University of Toronto, the Encyclopaedia Islamica Foundation, as well as the Library, Museum, and Document Center of the Iran Parliament. In addition, I am thankful to the Aga Khan University (ISMC-London) and the Encyclopaedia Islamica Foundation (Tehran) for awarding me scholarships during this program.

Last, but definitely not least, I would like to thank all of my family and friends who kindly supported and encouraged me during this study. In particular, I would like to express my deepest gratitude to my devoted parents, Zahra and Muhammad, my loving and loyal wife, Parisa, and my tolerant son, Masiha, who were warmly with me every step of this long way.

Note on transliteration and the citation style

- Arabic and Persian words are transliterated based on the Persian Romanization System approved by the Library of Congress. The table below shows the principal equivalent letters and vowels used in this system.

ʾ	ء	k	ک	ṣ	ص	kh	خ	[omit]	الف
ā	آ	g	گ	z̤	ض	d	د	b	ب
ī	اي	l	ل	ṭ	ط	z̲	ذ	p	پ
ū	او	m	م	ẓ	ظ	r	ر	t	ت
a	ـَ	n	ن	ʿ	ع	z	ز	s̱	ث
i	ـِ	v	و	gh	غ	zh	ژ	j	ج
u	ـُ	h	ه	f	ف	S	س	ch	چ
		y	ی	q	ق	Sh	ش	ḥ	ح

- The MHRA referencing style is used in this research. I consulted the third edition of the *MHRA Style Guide: A Handbook for Authors and Editors*, which was published in 2013 (London: Modern Humanities Research Association).

Introduction

I Rival conceptions of a concept in its formative years

The history of the concept of freedom in Iran from the encounter with modern European thought and lifestyle to the coup d'état of 1921 can be roughly divided into two phases: (1) from about 1815 (when the modern concept of freedom was first introduced to Iranian readers through the works of some writers who had visited and studied in Europe) to 1906; and (2) from 1906 (the Constitutional Revolution) to 1921. This research will mainly focus on the second phase as the most significant period in the history of the conceptualization of freedom in Iran.

In the first phase, the first group of Iranian students who were educated in Europe rendered an account of the political structure of Western countries and highlighted the concept of freedom as the pivotal difference between Western and Iranian societies. It was during the same period that a basic component of modern political thought, including a few chapters of J.S. Mill's *On Liberty*, were translated into Persian. To some members of the elite, freedom would necessarily result in rebellion, absolute license and chaos, and they were therefore puzzled by the existence of order and discipline in European countries. In their observation, 'law' was the master key of the paradox. Later on, intellectuals such as Mīrzā Malkam Khān Nāẓim al-Dawlah (1833–1908) and Mīrzā Yūsuf Mustashār al-Dawlah (1823–95) advised the monarch to codify and establish a *constitution.* They emphasized the right to freedom as one of the fundamental rights of the people.

In August 1906, popular demand for a limitation on royal power and the establishment of law finally forced Muẓaffar al-Dīn Shāh (r. 1896–1907) to issue 'the Constitutional Decree', promising to pave the way for the establishment of an elected parliament, or majlis. The decree heralded the second stage of the evolution of the concept of freedom: legislation. It was at this stage that the codification of freedom in the first parliament led to the development of different conceptions of freedom. During this formative 15-year period, revolutionary fervour and relative weakness of the central government provided an ideal situation for uncensored questioning and thinking about freedom.

In post-revolutionary Iran, the question of freedom was one of how to coordinate the activities of the members of a revolutionary and disorderly society.

This question is indeed, more or less, the serious concern of all human societies, as their members pursue their obligations and preferences in ways that can obstruct the pursuits of others. Prior to the constitutional era, however, Iranian society lacked reasonable mechanisms for making and implementing laws. The law was virtually the same as the ruler's will, and this very arbitrary will was the main obstacle to people's freedom. Iranian constitutionalism was a public demand to limit such will for the first time. Under the new circumstances, the main problem that logically would – and actually did – arise was the question of who would have the legitimacy to make laws and other types of social rules to control the freedom of individuals. Of equal importance was the question of whether imposing such laws on an individual's conduct would only aim to ensure that such activity not exceed certain bounds, or whether it would intend to ensure that the activity resulted in a certain outcome. The heated debate that took place over these questions represented what I call 'the struggle between different conceptions of freedom'. Here, I apply John Rawls's distinction between a 'concept' and its rival 'conceptions' to the case of freedom. To answer these questions, early modern Iranian thinkers presented rival conceptions of freedom that have affected most of the later discussions about the concept of freedom in Iran over the past century. Furthermore, the late Qajars witnessed the very first parliamentary laws with regard to freedom of the press, beliefs, and trade.

It is no exaggeration to claim that as far as fundamental theoretical debates over the concept of freedom are concerned, no other period can rival the year 1907/1325. In this year, Shaykh Faẕl Allāh Nūrī (1843–1909), who was a chief *mujtahid* of Tehran and a member of parliament, accompanied by a group of his followers, took sanctuary (*bast*) in the ʿAbd al-ʿAẕīm Shrine near Tehran to protest against the way freedom and equality were interpreted in the *Supplementary Fundamental Laws*. They published a set of leaflets, called *Lavāyiḥ*, to reject the 'offending' conceptions of freedom and equality and the secular laws in which they had been rooted. These *Lavāyiḥ* have been regarded as the classics of anti-liberty literature in Iran.

At the same time, Mīrzā ʿAbd al-Rahīm Ṭālibūf Tabrīzī (1834–1911) wrote the first monograph on freedom, entitled *Īẕāḥāt dar khuṣūṣ-i āzādī* (*Clarifications of Freedom*). Furthermore, in 1907 and 1908, a group of well-known politicians and respected clergy, including Muḥammad ʿAlī Furūghī (1878–1942), Ākhūnd Mullā Muḥammad Kāẓim Khurāsānī (1839–1911), Mīrzā Ḥusayn Nāʾīnī (1860–1936), and Shaykh Muḥammad Ismāʾīl Gharavī Maḥallātī (1853–1924), wrote treatises on political issues and further contributed to interpreting the concept of freedom and promoting the rival conceptions of freedom in the political discourses of both the elite and the populace.

II Methodology

The methodology of this research addresses two fundamental and interrelated questions: a general question about the historical approach, and a specific one about the philosophical approach in analyzing the concept of freedom. These two correlative questions could be briefly formulated as follows:

(1) When one wishes to study a given idea at a given time and within a given culture, (a) what is the object of inquiry and understanding? (b) what is the appropriate method for arriving at an understanding of this object?
(2) To what essential questions (if any) must a conception of freedom provide an answer in order to be intelligible?

Both questions address the problem of conditions of understanding and its methods. The former question asks what the understanding of an idea means and how it can be achieved, while the latter examines the conditions for the intelligibility of a conception of freedom. A short answer to the first question is that the object of inquiry in the historiography of an idea is not simply the statements uttered about that idea, but rather a complex consisting of these statements as answers and the questions to which they refer. It means that the history of an idea is the history of correlative questions and answers concerning the idea. It may also be argued that a proper method for understanding this object is a hermeneutical account of the logic of question and answer.

A brief answer to the second question is that every locution about freedom must at least answer to three essential questions about the agent, the constraint, and the purpose of freedom, otherwise it would not be clearly intelligible. Correspondingly, understanding a locution about freedom consists of understanding the author's formulation of these three questions and the author's responses to them.

Thus, the linkage between the intellectual history approach of this study and its philosophical approach can be seen not only in their shared problem of understanding, but also in their approach to solving this problem. A detailed explanation of these two approaches will make the point clear.

i Questioning and understanding in the historiography of ideas

My approach to the historiography of ideas innovatively consists of three theories of understanding: (a) R.G. Collingwood's logic of question and answer, (b) Hans-Georg Gadamer's hermeneutical considerations on the logic of question and answer, and (c) the theory of 'the unthought in contemporary Islamic thought'[1] by Mohammed Arkoun. Whereas each of these theories has previously been employed in a number of studies on the history of ideas, the application of a combination of them, particularly in the historiography of Iranian thought, is, to the best of my knowledge, unprecedented. It is necessary to accept the difficulties of the groundbreaking application of this new approach, since common methods applied in this field have often overlooked the particular cultural and sociopolitical conditions of the emergence of a thought in Iran as well as the differences between these conditions and those that operate in Western societies.

The main claim of this synthesized approach is as follows: when wishing to study a given idea at a given time and within a given culture, we must first consider the statement made on the idea at that time as a particular solution for a particular problem. To understand the statement, then, we must reconstruct the horizon in which the particular problem arose. Through this method, we will be also able to find out what questions and answers concerning that idea could and could not arise at that historical situation, what actually arose, and what did not arise despite its potential to do so. Accordingly, the history of an idea is the history of four things concerning the idea: the thinkable, the unthinkable, the thought, and the unthought. In the following subsections, this methodological approach will be illustrated.

In Collingwood's logic of question and answer, every statement uttered by an agent, as a part of 'unit of thought', must be considered as an answer to a question either explicitly formulated by the agent or implicitly present in his mind. The 'unit of thought'[2] is not 'any single proposition',[3] nor even a 'complex of propositions taken together'[4] but a 'complex of correlative question and answer'.[5] The principle of 'correlativity between question and answer' has two significant implications concerning (a) the process of thinking, and (b) the necessary conditions of understanding a given thought.

(a) To explain the process of thinking, this principle descriptively states that thinking without questioning is impossible. The absence of a question can be due either to the fact that the agent is forced not to ask a question about an issue, or that the agent decides voluntarily to avoid questioning that issue. Accordingly, if at a given time within a given culture, an issue is declared unquestionable (forbidden to be asked) or remains unquestioned, that issue remains unthinkable or unthought.
(b) To introduce a method for understanding a given thought, the principle of correlativity between question and answer normatively states that understanding is impossible without first finding out the *question* to which the thought has been uttered as the answer. Therefore, the task of understanding a text must start with the reconstruction of its correlative question.

In his *Truth and Method*, Hans-Georg Gadamer (1900–2002) explores the dialectic of question and answer inherent in the structure of hermeneutical experience.[6] His point of departure is that each text has been written as an answer to a question.[7] Rephrasing Collingwood, he states that 'we understand the sense of the text only by acquiring the *horizon* of the question – a horizon that, as such, necessarily includes other possible answers'.[8] Gadamer employs the notion of 'horizon' within the very tradition established by Nietzsche and Husserl:

> The horizon is the range of vision that includes everything that can be seen from a particular vantage point. Applying this to the thinking mind, we speak of the narrowness of horizon, of the possible expansion of horizon, of the opening up of new horizons, and so forth.[9]

For Gadamer, having no horizon means 'not seeing far enough' and accordingly 'over-valuing what is nearest' to the observer. By contrast, having a horizon is equivalent to 'not being limited to what is nearby but being able to see beyond it'.[10] In other words,

> a person who has a horizon knows the relative significance of everything within this horizon whether it is near or far, great or small. Similarly, working out the hermeneutical situation means acquiring the right horizon of inquiry for the questions evoked by the encounter with tradition.[11]

One who intends to understand a 'traditional text' must 'transpose [. . . himself] into the historical horizon from which [. . . it] speaks', otherwise he 'will misunderstand the significance of what it has to say to us'.[12] Indeed, discovering the other person's horizon makes that person's ideas intelligible.[13]

The Gadamerian account of the logic of question and answer can be summarized in the following points:

- *Main premises*:
  (1) A text is always written in the horizon of a question. This horizon includes, in addition to the text, other possible answers to that question.
  (2) Every reader/interpreter of a given text has his or her own horizon within which understanding takes place.
  (3) The question to which the text is intended as an answer (historical question) differs from the question to which the text is really an answer (philosophical question).
  (4) 'The text must be understood as an answer to a real question'.[14]
  (5) A real question is one that actually engages me as a reader and is understood by me. 'To understand a question means to ask it'.[15]
  (6) The real question stems from the text. We are perplexed by the encounter with 'traditionary word' and, in an effort to understand the text, begin a process of questioning.
- *Main conclusions*:
  (a) The meaning of the text goes beyond authorial intention. The interpreter's task is not to find out the question intended by the author (historical question).
  (b) The historical question can only be reconstructed by being merged with our own questioning, thereby evolving from 'the question of the other' to 'our question'.
  (c) 'The reconstructed question can never stand within its original horizon';[16] rather, it stands within the interpreter's horizon (the fusion of horizons).
  (d) 'It is a hermeneutical necessity to always go beyond mere reconstruction [of the historical question]. We *cannot avoid* thinking about what the author has unquestioningly accepted and hence has not considered'.[17]

A question cannot arise in a void. Each real question that actually engages the questioner arises within a horizon of meaning, a tradition of thought, a historical situation, after having supposed a particular presupposition.[18] A real question is not posed by the author but rather by the interpreter. Questions, as Gadamer states, 'always bring out the undetermined possibilities of a thing'[19] and allow the questioner to decide between these possibilities on the basis of reasoning.[20] If a question has only one possible answer, it will not expose any undetermined thing to determination, and accordingly will not be considered a real question.[21] Along the same line of analysis, if on the basis of any criterion other than an individual's own reasoning or free will, a questioner, in a particular historical situation, is not *actually* able to choose one of the possible answers within the questioner's horizon of meaning, then *free questioning* (and therefore *free thinking*) will not occur.

What could prevent us from asking a real question or from freely choosing one of the possible answers in practice (even if a real question has arisen)? A formulation of this question was posed by Mohammed Arkoun (1928–2010), Algerian thinker and expert in Islamic studies, in his project entitled *Critique of Islamic Reason*. Inquiring into the question of 'limits imposed by political and social pressures on the innovative and critical faculties of reason',[22] he asks: 'What does a tradition of thought allow us to think in a particular period of its evolution, concerning a particular subject?'[23]

Arkoun's answer to this question is grounded in the notion of 'tradition' or 'living tradition'. 'Tradition', for him, is 'the long-term historical evolution' that in Muslim societies often occurs 'according to dogmatic theological definitions'.[24] Controlled by political and religious powers, the living tradition determines the orthodox and accepted line of thinking. What stays within the boundary would be thinkable and in principle could be thought, but what is beyond the boundary would be regarded as unthinkable and remains unthought. Arkoun claims that all sources of religious and political power[25] 'exercise control over the **thinkable** and the **unthinkable**'.[26] In a traditional society, these authoritarian and intolerant political or religious powers expand the space of the unthinkable – especially in matters related to religion – through making or promoting rules and norms embodied in a 'dual censorship', imposed by both the state and public opinions from above and below. Arkoun adds that 'many intellectuals came to interiorize this dual control in the name of the nation, or religion, adding self-censorship to the censorship already imposed from outside'.[27]

Dual censorship is not the only obstacle in the way of free questioning and thinking; each language also imposes noticeable linguistic limits on the activities of thought. To explain these limitations, Arkoun uses the innovative concept of 'logosphere' identified as 'the linguistic mental space shared by all those who use the same language with which to articulate their thoughts, their representations, their collective memory, and their knowledge according to the fundamental principles and values claimed as a unifying *Weltanschauung*'.[28] A given language used by a number of people becomes a common logosphere. For instance, Persian, as the language used by different individuals of the late Qajar society, became a common and effective logosphere configuring their mental faculties. This in turn contributed to 'the creation of frontiers between the thinkable and the unthinkable, the thought and the unthought'.[29] The Arkounian point of view can explain how changes in social, economic, and political conditions open new possibilities for questions arising on 'the living tradition', and accordingly how Iranian intellectuals in the late Qajar period attempted to expand the space of the thinkable and started introducing the modern political thinkable into the Persian language, thereby challenging the religious and traditional political thinkable defended by monarchist and *pro-mashrūʿah* campaigners.[30]

Based on these methodological considerations, when we wish to study an idea, the objects of our inquiry are the 'units of thought' or complexes consisting of correlative questions and answers concerning the given idea. What actually exists before us is only one part of the unit of thought – i.e. the text as the answer. In order to understand this answer, the question which is correlative to the answer must be reconstructed based on the answer itself. We must find out which of the possible questions faced by the author within that historical horizon and in the 'situation' is the one that the text attempts to answer. Then we must consider the various solutions that might be offered for this question in such a horizon, and see why the author has chosen this specific solution over others.

In this approach, a historian of ideas must attach a lot of importance to the following issues: Within a particular historical horizon of meaning, what are the possible and impossible questions that arise on a given idea? What are the causes and reasons of possibility or impossibility? What are the possible answers to the arisen questions? Among the possible answers, what are the answers that are actually chosen? How are they presented? For a historian of ideas, the truth or fallacy of a given answer to a given question, the coherency or incoherency of two answers to the same question, and the similarities or dissimilarities of questions and answers – posed by the authors within the same horizon of thinking – about a given idea or a particular aspect of it, are all of secondary importance.

ii Freedom as a triadic relation

The above discussion introduces a proper method for studying the history of modern political ideas in societies where the force of tradition and political power impose strict controls over the field of the thinkable. Such a method can be applied to any political idea. Now we need a specific analytical framework to analyze the concept of freedom. This analytical framework should be consistent with the logic of question and answer so that it considers any interpretation of the concept of freedom as a specific answer to a specific question. In other words, it must consider rival conceptions of freedom as rival answers to more or less similar correlative questions. Let me illustrate this conceptual framework with an example.

In his travel account, Mīrzā Abū al-Ḥasan Khān Īlchī (d. 1846), Fatḥ ʿAlī Shāh's ambassador to London (1809–10), reported on 'the freedom of Londoners'. If, at that time, a Londoner were to say in Persian to an Iranian stranger '*man āzād hastam*' ('I am free'), his interlocutor, who would yet know nothing about the man's predicament, would ask him what he was free *from*; from prison, from his debts, from his wife, from his sins? Concerned about the same question, some theorists of freedom find it absurd to say 'I am free yet do not know what I am free from', almost as absurd as the claim of a German pupil of Martin Heidegger, who had learned the significance of 'the resolve' and proclaimed 'I am resolved, but I don't yet know to what' ('*Ich bin entschlossen, ich weiss nur nicht wozu*').[31]

Now, if again the Londoner were to respond 'I am free from the arbitrary interference of the state', the question of what he was free *to* do would remain: was he free to choose a career, to choose a religion or belief, to associate with others, to travel abroad? The use of the concept of freedom is not *precisely intelligible*, if this question remains unanswered.

This example briefly explains Gerard MacCallum's claim that freedom is always ***of*** something (an agent or agents), ***from*** something (conditions such as constraints, restrictions, interferences, or barriers), ***to*** do, not do, become, or not become something (actions or conditions of character or circumstance). To put it formally: '***x*** is (is not) free from ***y*** to do (not do, become, not become) ***z***'.[32] In order to be precisely intelligible, a discussion of freedom should not fail in explicitly referring to all three of these variables unless the reference can be grasped from the context of the discussion.[33] MacCallum left the interpretation of the three variables open to provide a frame of analysis which is not a theory about freedom but a meta-theoretical position about the differences between theories of freedom.[34]

Such an approach dismisses the distinction between positive and negative freedom as two fundamentally different concepts of freedom.[35] Theories of negative freedom (emphasizing 'freedom *from*' as the '*only*' kind of freedom) and theories of positive freedom (highlighting 'freedom *to*' as the '*truest*' freedom) all converge on one and the same triadic concept of freedom. Indeed, their differences stem from the ways in which they interpret and extend each of the three variables of agent, constraints, and purposes.[36] Theorists of negative freedom tend to think of the freedom of an agent as 'the absence of obstacles external to the agent' or, as Isaiah Berlin says, they attempt to answer the question of 'what is the area within which the subject – a person or group of persons – is or should be left to do or be what he is able to do or be, without interference by other persons?' Theorists of positive freedom, on the other hand, tend to think of the freedom of an agent as 'the presence of control on the part of the agent' or, in Berlin's words, they are answering the question of 'what, or who, is the source of control or interference that can determine someone to do, or be, this rather than that?'[37] Both views can be translated into the triadic format, though there is noticeable difference in the degree of precision with which they identify x, y, and z. In Table 0.1, I briefly compare both sides of the debate while considering the differences between their interpretations and extensions of the three variables.

Whether or not MacCallum's frame of analysis is applicable to a study on the idea of freedom in nineteenth-century Iran remains to be seen. It is mentioned above that MacCallum's triadic structure is a meta-theoretical position; thus, it can be generally used for analyzing all utterances concerning the freedom of agents regardless of specific cultural and historical contexts. Admittedly, this does not mean that all pronouncements on freedom clearly identify the three variables of agent, constraints, and purpose, but rather it means that the utterances are not intelligible unless they can be translated into the triadic formula.

Table 0.1 Negative and positive conceptions of freedom translated into MacCallum's triadic formula

Approaches to the concept of freedom based on Berlin's categorization	*Interpretations and extensions of the three variables*		
	agent (x)	*constraint (y)*	*purpose (z)*
Negative conception of freedom	an individual human being with all the individual's empirical beliefs and desires	only external obstacles	whatever the agent might desire to do or become
Positive conception of freedom	a real, moral, or rational person with only that person's authentic, virtuous, or rational beliefs and desires	not only external obstacles but also internal factors such as irrational desires, fears, or ignorance	only authentic, virtuous, or rational actions or states that help to take control of the agent's own destiny in the agent's own interests

III The research questions

Considering the methodological framework, the research questions to be considered in this book are formulated as follows:

(1) What was the historical situation and the horizon of meaning in which the question of freedom emerged in nineteenth- and early twentieth-century Iran?
(2) How were the three variables of freedom (i.e. the agent, the restraint, and the purpose of freedom) introduced and interpreted in nineteenth-century Iranian travellers' accounts of European freedoms?
(3) How did late Qajar interpretations of the three variables of freedom manifest themselves in the sociopolitical life of early twentieth-century Iran? Particularly:

    (3.1) Concerning the agent of freedom: According to the interpretations of Qajar thinkers, who was to be deemed as an eligible agent of freedom? To what extent did this eligibility vary with reference to the person's gender, religion, or social class? (The question of eligibility and equality.)
    (3.2) Concerning legal restraints on or interferences in freedom: To what extent and wherefore was the majlis considered as a legitimate authority to make laws which imposed limitations on the freedoms of individuals? What freedoms were recognized for the people of Iran in these parliamentary laws, and which of the governments' interferences in the people's freedoms were allowed? Did these legal interferences aim to ensure that an activity would not go beyond certain bounds, or were they intended to ensure that the activity would also result in certain

consequences? What legal mechanisms were enacted to protect a person's freedom against the interferences of the state and other people? (The question of legislation.)

(3.3) Concerning the purpose of freedom: What freedoms were recognized for the people of Iran in parliamentary laws? What freedoms were actually tolerated in late Qajar Iran? (The question of permissibility.)

I will address these research questions in five chapters. Chapter 1 illustrates the application of my intellectual history approach by reconstructing the historical situation and the horizon of meaning in which the question of freedom emerged in nineteenth-century Iran. It investigates how the Iranian elite of that time formulated and answered the question of the decline of Iran, and shows that the texts written on freedom in the last century of the Qajar period can be understood as an answer to the question of decline.

Chapter 2 addresses the second question and shows how the application of MacCallum's conceptual framework of freedom assists in arriving at a more accurate understanding of the text. It first provides the Persian terminology of freedom and the usage of the three words *āzādī*, *ḥurrīyat*, and *ikhtiyār* for explaining the new meanings of freedom. It then employs the triadic formula for analyzing a number of Iranian travellers' explanations of European freedoms, and shows how these reports expanded the meaning of freedom in the Persian language and highlighted four significant themes concerning the new conceptions of freedom: the limitations of the King's freedom to impose his arbitrary will, the parliamentary freedoms to establish laws and criticize the government, the freedom of religion, and the freedom of male-female relationships.

Chapter 3 discusses the linkage between law and freedom. Assessing the parliamentary proceedings and the laws enacted by the first two Parliaments, it compares the first constitutional period (August 1906–June 1908) with the second one (July 1909–February 1921), addressing the questions related to different aspects of the issue of the imposition and enforcement of legal obligations on a person's activities (i.e. research questions, group 3.2 above). Answering such questions will clarify the Iranian elites' understandings of the second variable of the triadic formula of freedom.

The main purpose of Chapter 4 is to reconstruct the questions and answers which addressed the aim of freedom during the first constitutional period as well as the second one. It shows that freedom in the following four realms were of particular importance to Iranian constitutionalists: freedom of assembly, freedom of expression, freedom of work and commerce, and freedom of thought and lifestyle. The chapter also argues that for most thinkers of the time, freedom was instrumentally valuable, and therefore 'the right to be wrong', even if it harmed no one, was never defended by them.

Chapter 5 discusses two significant aspects of the first variable of the triadic relation of freedom: the eligibility of the agent of freedom, and the equality of agents in having freedom. Besides addressing these two issues, it will also discuss the actual effects of religion and gender upon the agents' freedom in late Qajar Iran.

It could be asked why the organization of chapters in this book does not maintain the order of the three components of MacCallum's triadic concept of freedom [namely, (1st) Agent, (2nd) Constraint, and (3rd) Purpose]. To avoid a 'potential performative contradiction', isn't it better to make a rearrangement in the chapters' order and change the book's narrative structure by repositioning Chapter 5 before Chapters 3 and 4? I do not believe so. To my understanding, there is no logical or philosophical order between the three variables in MacCallum's triadic relation of freedom. According to MacCallum, every statement about freedom could be formulated in the following triadic format: 'x is (is not) free from y to do (not do, become, not become) z'. However, the grammatical (or rhetorical) order of x, y, and z does not necessarily lead to any logical or philosophical precedence.

The line of argument in my research started from the linkage between law and freedom (addressing the questions related to different aspects of the issue of the imposition and enforcement of legal obligations on a person's activities); then it passed to the question of permissibility (asking if freedom was intrinsically valuable for Iranians or if it was only instrumentally valuable, and asking about different types of freedoms). The last stage of my inquiry is to reconstruct the question of eligibility and equality of the agents of freedom (What person is entitled to be free? And must all people equally benefit from freedom?). To address this questions, the reader should already have a well-articulated understanding of the constraint and purpose of freedom. It is worth mentioning that the agent of freedom is not the variable that makes a distinction between the theories of so-called 'negative' and 'positive' freedoms. Moreover, in my understanding, the interpretations and expansions of the agents of freedom (particularly the question of the equality of the agents) could be considered as a turning point to conclude a theory of freedom and to lead the discussion to a theory of justice.

IV Review of previous scholarship

i Studies on the history of freedom in Iran

There have been, as yet, few systematic studies on 'the history of philosophical ideas in Iran', since in general little attention has been paid to the historiography of ideas in the Iranian context. The existing literature on intellectual history often confuses the historiography of ideas with the biography of the thinkers. For instance, Farīdūn Ādamīyat, who is often considered the founder of modern historiography in Iran and who has contributed more than any other historian to studies on the Constitutional Revolution, wrote several noteworthy monographs on a number of outstanding thinkers of the Qajar period, such as Mīrzā Āqā Khān Kirmānī, Ākhūnd'zādah, and Ṭālibūf. He also conducted two studies on the history of modern thoughts and ideas in the Qajar period: the first was *Fikr-i āzādī va muqaddamah-i nihẕat-i mashrūṭīyat* (*The Idea of Freedom and the Emergence of the Constitutional Movement*),[38] and the second, *Andīshah-ʾi taraqqī va ḥukūmat-i qānūn: ʿaṣr-i Sipahsālār* (*The Idea of Progress and the Rule of Law: The Age of Sipahsālār*).[39]

The first book seems relevant to the present research, but it is in fact a brief history of the lives and thoughts of Mīrzā Malkam Khān and Mustashār al-Dawlah. The introductory chapter of this book provides a short history of the idea of freedom and democracy in Europe. The last chapter is about '*jāmi'-i ādamīyat*', an association modelled after European Masonic lodges. Therefore, the book consists of three monographs on two intellectuals and a political group, as they all share the same social and political views. The second book is about the political life and thought of Mushīr al-Dawlah Mīrzā Ḥusayn Khān Sipahsālār, the outstanding prime minister who served under Nāṣir al-Dīn Shāh. The book depicts the events that took place during his ministry, a period when the idea of progress was being promoted in Iran. This book likewise cannot be considered 'a history of the idea of progress in the age of Sipahsālār'. Nevertheless, both studies are valuable as they cite a set of important primary sources, and can be used to trace the conceptions of freedom as it was interpreted prior to the Constitutional Revolution.

Two other studies on the history of freedom in a Muslim context have been published in the *Encyclopaedia of Islam* under entries '*Āzādī*'[40] and '*Ḥurrīya*'.[41] Written by ʿAbd al-Hādī Ḥāʾirī, the article under '*Āzādī*' is an introductory study on the modern sense of *āzādī* and investigates the impact of Western ideas on Persian culture. This article is important as it provides an overview of a number of early Persian accounts on 'new' European political ideas written since 1732. Ḥāʾirī briefly discusses three approaches to the idea of freedom in the course of the Constitutional Revolution of 1905–11 and simply categorizes the thinkers as follows: (a) those thinkers who were proponents of freedom, but a type of freedom compatible with Islam; (b) a group of intellectuals who had better familiarity with European ideas and thus interpreted freedom in a more 'Western sense'; and (c) those thinkers who supported the old régime, opposed *mashrūṭah*, and saw freedom as detrimental to Islam.[42] Written by F. Rosenthal and B. Lewis, the article under '*Ḥurrīya*' focuses on the notion of freedom in the Ottoman Empire, the terminology of the word *ḥurrīya* in Arabic, as well as a brief history of this notion during the first centuries of the Islamic era. Both Rosenthal and Lewis have conducted a number of inquiries on the history of political concepts in the Muslim world; however, they have noticeably overlooked the Persian case.[43]

I have also consulted Homa Katouzian's works on this issue. His intellectual attempts to develop theories and conceptual frameworks for the study of Iranian history and society include analyses regarding law and freedom. Casting doubt on the accuracy of uncritically applying the theories developed for the study of European society to the Iranian case, he has put forward a number of thoughtful ideas, such as his notions of 'arbitrary rule and chaos',[44] 'the fundamental conflict between state and society in Iranian history',[45] 'Iran as a short-term society',[46] and 'liberty and license in Iranian history'.[47] These ideas are useful in recapturing the historical situation in which questions of freedom arose.

ii Similar philosophical approaches to the study of Western theories of freedom

Existing literature that has employed the approach of this research in the study of other periods/areas/topics is worth mentioning here, as it will deepen the contextualization of my work within the secondary sources. My philosophical approach to the concept of freedom has been used several times in earlier studies: First, in the very same essay in which he introduced his triadic frame of analysis, MacCallum attempted to invalidate Berlin's analytical and historical claims in making a distinction between positive and negative freedom as two fundamentally different concepts. Unlike Berlin, he did not frequently refer to specific historical examples, but rather discussed almost all possible situations and typical locutions that could have been uttered by adherents of so-called 'positive' or 'negative' freedom in order to prove that all intelligible locutions about freedom could be translated into the triadic formula. As MacCallum attempted to defend his theory against probable challenges, his detailed and comprehensive analysis has provided a good model for particular historical studies.

In the next development, John Rawls (1971) applied his distinction between a 'concept' and its rival 'conceptions' to the case of freedom, and reemphasized that the triadic formula is applicable to all *complete* explanations of freedom. Rawls's analysis is of particular interest for his view on the relationship between freedom and constitutional and legal restrictions:

> [L]iberty is a certain structure of institutions, a certain system of public rules defining rights and duties. Set against this background, persons are at liberty to do something when they are free from certain constraints either to do it or not to do it and when their doing it or not doing it is protected from interference by other persons.[48]

In other words, Rawls maintains that a particular freedom as defined by law simultaneously indicates that a person has a legal right to do a certain action and that other persons have a legal duty not to interfere. I will employ this analysis in the explanation of the linkage between law-seeking and freedom-seeking in the Constitutional Revolution era.

Since Rawls's analysis, quite a few studies have employed the triadic framework in analyzing Western theories of freedom. Here I only refer to three significant works. In *Marxism and Morality* (1985), Steven Lukes provided a concise overview of the spectrum of possible interpretations of the three variables of freedom and developed the analytical dimension of MacCallum's formula.[49]

The second research, conducted by Eric Nelson, attempts to reject Berlin's historical claim rather than defend MacCallum's analytical claim. He argues that for all theorists of liberty, even the so-called positive freedom theorists, freedom is the absence of some constraint; he maintains that 'within this broad set, however, there are substantially different claims about the ends of human life, the character of human beings, and the elements that can constrain us'.[50]

Another important development took place in Ian Carter's work. He reminds us that, both in everyday discourse and in contemporary political philosophy, we sometimes talk about 'the level of freedom', which refers to 'the concept of overall freedom' rather than 'a particular meaning of freedom'. According to Carter, this overall freedom is quantitative rather than triadic.[51] Nonetheless, MacCallum's framework is particularly well-suited to the clarification of the possibility of measuring, either comparatively or absolutely, a person's degree of overall freedom. Because what is involved in this measuring is not the distinction between positive and negative freedom, but the question of 'how an agent's available actions are to be individuated, counted, and weighted, and that of comparing and weighting different types (but not necessarily different sources) of constraints on freedom (such as physical prevention, punishability, threats, and manipulation)'.[52]

Each of these studies examines some of the capabilities of MacCallum's triadic formula in analyzing conceptions of freedom. Employing these examinations, my research attempts to make a new contribution. Firstly, I use MacCallum's metatheory, this time not for analyzing Western theories of freedom but for analyzing a number of Iranian explanations of freedom. Secondly, I attempt to show that the triadic frame of analysis can be systematically used even in analyzing incomplete locutions about freedom so that in addition to the thought, the unthought of the locutions may be found out.

iii Similar historiographical approach to the study of other ideas

Let us now turn to see whether the historiographical approach of this research has been employed in previous studies. Collingwood's logic of question and answer and his method for systematic questioning in historiography have been developed in various ways. The main difference between these developments lies in the question that must be reconstructed for understanding the text. Following Collingwood, Quentin Skinner (b. 1940), a founder of the 'Cambridge School' in the history of political thought, claims that understanding the meaning of an utterance is impossible unless the correlative *historical* question intended by its author is reconstructed and the 'illocutionary force' which the author meant to communicate within the linguistic conventions available to him and his audiences is grasped.[53] However, as Skinner's critics point out, there is doubt as to whether he has been successful in demonstrating how one can 'arrive at a historically valid ascription of intention behind historical action' with regard to the examples provided in his research.[54]

I tend to agree with those critics who believe that grasping authorial intention is hardly possible. Pointing out the hermeneutical theme missed in Skinner's account, John Keane persuasively states that 'not only those whose utterances are to be interpreted, but interpreters themselves are always situated within a field of historically bound convention and practices mediated by ordinary language'.[55] Accordingly, through the medium of a common language, the interpreter and the interpreted negotiate as two 'situated (if unequal) partners'.[56] This is what Gadamer has called 'the fusion of the horizons' (*Horizontverschmelzung*) of the reader and the writer. From this point of view, even the meaning of the author's intention 'must be co-determined by the interpreter'.[57] The application of this hermeneutical doctrine has been illustrated through Gadamer's historical examples in his *Truth and Method*, and John Keane's comprehensive work *The Life and Death of Democracy*.[58]

It is worth noting that, in analytical philosophy, the notion of horizon can be equated with the notion of situation. In his works, Karl Popper (1902–94) describes his method of historiography of thought under the name of 'situational logic' or 'situational analysis'. Following Collingwood, he states that in order to understand a passage of a philosophical work, the historian (1) 'must know the language in a philosophical sense', (2) 'must see what the philosophical problem was, of which this author is here stating his solution', (3), 'must think that problem out for himself, see what possible solutions of it might be offered', and (4) must 'see why this particular philosopher chose that solution instead of another'.[59] As Popper himself points out, there is a difference between Collingwood's theory and his own theory: while Collingwood emphasizes 'the historian's mental process of re-enactment', Popper suggests that the historian must 'reconstruct the problem situation in which the acting person finds himself', though he admits that the psychological process of re-enactment may only be used as an 'intuitive check of the success of his situational analysis'[60]. In Popperian situational analysis, the central problem that the historian attempts to solve is the following question: 'What were the important or operative elements in the situation? [. . .] to the extent that he solves it, he has understood the historical situation and the piece of history that he tries to recapture'.[61] Popper has presented good examples for the application of 'situational analyses' in his works, especially in his renowned work, *Open Society and its Enemies*.[62]

iv Primary sources

Historical research materials in this field are very heterogeneous. To trace the conceptions of freedom, I consulted not only books and treatises produced by the elite of late Qajar Iran, but also sources such as governmental decrees (like 'the Royal Proclamation on preserving peoples' freedom' issued by Nāṣir al-Dīn Shah in Ramadan 1305/May 1888), proceedings of the parliaments (first: 1906–09, second: 1909–11, third: 1914–15), legislative texts (such as *The Constitution* and *The Supplementary Fundamental Laws*), court judgments (like *Sharḥ- i muḥākimah-ʾi Shaykh Fazl Allāh Nūrī*), written records of minutes and memos (like *Asnād-i Khān Malik Sasānī*), as well as the memoirs, diaries, correspondence, and autobiographies of individuals (such as *Khātirāt-i Yaḥyá Dawlat'ābādī* and *Tārīkh-i bīdārī-i Irānīyān*). This mass of source material makes the task of researchers difficult, as they have to identify and select the most appropriate sources.

Most of the primary sources used in this study were produced in the decade after the triumph of the Constitutional Revolution. Here I only name a few of them. As mentioned above, after the deliberations on *The Supplementary Fundamental Laws* in the first parliament, Shaykh Fazl Allāh Nūrī (d. 1909), along with a number of his followers, produced a set of statements (*Lavāyiḥ*, published in 1325/1907) which, as mentioned before, can be regarded as classics of anti-liberty literature in Iran. On the other hand, as noted, a contemporary to Nūrī, Mīrzā ʿAbd al-Raḥīm Ṭālibūf Tabrīzī (1834–1911) wrote the first monograph on freedom, titled *Īzāḥāt dar Khuṣūṣ-i Āzādī* (*Clarifications of Freedom*). Ṭālibūf was a well-known intellectual in his time and was familiar with Western sciences and humanities as well as Russian revolutionary ideas. In the same year, Muḥammad ʿAlī Furūghī

(1878–1942), director and lecturer at the Tehran School of Political Science, published his *Ḥuqūq-i asāsī ya'nī ādāb-i mashrūṭīyat-i duval* (*Constitutional Rights i.e. Rules of the Constitutional States*) as the first Persian book on constitutional rights. Furūghī was a Europhile with strong inclination for European philosophy.

Five books produced in 1327–28/1909–10 merit careful consideration and were used in the present study. Among others, *Sarmāyah-'i sa'ādat yā 'ilm va āzādī* (*The Wealth of Happiness or Knowledge and Freedom*) published in 1327/1909 has received very little attention. The author, Abū al-Ḥasan Khān Furūghī, younger brother of Muḥammad 'Alī, was a lecturer in geography and history of Greece at the School of Political Science. Other books were written by four clerics: *Al-làālī al-marbuṭa fī wujūb al-mashrūṭa* (*Related Pearls on the Necessity of Constitutionalism*) by Shaykh Isma'īl Mujtahid Gharavī Maḥallātī, *Tanbīh al-umma wa tanzīh al-milla*[63] (*Awakening the Community and Purifying the Religion*) by Shaykh Muḥammad Ḥusayn Nā'īnī (1860–1936), *Ḥurmat-i mashrūṭah* (*Illegitimacy of Constitutionalism*) by Shaykh Fazl Allāh Nūrī (all published in 1327/1909), and *Risālah-'i inṣāfīyah* (*The Treatise on Fairness*) by Mullā 'Abd al-Rasūl Madanī Kāshānī (published in 1328/1910). Among these four clerics, only Nūrī was an opponent of constitutionalism. Maḥallātī's and Nā'īnī's works were published with the approval of the leading *marāji'* of Najaf, Akhūnd Mullā Kāẓim Khurāsānī[64] and Shaykh 'Abd Allāh Māzandarānī. Thus, their works were regarded as religious responses to anti-constitutionalism, especially to Nūrī's works on the illegitimacy of constitutionalism and freedom.

Notes

1 Mohammed Arkoun, *The Unthought in Contemporary Islamic Thought* (London: Saqi, 2002).

2 The 'unit of thought', as Collingwood conceived it, is that which 'any of [. . . its] parts taken singly is not a complete thought, that is, not capable of being true or false' (Robin George Collingwood, *An Autobiography* (London; New York, etc.: Oxford University Press, 1939), p. 34.). Establishing his 'logic of question and answer', Collingwood rejects the central doctrine of propositional logic in which the proposition is regarded as the 'unit of thought'.

3 As it is maintained in propositional logic (Collingwood, *An Autobiography*, p. 34).

4 As coherence-theorists maintain (ibid., p. 37).

5 Collingwood (ibid., p. 32) calls it the 'principle of correlativity between question and answer'.

6 Hans-Georg Gadamer, *Truth and Method*, trans. by Joel Weinsheimer and Donald G. Marshall (London: Continuum, 1975), pp. 363–71.

7 Acknowledging Collingwood, Gadamer says: 'In a brilliant and telling critique of the Oxford "realist" school, he developed the idea of a logic of question and answer, but unfortunately never elaborated it systematically' (ibid., p. 363).

8 Ibid.

9 Ibid., p. 302.

10 Ibid., p. 301.

11 Ibid., pp. 301–2.

12 Ibid., p. 302.

13 Setting aside Schleiermacher's ideas on subjective interpretation, Gadamer points out that 'when we try to understand a text we do not try to transpose ourselves into the

author's mind but, if one wants to use this terminology, we try to transpose ourselves into the perspective within which the author has formed his views. But this simply means that we try to understand how what he is saying could be right' (ibid., p. 292).

14 Ibid., p. 367.

15 Ibid., p. 368.

16 Ibid., p. 367.

17 Ibid., my italic.

18 In Collingwood's words, 'to say that a question "does not arise" is the ordinary English way of saying that it involves a presupposition, which is not in fact being made' (Robin George Collingwood, *An Essay on Metaphysics* (Oxford: Clarendon Press, 1940), p. 26).

19 Gadamer, p. 368.

20 Gadamer does not regard problems as real questions that arise of themselves. For 'part of the concept of the problem is that there can be no clear decision on the basis of reasons. That is why Kant sees the rise of the concept of the problem as limited to the dialectic of pure reason' (ibid., p. 369).

21 For example, if a Muslim theologian asks himself 'is Muhammad a divine prophet?', this is a real question as long as he equally considers all possible answers.

22 Mohammed Arkoun, *The Unthought in Contemporary Islamic Thought* (London: Saqi, 2002), p. 22.

23 Ibid., p. 11.

24 Ibid.

25 These sources of controlling power vary 'from clan leader, tribal chief or village mayor to king, caliph, sultan, emperor or president, from the smallest republic or kingdom to today's United States; from bishop, rabbi, village imam to pope, chief mufti or chief rabbi' (Arkoun, pp. 20–1).

26 Ibid., p. 21.

27 Ibid., p. 13.

28 Ibid., p. 12.

29 Ibid.

30 To adapt it to my case, I am reformulating Arkoun's original example of introducing the Greek philosophical thinkable into the Arabic language by the Arab Philosophers (for this example, see Arkoun, p. 12).

31 Maurice Cranston, *Freedom: A New Analysis*, 3rd edn. (London: Longmans, 1976), pp. 3–4.

32 Gerald C. MacCallum, 'Negative and Positive Freedom', *The Philosophical Review*, 76 (1967), 312 (p. 314) <http://dx.doi.org/10.2307/2183622>.

33 Ibid., p. 314.

34 See Ian Carter, 'Positive and Negative Liberty', in *The Stanford Encyclopedia of Philosophy*, ed. by Ian Carter and Edward N. Zalta, Spring 2012, <http://plato.stanford.edu/archives/spr2012/entries/liberty-positive-negative/> [accessed 21 June 2014].

35 MacCallum (p. 313) points out that fruitless concentration on 'kinds' of freedom has drawn attention away from the truly significant questions related to the presence or absence of freedom in a society. For him, all social and political disputes over the ranking of freedom among possible social benefits, the reasonable way of realizing and attaining freedom, as well as the relationships between attaining freedom and realizing other social goals and values, may stem from or turn into a dispute over the nature of freedom itself.

36 For a brief study on the history of the debates between positive and negative camps of liberty, see Carter, 'Positive and Negative Liberty'; for a selection of the key literatures written by positive and negative theorists of liberty as well as the critics of such dichotomy, see *Freedom: A Philosophical Anthology*, ed. by Ian Carter, Matthew H. Kramer, and Hillel Steiner (Malden, MA: Blackwell Pub., 2007), pp. 6–80.

37 Isaiah Berlin, 'Two Concepts of Liberty', in *Four Essays on Liberty* (Oxford: Oxford University Press, 1969), pp. 118–72 (pp. 121–2).

38 Farīdūn Ādamīyat, *Fikr-i āzādī va muqaddamah-i nihẕat-i mashrūṭīyat* (Tehran: Sukhan, 1961).

39 Farīdūn Ādamīyat, *Andīshah-i taraqqī va ḥukūmat-i qānūn: ʻaṣr-i Sipahsālār* (Tehran: Shirkat-i Sihāmī-i Intishārāt-i Khvarazmī, 1351).

40 See ʿAbd al-Hādī Ḥāʾirī, ʻĀzādī', in *The Encyclopaedia of Islam*, ed. by P.J. Bearman and others (Leiden: Brill, 2004), vol. 2.

41 See Franz Rosenthal and Bernard Lewis, 'Ḥurrīya', in *The Encyclopaedia of Islam*, ed. by B. Lewis and others (Leiden: Brill, 1971), vol. 2.

42 Hāʿirī has developed his study in his work entitled ʻAbd al-Hādī Ḥā'irī, *Azādīhā-yi siyāsī va ijtimāʻī az dīdgāh-i andīshah'garān: guẕarī bar nivishtah'hā-yi pārsī dar dū sadah-'i vāpasīn* (Mashhad: Jihād-i Dānishgāhī-i Mashhad, 1374).

43 See, for instance, Bernard Lewis, *Race and Slavery in the Middle East: An Historical Enquiry* (New York: Oxford University Press, 1990); B. Lewis, 'Democracy in the Middle East: Its State and Prospect', *Middle Eastern Affairs*, 6 (1955), 101–8; Bernard Lewis, *The Political Language of Islam* (Chicago: University of Chicago Press, 1988); Franz Rosenthal, *The Muslim Concept of Freedom prior to the Nineteenth Century* (Leiden: Brill, 1960).

44 See Homa Katouzian, 'Arbitrary Rule: A Comparative Theory of State, Politics and Society in Iran', *British Journal of Middle Eastern Studies*, 24 (1997), 49–73.

45 See Homa Katouzian, *Iranian History and Politics: The Dialectic of State and Society* (London; New York: Routledge; Curzon, 2003).

46 See Homa Katouzian, 'The Short-Term Society: A Study in the Problems of Long-Term Political and Economic Development in Iran', *Middle Eastern Studies*, 40 (2004), 1–22.

47 See Homa Katouzian, 'Liberty and Licence in the Constitutional Revolution of Iran', *Journal of the Royal Asiatic Society*, 8:3 (1998), 159–80.

48 John Rawls, *A Theory of Justice* (Cambridge, MA: Belknap Press of Harvard University Press, 1971), p. 177.

49 See Steven Lukes, *Marxism and Morality* (Oxford; New York: Clarendon Press; Oxford University Press, 1985), pp. 72–5.

50 Eric Nelson, 'Liberty : One Concept Too Many?', *Political Theory*, 33:1 (2005), 58–78 (pp. 73–4).

51 This means that we interpret the third variable of freedom in a non-specific way and value 'being free to do things' in a general, rather than in any specific sense. See Ian Carter, *A Measure of Freedom* (New York: Oxford University Press, 1999), p. 32.

52 Ian Carter, 'Positive and Negative Liberty', in *The Stanford Encyclopedia of Philosophy*, ed. by Edward N. Zalta, Spring 2012, <http://plato.stanford.edu/archives/spr2012/entries/liberty-positive-negative/> [accessed 18 July 2014].

53 Quentin Skinner, 'Meaning and Understanding in the History of Ideas', *History and Theory*, 8:1 (1969), 3–53 (p. 46).

54 For an instance of these criticisms, see Lotte Mulligan, Judith Richards, and John Graham, 'Intentions and Conventions: A Critique Quentin Skinner's Method for the Study of the History of Ideas', *Political Studies*, 27:1 (1979), 84–98.

55 John Keane, 'More Theses on the Philosophy of History', in *Meaning and Context: Quentin Skinner and His Critics*, ed. by James Tully (Cambridge; Oxford: Polity Press & Basil Blackwell, 1988), pp. 204−17 (pp. 209–10).

56 Using this metaphor, Gadamer states that 'just as each interlocutor is trying to reach agreement on some subject with his partner, so also the interpreter is trying to understand what the text is saying' (Gadamer, p. 370).

57 Keane, 'More Theses on the Philosophy of History', p. 212.

58 John Keane, *The Life and Death of Democracy* (New York: W.W. Norton & Co., 2009).

59 Karl R. Popper, *The Myth of the Framework: In Defence of Science and Rationality* (London; New York: Routledge, 1994), p. 146.

60 Ibid., p. 147.
61 Ibid.
62 Karl R. Popper, *The Open Society and Its Enemies* (London: G. Routledge & Sons, Ltd., 1945).
63 The Arabic word *'Milla'* derived from the Qur'ānic term (*millata Ibrāhīma ḥanīfā*) (see Q.:135) means the sharia and its follower. It is currently used in Persian to mean 'nation'. However, the combination of *al-millah* with *tanzih* (purifing) in the book title shows that the traditional meaning of the word was meant by Nā'īnī.
64 See also Muḥammad Kāẓim Khurāsānī, *Siyāsat'nāmah-'i Khurāsānī: qiṭa'āt-i siyāsī dar āsār-i Ākhūnd Mullā Muḥammad Kāẓim Khurāsānī ṣāḥib-i Kifāyah (1255–1329 Hijrī Qamarī)*, ed. by Muḥsin Kadīvar (Tehran: Kavīr, 1385).

1 The horizon of the question of freedom in nineteenth-century Iran

A version of this chapter has been published previously in *Iran Nameh* quarterly journal as: Ahmad Hashemi, "Freedom as a Remedy for the Decline: The Horizon of the Question of Freedom in Nineteenth Century Iran", *Iran Nameh*, vol. 30:4, Winter 2016.

The intellectual elite in nineteenth- century Iran gradually found the opportunity to become familiar with a new concept of freedom. Their discovery of this new meaning was less the result of abstract philosophical reflections and more the consequence of the observation of European social and individual lifestyles. They realized that Westerners (*farangiyān*) lived free from many restraints, while in Iran such restraints, according to a long-lasting cultural and political tradition, had been unquestionably regarded as necessary conditions to preserve order and security and to provide happiness in this world and the afterlife. A number of the Iranian elite came to believe that Europeans, free from these restraints, were successful in building ordered societies, decent and secure citizenship, powerful and lawful states, and ultimately, developed countries; on the contrary, the lack of this freedom had left Iranians as unfortunate and insecure subjects in a disordered society with an army defeated at the hands of 'infidels' in the two Russo-Persian wars (1803–13 and 1826–28), in a critically weakened country ruled by an arbitrary state. This chapter aims to examine the various aspects of this new awareness through studying Iranian travelogues and reformist writings of the nineteenth and early twentieth centuries, in order to argue that the concept of freedom was understood in the horizon of the question of decline.

The chapter is divided into two parts. As an application of my intellectual history approach, the first part reconstructs the horizon of meaning in which the question of freedom arose. It investigates how the Iranian elite of that time formulated and answered the question of the decline of Iran, and to what extent their formulations differ from those of earlier writers. They also wondered about the causes behind the 'decline and fall' of dynasties in times of crisis, as well as Iran's defeat throughout history (for instance, the causes of the Safavids' decline was the subject of several treatises written after the fall of Isfahan in 1722). However, in the nineteenth century the new awareness of the gap between Iran and the West focused on new issues and departed from a novel worldview. Unlike the traditional *Weltanschauung* of political thought and *andarz'nāmah* literature, this elite posed the question of 'decline and fall' within a new horizon of meaning and became attracted to a new set of social and cultural aspects, such as the linkage between decline on the one hand and factors like the Arabic alphabet, the absence of law, and the dominance of Islam.

The second part of the chapter shows how most locutions about freedom uttered in the last century of the Qajar period were formed within the horizon of the question of decline and were somehow related to remedy such situations. They identified lawlessness and arbitrary rule as the chief cause of Iran's decline. The linkage between arbitrary rule and freedom will be better understood when one uses the triadic format to formulate arbitrary rule: the ruler is free *from* all restraints *to* do whatever the ruler desires. On the contrary, the Iranian reformists of the time often aimed to establish the rule of law and to form a society in which civilized people were free *from* the arbitrary interferences of the state *to* do whatever led them to progress and happiness.

1.1 Awareness of the decline

When Āghā Muḥammad Khān (r. 1794–97) put an end to chaos and reunited Iran in 1796, the issue of the decline and fall of the Safavids in 1722 was still disputed by a number of the Iranian elite: what caused the sudden decline of this glorious empire and its humiliating defeat at the hands of an Afghan tribe of a far-flung corner of the country?

These thinkers inquired into the issue of decline within the Perso-Islamic tradition of political thought.[1] Their analysis, both in perceiving decline and seeking remedies, often remained within the framework of this tradition with no comparison to other countries. To illustrate this point, I consider two significant diagnoses of the fall of the Safavids.

The first diagnosis comes from Quṭb al-Dīn Nayrīzī Shīrāzī (1688–1759), a master of *zahabī ṭarīqah* (a chain in Sufism). Having witnessed the fall of Isfahan, he wrote two treatises on the Afghan *fitnah* (rebellion): *Ṭib al-mamālik* (in Arabic)[2] and *Faṣl al-khiṭāb* (in Persian).[3]

Ṭib al-mamālik was probably written after Isfahan was recaptured by Nādir Shah Afshār in 1729 and Safavid princes returned to the capital hoping to restore the Safavid throne.[4] Referring to the Qur'ān and Shīʿī traditions, especially Imam ʿAlī's *Nahj al-balāgha*, Nayrīzī introduces five causes and symptoms for decline and social illness (*iʿtilāl*): breach of the divine and the prophetic promise, abandonment of the duty of commending the right and forbidding the wrong (*amr bi-lmaʿrūf wa nahy ʿan-lmunkar*), the *ʿulamā's* worldliness and their submission to the sultan, the sultan's ignorance and his lack of willpower, and the governors' corruption.[5]

Despite such a traditional approach in perceiving the causes of decline, his proposal for resolving the crisis was innovative within the framework of the premodern tradition of political thought. He proposed that, in order to remedy the decline, rational members of the society, namely *ʿulamā*, should mediate between the king and his subjects. By drawing lots, they should reach a consensus on the kingship of one of the Safavid princes. Then, they must obtain the new shah's commitment to follow what ʿAlī ibn abī Ṭālib, the first Shīʿī Imam, commanded his governor, Mālik Ashtar, to do in issues such as collecting taxes, fighting enemies, improving people's affairs, and improving the cities. Finally, a just scribe must document the agreement between the shah, the *ʿulamā*, and the subjects. This endorsed agreement should be sent to all cities.[6]

Accordingly, it can be said that in Nayrīzī's view, the ultimate remedy for decline is to place limits on the sultan's power by obligating him to obey a set of regulations and making the legitimacy of his authority conditional on a written undertaking based on the religious command of Imam ʿAlī to Mālik Ashtar.

The connection between lawlessness and decline has been better addressed in the second diagnosis attributed to Karīm Khān Zand (r. 1759–1779).[7] Muḥammad Hāshim Āṣaf, known as Rustam al-Ḥukamā (d. 1841), provides a detailed quotation from Karīm Khān on the causes of the decline and fall of the Safavids. Karīm Khān compared Iran with the Ottoman Empire, Europe, China, Cathay, and Transoxiana, and asserted that what had made these foreign countries stable, prosperous, and powerful was that they had righteous laws (*qavānīn-i sharīfah*) and acted as required by wisdom, prudence, and justice. He went on to add

> what can I say about ruined Iran where calculation and planning are as futile as writing on water, and where appropriate customs and fascinating laws are rare? Iran is always in a state of chaos due to the coercion and oppression of tyrants, and it is constantly destroyed by the conflict between despots.[8]

Even if such a quotation was post-constructed by Rustam al-Ḥukamā's historiographical imagination in the early years of the nineteenth century, it indicates that in the light of comparing Iran with other countries, an awareness of the causal relationship between lawlessness and decline began to arise.

The establishment of a new and relatively strong state by the Qajars did not effectively improve the situation within which the question of decline and backwardness had arisen. On the contrary, the domestic and international conditions of nineteenth-century Iran made the situation even more critical. The long military conflicts with Russia over the control of neighbouring territories resulted in two humiliating defeats and bitter treaties. These defeats cast doubt not only on the country's military power, but also on the efficiency of the whole sociopolitical structure of Iran.

This new perception of decline has a comparative nature. The Iranian elite of the time perceived the country's weakness and deficiency in comparison with Europe.[9] To go into the details of this newly emerged awareness is beyond the scope of this study. An outline of the innovative formulations of and solutions for the question of decline is, however, necessary in order to reconstruct the horizon of meaning within which the new Iranian sociopolitical thought emerged and a paradigm shift in approaching the question of decline occurred. By the horizon of meaning, I mean the essential part of the concept of historical situation, since as Gadamer says 'situation . . . represents a standpoint that limits the possibility of vision'.[10] This range of vison or horizon of meaning was expanded through comparisons with and evaluations of Europe; for the comparisons constructed the 'other', and shifted the standpoint from which the Iranian elite comprehended and evaluated the 'self'. The progress and success of the 'other' were juxtaposed with the deficiency of the 'self', yet in different ways. The perception of Iran's deficiency or even Iran's decline did not necessarily mean that a mood of despondency about the condition of the country had set in among all elite. Many of them, rather, simply admired the achievements of the West and argued that it was essential for Iran to undergo a set of European-style reforms.

Admittedly, ʿAbbās Mīrzā (1789–1833), Prince Regent and governor-general of Azerbaijan and the Iranian military commander in Russo-Persian wars, was one of the first who intuitively perceived that the military defeats were indicative of a greater problem. He naïvely framed such a multifaceted and critical situation in a question addressed to Napoleon's secret agent, Pierre Amédée Jaubert, who visited the Prince Regent in 1805 at his court in Tabriz:

> What is the power that gives (Europe) so great a superiority over us? What is the cause of your progress and of our constant weakness? You know the art of governing, the art of conquering, and the art of putting into action all human faculties, whereas we seem condemned to vegetate in shameful ignorance.[11]

To rectify the situation, ʿAbbās Mīrzā, along with his reform-minded ministers, Mīrzā ʿĪsā and his son Mīrzā Abū al-Qāsim (*Qāʾim'maqām* I and II), brought about a series of reforms. Similar to the process of reform that under Sultan Selīm III (r. 1789–1807) was already in progress in the Ottoman Empire, these efforts aimed primarily to form a new army, *niẓām-i jadīd*, along European guidelines.[12] The first steps were taken by translating French military books on artillery and war technique, as well as hiring European advisors to train Iranian troops. At the same time, ʿAbbās Mīrzā dispatched two student missions to Europe in 1811 and 1815.[13] All these measures stemmed from admiration and emulation of Europe as the pioneer of progress and a model for change.

The Prince Regent's enthusiasm to know the history of European progress and the causes behind the decline of great powers also led to the translation and writing of a number of books and treatises. In 1807, Muḥammad Raẕī Tabrīzī translated *Ḥavādis'nāmah* from Turkish into Persian as an account of the defeat of Russia in the Battle of Austerlitz, which occurred in 1805 between Napoleon's army and the Russo-Austrian army.[14] *Tārīkh-i Iskandar*, a biography of Alexander the Great, was collected and translated by 'James Camel' (جیمز کمل?) for the Prince Regent in 1813.[15] Furthermore, Mīrzā Ṣāliḥ Shīrāzī, a student dispatched to England, wrote his travelogue around 1819. He not only presented his observations on the sociopolitical system of 'the new world' (*jahān-i jadīd*) but also spent a chapter on the history of the kings of England in order to show 'the path of the progress of that country' (*ṭarīq-i taraqqī-i īn valāyat*).[16] Likewise, Mīrzā Riẕā Muhandis translated a number of historical books for ʿAbbās Mīrzā, including the first chapter of Edward Gibbon's *The History of the Decline and Fall of the Roman Empire* (*Tārīkh-i tanazzul va kharabī-i dawlat-i Rūm*) circa 1831.[17] Each of these works in its own way helped the ruling elite to perceive the situation of decline.[18]

The Prince Regent died in 1833 before acceding to the throne, but his question echoed throughout the century. The root of almost all reformist thought, until the triumph of the Constitutional Revolution, was the question of decline. Two changes took place in this era. First, formulations of the issue of decline were now founded on comparisons of Iran with Europe. Second, solutions for the crisis were sought beyond the framework of tradition and by reference to Western achievements and experiences in science, technology, politics, and culture.

As time went by, efforts to diagnose the causes of decline became more intense as superficial reformist measures met with increasing failure. Soon after playing a key role in putting down the succession crisis and helping Muḥammad Mīrzā (r. 1834–1848), the eldest son of ʿAbbās Mīrzā, to succeed to the throne, the enlightened chief minister, Mīrzā Abū al-Qāsim Qāʾim'maqām (d. 1835), was executed by the shah's arbitrary order. Fourteen years later, Amīr Kabīr, the reform-minded politician trained by Qāʾim'maqām, loyally assisted young heir-designate Nāṣir al-Dīn Mīrzā to come to power. He became chief minister as well as army commander, and attempted to conduct a reform program. However, once again, the shah arbitrarily took his life and brought the reformist measures to a halt.[19] Such determining events uncovered the arbitrary nature of Iranian rule; hence, many of the elite arrived at the conclusion that the country's decline could not be remedied without changing the political culture.

In such a situation, the idea of the absence of the rule of law or, in other words, 'arbitrary rule' (*istibdād*) being at the root cause of decline, was gradually constructed.[20] From the early nineteenth century onward, European law and order were wonderingly and enviously pointed out in almost all Iranian travel accounts. The most renowned messenger of the idea of the necessity of law was Mīrzā Malkam Khān Nāẓim al-Dawlah (1833–1908).

Around 1859, young Malkam Khān submitted a constitutional proposal entitled *Daftar-i tanẓīmāt yā Kitābchah-ʾi ghaybī* to the chief minister, Mīrzā Jaʿfar Mushīr al-Dawlah Mīrzā Ḥusayn Khān Sipahsālār (d. 1862).[21] In the introduction of the proposal, Malkam wrote:

> We have not yet perceived how far ahead of us Europeans are. We assume that their progress is as much as we see in their industries, whereas their main progress has appeared in the rules of civilization (*āʾīn-i tamaddun*). And it is impossible for those who have never travelled abroad to perceive the extent of this type of European advancement.[22]

Using the metaphor of 'the human factories of Europe' (*kārkhānijāt-i insānī-i farang*) and expressing the significance and priority of these factories over industrial factories, he added that 'what we need in Iran is these human factories such as the tax factory, the army factory, the justice factory, the science factory, the security factory, the regulation factory and so on'.[23] He went on to emphasize that 'to regulate the state is not to deny any religion but the religion of those whose greatness requires the perpetuation of chaos'.[24]

In the third law of *Daftar-i tanẓīmāt*, Malkam Khān introduced eight articles of the rights of the people, highlighting their significance by footnoting that to understand these few lines would take ten years: 'The French state has killed four million human beings for these very lines'.[25] Malkam Khān spent the rest of his life explaining the same rights and promoting the idea of the rule of law by various means, such as establishing the *farāmūsh'khānah* (House of Oblivion, an association modelled after European Masonic lodges), writing several effective works, correspondences and debates with the intellectual and political elite, and publishing the *Qānūn* newspaper in which he called on commoners and nobles to claim the rule of law.

Many times in his works, Malkam Khān identified arbitrary rule and lawlessness as the fundamental causes of decline. The crux of the problem, in his words, is that 'today, all of Iran's affairs are run by the arbitrariness of rulers (*dil'bikhvāh-ʾi ruʾasā*)'.[26]

It is worth mentioning that Malkam Khān tried to place his solution within traditional values. Distinguishing between the legislation and the implementation of law, he wrote that

> We are not saying that we demand the law of Paris, Russia or India. The principles of good laws are always the same, and the best laws are those which we learn from the sharia of God. However, we have been so deeply wronged due to the lack of implementation of these principles . . . that we are content with any kind of law, be it Turkmen law, because even the worst laws are better than lawlessness.[27]

He went on to add that 'good laws, whether divine or rational, from whatever source and language' would not be implemented by themselves, and would require the 'special measures' (*tadābīr-i makhṣūṣ*) which were discovered by the developed nations through hundreds of trials and errors. He persistently concludes by saying, 'yet Iranians have no idea about the contents and functions of these measures'.[28]

Another famous proponent of the rule of law was Yūsuf Khān Mustashār al-Dawlah[29] (1823–95). He also posed the question of decline in the introduction to his book *One Word* (*Yik Kalamah*) (published in 1278/1861), asking his countrymen: 'why are you sitting so unaware and idle? Why are you not thinking about the progress of other nations?'.[30]He bemoaned the fact that not only Europe but also even Iran's neighbour (Ottoman) had overtaken Iran in constructing hospitals, schools, roads, and railways, in the court of law (*dīvān'khanah*), and in regularizing taxation. Although he had once advocated the importation of European science and technology, especially railways, he maintained that 'telegraphs and steam ships and catapults and war instruments' were 'the results and not the preliminaries'.[31] Mustashār al-Dawlah criticized the elite who focused on 'the history and technology of Europe' and neglected its 'principles and foundations of administration' (*bunyān-i ʿamal-i idārah*). He described them as men who only looked at the surface and overlooked the undercurrent (*qaṣr-i naẓar kardan bih naẓarīyāt-i sādah* and *ṣarf-i naẓar nimudan az ʿamalīyāt-i ʿumdah*)'.[32] Instead, he summarized the source of Europe's progress and orderly system in one word: 'the book of law' (*kitāb-i qānūn*).

The other tendency in diagnosing the decline identified 'religion' as the chief cause. Without doubt, the figure most representative of this trend was Fatḥ ʿAlī

Ākhund'zādah (1812–78), who described himself as a 'liberal' and 'a wayfarer of the path of progress and a proponent of civilization' (*az sālikān-i maslak-i puruqrah va ṭālibān-i sīvīlīzah*). He had once believed that 'the instinctive (i.e. immanent) capability of the Muslim people' (*qābilīyat-i jibillī-i millat-i Islām*) was greater than that of Europeans, and that the only cause of their backwardness was the insufficiency of the Arabic script.[33] However, when his insistence on replacing a new alphabet[34] did not succeed, he located the source of this failure in Muslim fanaticism (*fināṭīzm-i millat-i Islām*) and began to write his criticism, *Maktūbāt-i Kamāl al-Dawlah* (written in 1280/1863), in order to 'destruct the foundation of this religion (Islam), to remove fanaticism, to waken the Asian nations from carelessness and ignorance, and to prove the necessity of Protestantism in Islam'.[35] In his view, the expansion of science is conditional on progress, progress is conditional on being liberal, and being liberal is conditional on release from wrong beliefs. Yet religion prevents release from wrong beliefs.[36]

Such bitter criticism could certainly not be widely welcomed in the religious and traditional atmosphere of Iran. But a mild account of this diagnosis captured some attention. In such an account, the cause of decline referred not to Islam itself but to the assaults of the Arabs and the sociopolitical role of the *ʿulamā*. The anti-Arab prejudice and accusing Arabs of Iran's thousand-year decline was not a new phenomenon, but Ākhund'zādah's opinion on the role of clerics in catalysing the crisis seemed innovative. For instance, in a letter (written in March 1871) to Mustashār al-Dawlah, who was recently appointed minister of the newly established justice ministry (*vizārat-i ʿadlīyah*), Ākhūnd'zādah reminded him of the necessity of deposing the *ʿulamā* from judicial affairs. He also pointed out that the gap and the conflict between the state and society in the Shiite community stemmed from the *ʿulamā* convincing the people that governors were agents of injustice (*ahl-i ẓalamah*) and that *ʿulamā* were the judges and protectors of the people (*marjaʿ-i millat*).[37] The innovation and the 'heresy' of Ākhūnd'zādah's opinion becomes clear by comparison to Quṭb al-Dīn Nayrīzī, who had lived a century before him. Within the framework of the Perso-Islamic political thought, Nayrīzī believed that the cause of the Safavids' decline was the breach of the divine and the prophetic promise. He also believed that the ultimate remedy would be the mediation of the *ʿulamā* between state and society in order to select a shah and commit him to obeying the religious commands of Imam ʿAlī.[38]

1.2 Freedom and law as the answers to the question of decline

In almost all of the diagnoses of Iran's decline by the nineteenth-century Iranian reformist thinkers, lawless and arbitrary rule was identified as the chief cause of decline. For these reformist thinkers, the term 'arbitrary rule' described the following triadic relation of freedom: the ruler is free *from* all restraints *to* do whatever he desires. Such arbitrary exercise of power by both central and provincial rulers constrained people's freedoms and threatened the security of their life and property. Needless to say, the rulers' power was not absolute. On the surface, even the king, as the sultan of Islam, pretended to observe the sharia. The *ʿulamā*, who were considered by the people as the guardian of Islam and countervailing power to the state, particularly after the Tobacco Revolt of 1891–2, used their power and authority to limit the shah's arbitrary rule.[39] Yet the sharia was not always an insurmountable law, as the *ʿulama* had their own inter-personal rivalries for which many of them did not refuse to be reconciled with the state.

A description of such a lawless society has been effectively presented by Mīrzā Abū Ṭālib Bihbahānī in a short passage of his *Minhāj al-ʿulā*, written in 1877:

> disorder and chaos in the administrative apparatus; constant abrogation of decrees; indecisiveness and hesitant decision-making; unnecessary and unfounded modifications; contradictions and falsifications in the words of the government; and the oppression of the poor, the weak and the defenseless by the staff and employees of the government administration as well as the men of power and wealth.[40]

Under such circumstances, reformist thinkers sought freedom *from arbitrary rule* through a revolt for law. Unlike European revolutions, such as the French Revolution of 1789, which aimed to make existing laws fairer and to remove the legal restraints on the freedom of individual, the Constitutional Revolution of 1906 was indeed a revolt for establishing law which sought to achieve freedom and other social rights.[41] Western classical liberals of the eighteenth and nineteenth centuries, especially proponents of the individualist or negative concept of liberty, tended to think of liberty as freedom from legal restraints. This concern is echoed in a famous definition of freedom suggested by Thomas Jefferson (1743–1826), one of the Founding Fathers of republicanism in the United States:

> Rightful liberty is unobstructed action according to our will within limits drawn around us by the equal rights of others. I do not add 'within the limits of the law', because law is often but the tyrant's will, and always so when it violates the rights of the individual.[42]

In the absence of law in nineteenth-century Iran, however, the fact that the law itself could restrict the freedom of the individual was not seen as a real question and accordingly was not considered as such. For instance, as mentioned above, Mīrzā Malkam Khān emphasized the significance of the implementation of law in saying that 'we are content with any kind of law, be it Turkmen law, because even the worst laws are better than lawlessness'.[43] It was only after the Constitutional Revolution that disputes over the legislation of freedom arose in the first Parliament and the simplistic idea of 'law as freedom' was re-examined.

Let us return to the pre-constitutional era in order to examine what made reformist thinkers lose their hope in reform from above, leading them to call for revolt against arbitrary rule. It was not only the reformist thinkers, but also Nāṣir al-Dīn Shāh, who realized that lawlessness was the main obstacle to the freedom of the people. It is often pointed out that he returned from his third European tour (first in 1873, another in 1878, and the third in 1889) with the idea of introducing law and responsible government.[44] Nonetheless, it was not until the year before his third visit to Europe that the shah attempted to take the main step in preserving peoples' freedom. In Ramadan 1305/May 1888, he issued the following Royal Proclamation:

> Forasmuch as Almighty God has endowed our blessed nature with the attributes of justice and benignity and ordained us as the manifestation of his ordinances and power, and has especially committed to our all-sufficient guardianship the lives and property of the subjects of the divinely guarded Empire of Iran; in gratitude for this great gift, we consider it incumbent on us, in discharge of the duties it imposes on us, to relax nothing in ensuring to the people of this kingdom the enjoyment of their rights and the preservation of their lives and property from molestation by oppressors, and to spare no efforts to the end that the people, secure in their persons and property, shall, in perfect ease and tranquility, employ themselves in affairs conductive to the spread of civilization and stability. Therefore, for the information and re-assurance of all the subjects and people of this kingdom generally, we do proclaim that all our subjects are free and independent as regards their persons and property; it is our will and pleasure that they should, without fear or doubt, employ their capital in whatever manner they please, and engage in any enterprises, such as combination of funds, formation of companies for construction of factories and roads, or in any measures for the promotion of civilization and security. The care of that is taken on ourselves; and no one has the right or power to interfere with, or lay hands on, the property of Persian subjects, nor to molest their persons or property, nor to punish Persian subjects except in giving effect to decrees of the civil or religious law.[45]

In this decree, the shah is a lawgiver who 'epitomizes the divine ordinances and power' (not as a representative of the people) and believes that he is committed to preserving the lives and property of subjects and protecting their economic freedom. He thereby proclaims that the people of Iran are free *from* fear of oppressors' molestations and invasions of their lives and property *to* 'employ their capital in whatever manner they please', *to* 'engage in any enterprise', and *to* 'take any measures for the promotion of civilization and security'. Along the same lines, no one is free *from* the restraint of this proclamation *to* 'interfere with, or lay hands on, the property of Persian subjects, nor *to* molest their persons or property, nor *to* punish Persian subjects except in giving effect to decrees of the civil or religious law'.

The Royal Proclamation on freedom was telegraphed to all the provincial governors, but it was fruitless. In fact, during his 48-year reign, Nāṣir al-Dīn Shāh sometimes gave people a number of privileges and freedoms in order to appease them. However, soon after each decree, a group of governors or *ʿulamā* often resisted the decrees, complaining that freedom would result in chaos and indecency. This would often lead to the shah's withdrawal of the decree. Regarding the Royal Proclamation of May 1888, Muhammad Ḥasan Khān Iʿtimād al-Salṭanah (1259–1313/1843–95), the minister of publications and the shah's private secretary, wrote in his diary:

> I respectfully informed [the shah] that the published proclamation of the freedom of the people was untimely, bad and inappropriate (*bī-mawqiʿ, bad, nā'munāsib*). Perhaps on the occasion of the 41st anniversary of the crown, and in gratitude for this divine gift, you intended to provide the subjects with ease and tranquility. However the content of the proclamation shows that you were either forced or dreaming when publishing it. The shah did not like what I was saying, and replied that since Ẓil al-Sulṭān [his son and the governor of Isfahan] treated people very oppressively, I dismissed him and judged the proclamation necessary.[46]

Such resistance to freedom can also be traced in the first and second phases of Nāṣir al-Dīn Shāh's rule. Once, in the early second decade of his reign, he issued a decree on the establishment of the *majlis-i maṣlaḥat'khānah* (House of Consultation, a preliminary parliament composed of 25 elite members who would be free in criticizing governmental affairs) and permitted Malkam Khān to set up the *farāmūsh'khānah*. However, soon after in 1278/1861, both institutions were dissolved according to the shah's order. A member of the *maṣlaḥat'khānah*, Mīrzā Ibrāhīm Badāyiʿ'nigār (1240–99/1825–82), expressed his disappointment at the dissolution of the *maṣlaḥat'khānah*, saying that 'Alas, they did not tolerate it and swayed the royal might from such a noble freedom (*rày-i aʿlā rā az īn ikhtiyār-i fāẕil bar'tāftand*)'.[47]

An instance of the *ʿulmā's* resistance to such reforms is the case of Ḥāj Mullā ʿAlī Kanī (1220–1306/1805–89), the leading *mujtahid* of Tehran. In a letter addressed to the shah in 1873, he complained about the chaotic situation caused by 'the pernicious concept of freedom' (*kalamah-ʾi qabīḥah-ʾi āzādī*) based on which 'anyone can say whatever he desires' while claiming that 'this is freedom and the supreme person of the country has liberated everyone'.[48] Although none of the reputable thinkers of the time defined 'freedom' as the absence of all constraints, they were always susceptible to such accusation by Ḥāj Mullā ʿAlī Kanī. As is evident from the following argument, he tended to think of freedom as the absence of all constraints and therefore against the sharia as well as the raison d'etre of the government:

> The sharias and religions as such have always been the firm restraints which prevented people from committing prohibited deeds and sins and from molesting people's property and honour. Likewise, it is against the aims and regulations of government and kingship for anyone to say whatever he desires and to plunder wealth through fraud and corruption.[49]

These complaints distorted the reformist thinkers' conceptions of freedom and reduced it to absolute license,[50] but Nāṣir al-Dīn Shāh often lacked the motivation to withstand such objections. Despite this distortion, it can be argued that the common understanding of freedom among most of the Iranian elite of the time can be formulated as follows: civilized people are free *from* the arbitrary interferences of the state *to* do whatever leads them to progress and happiness. Such a formulation, of course, cannot be precisely found in any text of the time; rather, it can only be inferred after a conceptual analysis of the ambiguous passages on freedom here and there. Nevertheless, one must avoid a reductionist account. For instance, freedom in a number of these passages means freedom from superstition and ignorance embodied in some parts of Islamic law (*shar'*) and social customs (*'urf*).

A comprehensive analysis of this issue will be the objective of the following chapters. In the meantime, it is worth noting that in the Constitutionalist Movement, freedom from arbitrary rule emerged as a rising public demand for the introduction of a set of fundamental laws to limit the monarch's power.[51] Once the first parliament convened and the constitutional government was formed, some new concerns about freedom emerged and were carefully examined. Then rose an awareness that freedom in its legal expression must define not only the rights but also the duties to protect persons from interferences by both the state and other persons – in other words, from both arbitrary rule and license (*istibdād* and *harj-u-marj*).

Notes

1 The central doctrine of this tradition is that the right to rule directly comes from the will of God. Possessing *farr* or Divine Grace, a shah has legitimacy to rule. As long as he is just, he will hold his Divine Grace and hence remain legitimate. For more information on the myth of Divine Grace, see Homa Katouzian, *The Persians: Ancient, Mediaeval, and Modern Iran* (New Haven: Yale University Press, 2009), pp. 396–7.

2 See Quṭb al-Dīn Nayrīzī Shīrāzī, 'Ṭib al-mamālik', in *'Ilal-i bar'uftādan-i Ṣafavīyān: mukāfāt'nāmah*, ed. by Rasūl Ja'farīyān (Tehran: Sāzmān-i Tabīghāt-i Islāmī, 1993), pp. 217–34.

3 *Faṣl al-khiṭāb* has not yet published. For a summary of this verse treatise, see Rasūl Ja'farīyān, 'Darbārah-'i faṣl al-khiṭāb', in *'Ilal-i bar'uftādan-i Ṣafavīyān: mukāfāt'nāmah*, ed. by Rasūl Ja'faīiyān (Tehran: Sāzmān-i Tabīghāt-i Islāmī, 1993), pp. 257–81.

4 See Rasūl Ja'farīyān, 'Darbārah-i risālah-'i ṭib al-mamālik'', in *'Ilal-i bar'uftādan-i Ṣafavīyān: mukāfāt'nāmah*, ed. by Rasūl Ja'farīyān (Tehran: Sāzmān-i Tabīghāt-i Islāmī, 1993), pp. 201–13 (p. 202).

5 Nayrīzī Shīrāzī, pp. 219–26.

6 Ibid., pp. 226–7.

7 Adding legitimacy to his claim, Karīm Khān pretended to rule on behalf of the infant Shāh Ismā'īl III (d. 1773), the grandson of the last Safavid sultan, who was placed on the throne in 1757 by him.

8 Karīm Khān Zand, quoted in Muḥammad Hāshim Āṣaf, *Rustam al-tavārīkh* (Tehran: Amīr Kabīr, 1973), pp. 395–6.

9 For a study on the perception of Iran's deficiency in early Qajar travel literature, see Monica M. Ringer, *Education, Religion, and the Discourse of Cultural Reform in Qajar Iran* (Costa Mesa, CA: Mazda Publishers, 2001), pp. 53–65.

10 Gadamer, p. 302.

11 Pierre Amédée Émilien Probe Jaubert, *Voyage En Arménie et En Perse, Fait Dans Les Années 1805 et 1806* (Paris: Pélicier [etc.], 1821), pp. 175–7, quoted in Ringer, p. 1.

12 For a helpful study on the reform from 1800 to 1848, see Vanessa Martin, 'An Evaluation of Reform and Development of the State in the Early Qājār Period', *Die Welt des Islams*, 36 (1996), 1–24.

13 For an in-depth study on *niẓām-i jadīd* under 'Abbās Mīrzā and his son Muḥammad Shāh, see Ringer, pp. 15–51.

14 'Ḥavādis'nāmah', trans. by Muḥammad Raẓī Tabrīzī (Tehran), MS Farsi / 80, The Iranian National Library. See Kitābkhānah-ʾi Millī-i Īrān, *Fihrist-i nusakh-i Khaṭṭī-i Kitābkhānah-i Millī-i Īrān*, ed. by 'Abd Allāh Anvār (Tehran: Kitābkhānah-i Millī-i Īrān, 1365), vol. 1, pp. 68–9.

15 'Tārīkh-i Iskandar', trans. by James Camel [?] (Tehran), MS Farsi/1680, the Iranian National Library. See Kitābkhānah-i Millī-i Īrān, vol. 4, pp. 155–6.

16 This is comparable with *The History of Persia* written by British Major-General Sir John Malcolm (1769–1833), which was published in India in 1815. This was the first nationalistic history of Iran in which the conquest of Iran by the Arabs was introduced as the cause of Iran's decline.

17 Edward Gibbon, 'Tārīkh-i tanazzul va kharabī-i dawlat-i Rūm', trans. by Mīrzā Riẓā Muḥandis (Tehran), Ms Farsi/66, The Iranian National Library. See Kitābkhānah-i Millī-i Īrān, vol. 1, pp. 56–7.

18 For further information about translations in Qajar Iran, see Seyed Ahmad Hashemi, 'Tarjumah: Tarjumah-i Fārsī dar Dawrah-i Muʿāsir: Qājār, Pahlavī, pas az inqilāb-i Islāmī', *Dānish'nāmah-i jahān-i Islām* <*Encyclopaedia of the World of Islam*> (Tehran: Kitāb-i Marjaʿ, 2002); Iraj Afshar, 'Book Translations as a Cultural Activity in Iran 1806–1896', *Iran*, 41 (2003), 279–89 <http://dx.doi.org/10.2307/4300649>.

19 Abbas Amanat discussed the significance of the dismissal, and later execution, of Amīr Kabīr in demonstrating the inherent weaknesses of ministerial power, and elaborated how such reformist attempts from above faced structural resistance from within and diplomatic pressure from without; see Abbas Amanat, 'The Downfall of Mirza Taqi Khan Amir Kabir and the Problem of Ministerial Authority in Qajar Iran', *International Journal of Middle East Studies*, 23 (1991), 577–99.

20 This point has been comprehensively discussed in Homa Katouzian's works, especially in his thoughtful study on the history of Iran, *The Persians*. In his words, 'for the first time in Iranian history they struck upon the most ancient and fundamental problem of the state and society, that is, arbitrary rule (*estebdad*), which revealed the *differentia specifica* between Iran and Europe: in the latter, lawful government and orderly society had been the rule rather than the exception.'(Katouzian, *The Persians*, p. 157). For further discussion on the theory of arbitrary rule as an approach to the study of Iranian society, see Katouzian, 'Arbitrary Rule'.

21 Mushīr al-Dawlah is Mīrzā Jaʿfar Muhandis, who was dispatched by ʿAbbās Mīrzā to England along with Mīrzā Ṣāliḥ Shīrāzī and three other students. He was also Iran's ambassador to the Ottoman Empire during 1252–59/1836–43.

22 Mīrzā Malkam Khān, 'Daftar-i tanẓīmāt yā kitābchah-ʾi ghaybī', in *Risālah'hā-yi Mīrzā Malkam Khān Nāẓim al-Dawlah*, ed. by Ḥujjat Allāh Aṣīl (Tehran: Nashr-i Nay, 1381), pp. 23–59 (p. 28).

23 Ibid., p. 29.

24 Ibid., p. 31.

25 Ibid., p. 39.

26 Mīrzā Malkam Khān, '[Īrān mamluvv ast az naʿamāt-i khudādād]', *Qānūn* (London, 1 Rajab 1307 / [21 February 1890]), no. 1, pp. 1–2 (p. 2).

27 Mīrzā Malkam Khān, '[Yikī az ḥarf'hā-yi tāzah-ʾi mā]', *Qānūn* (London, 1 Rajab 1307/ [28 February 1890]), no. 1, pp. 2–4 (p. 4).

28 Ibid., p. 2.

29 Mustashār al-Dawlah was closely familiar with the European lifestyle and its political system: he lived abroad and worked as a consul for almost 15 years (eight years in Ästerxan, four years in Tbilisi, and three years in Paris) and travelled to London four times.

30 Mīrzā Yūsuf Khān Mustashār al-Dawlah Tabrīzī, *Yik kalamah va yik nāmah* (Tehran: Intishārāt-i Ṣabāḥ, 1382), p. 38.

31 Ibid.

32 Ibid.

33 Fatḥ ʻAlī Ākhund'zādah, '[Letter to Mīrzā Yūsuf Khān Mustashār Al-Dawlah Tabrīzī (1872)]', in *Alifbā-yi jadīd va maktūbāt*, ed. by Ḥamīd Mūhammad'zādah (Tabriz: Nashr-i Iḥyāʾ, 1357), pp. 270–7 (p. 276).
34 He suggested his new script in 1875. See Fatḥ ʻAlī Ākhund'zādah, '[Autobiography]', in *Alifbā-yi jadīd va maktūbāt*, ed. by Ḥamīd Mūhammad'zādah (Tabriz: Nashr-i Iḥyāʾ, 1357), pp. 349–55 (p. 352).
35 Ākhund'zādah, '[Autobiography]', p. 354.
36 Fatḥ ʻAlī Ākhund'zādah, *Maktūbāt-i Kamāl al-Dawlah* ([n.p.]: Intishārāt-i Mard-i Imrūz, 1364), p. 61.
37 Fatḥ ʻAlī Ākhund'zādah, '[letter to Yūsuf Khān Mustashār al-Dawlah Tabrīzī (Mar. 1871)]', in *Alifbā-yi jadīd va maktūbāt* (Tabriz: Nashr-i Iḥyāʾ, 1357), pp. 199–202.
38 A counter approach was suggested by Sayyid Jamāl al-Dīn al-Afghānī (1838–97), the well-known reformist cleric. Instead of questioning Iran's decline, he always posed the question of Islam's decline. Examining his important diagnosis is beyond the scope of this paper. For an analysis of one of his essays on this issue, entitled *Chirā Islam ẕāʿīf shud?* [*Why has Islam become weak?*], see ʿAbd al-Hādī Ḥāʾirī, 'Afghani on the Decline of Islam', *Die Welt des Islams*, 13 (1971), 121–5; and ʿAbd al-Hādī Ḥāʾirī, 'Afghani on the Decline of Islam: A Postscript', *Die Welt des Islams*, 14 (1973), 116–28.
39 The Tobacco Revolt, as Katouzian pointed out, was an exceptional event in Iranian history. It was the first time that 'the arbitrary state had given in to a public demand rather than either suppressing it or being overthrown violently' (see Katouzian, *The Persians*, pp. 164–5; for a history of the revolt, see Nikki R. Keddie, *Religion and Rebellion in Iran: The Tobacco Protest of 1891–1892* (London: Cass, 1966)).
40 Mīrzā Abū Ṭālib Bihbahānī, 'Minhāj al-ʿUlā', in *Rasāʾil-i siyāsī-i ʿaṣr-i Qājār*, ed. by Ghulām Ḥusayn Zargarī'nizhād (Tehran: Kitābkhānah-i Millī-i Jumhūrī-i Islāmī-i Īrān, 2001), vol. 1, p. 276.
41 For an in-depth discussion of this point, see Homa Katouzian, 'The Revolution for Law: A Chronographic Analysis of the Constitutional Revolution of Iran', *Middle Eastern Studies*, 47 (2011), 757–77.
42 Thomas Jefferson to Isaac H. Tiffany, April 4, 1819, in Thomas Jefferson, *Political Writings: Representative Selections* (New York: Liberal Arts Press, 1955).
43 Mīrzā Malkam Khān, '[Yikī az ḥarf'hā-yi tāzah-ʾi mā]', pp. 2–4 (p. 4).
44 Homa Katouzian distinguishes three phases for Nāṣir al-Dīn Shāh's rule (1848–58, 1858–73, and 1973–96). In phase III, the shah 'contented himself with maintaining his own authority at home, managing foreign relations as best he could and continuing to enjoy hunting and women'. After his third European tour, as his brother ʿAbbās Mīrzā Mulk Ārā reported, the shah said to a group of the ruling elite: 'All the order and progress which we observed in Europe in our recent visit is due to the existence of law. Therefore, we too have made up our mind to introduce a law and act according to it' (see Katouzian, *The Persians*, p. 162).
45 See Nāṣir al-Dīn Shāh, 'Iʿlān-i rasmī-i dawlatī', *Īrān* (Tehran, 19 Ramadan 1305/ [30 May 1888]), p. 1. The English translation is quoted in George Nathaniel Curzon, *Persia and the Persian Question* (London: Longmans, Green, and Co., 1892), pp. 460–1.
46 Muḥammad Ḥasan Khān Iʿtimād al-Salṭanah, *Rūznāmah-ʾi khāṭirāt-i Iʿtimād al-Salṭanah*, ed. by Īraj Afshār (Tehran: Amīr Kabīr, 1343), p. 649.
47 Mīrzā Ibrāhīm Badāyiʿ'nigār, quoted in Khān Malak Sasānī, *Siyāsatgarān-i dawrah-ʾi Qājār* (Tehran: Kitābkhānah-ʾi Ṭuhūrī, 1338), p. 107.
48 Ḥāj Mullā ʿAlī Kanī's letter, Quoted in Ādamīyat, *Andīshah-ʾi taraqqī va ḥukūmat-i qānūn*, pp. 200–1.
49 Ādamīyat, *Andīshah-i taraqqī va ḥukūmat-i qānūn*, pp. 200–1.
50 For details, see Katouzian, 'Liberty and Licence in the Constitutional Revolution of Iran'.
51 See Katouzian, 'The Revolution for Law: A Chronographic Analysis of the Constitutional Revolution of Iran'.

2 The expansion of the meaning of freedom in the Iranian travelogues

The two near synonyms *āzādī* and *ḥurrīyat* are words that have been used in Persian poetry and prose for centuries. However, as late as 1907, when not only the elite but also common people congratulated themselves on the blessing of freedom, Ṭālibūf Tabrīzī called these words 'newly emerged' (*naw'ẓuhūr*) to emphasize that this '*āzādī*' was not the same as the old word that Iranians used to use in order to convey the sense of being free from jail and slavery.

> They said that Iranians have been given freedom (*ḥurrīyat*). I cannot understand the meaning of this newly emerged notion. Were we slaves that they liberated us (*azād kardand*)? Were we in jail that they released us?[1]

For him, 'the newly emerged word' of freedom was beyond Iranian narratives (*manqūlāt*). He asserted that 'no explanation has yet been written about this abstract word (*kalamah-ʾi mujarradah*) in our books . . . and obviously what is beyond our narratives seems to be beyond our reasoning (*maʿqūlāt*)'.[2] Nonetheless, since the early nineteenth century, Iranian travellers to Europe had employed the same word to report sociopolitical European freedoms. Encountering the new senses of freedom, they were also perplexed. They were not aware that using a familiar word to express new and unfamiliar contents might lead to misunderstanding and fallacious reasoning.

Through analyzing a selection of the Iranian travellers' reports on European freedoms in the nineteenth century, this chapter has two objectives: (1) to explore the expansion of sociopolitical conceptions of freedom in the Persian logosphere and everyday language; and (2) to illustrate the application of MacCallum's triadic frame of analysis to better understand the locutions of freedom.

The chapter pursues its aims in two parts: the first part provides the Persian terminology of freedom and the usage of the three words *āzādī, ḥurrīyat*, and *ikhtiyār* for explaining the new meanings of freedom in the late Qajar period. The second part, consisting of five sections, will focus on the expansion of the meaning of freedom. First, it analyzes an important report of European freedom in an Iranian travelogue written by Abū al-Ḥasan Khān Īlchī, Fatḥ ʿAlī Shāh's ambassador to London (1809–10), in order to show how the triadic frame assists in arriving at a more accurate understanding of the text. In the last section, this chapter studies more reports and explores four themes to which they attached importance: the limitations of the king's freedom to impose his arbitrary will, the parliamentary freedoms to establish laws and criticize the government, the freedom of religion, and the freedom of male-female relationships. These themes were also noticeably present in the disputes over freedom which occurred during the Constitutional Revolution.

2.1 The Persian terminology of freedom

Most linguists believe that the Persian word *āzādī* comes from the Avesta word *ā-zāta* and the Pahlavi word *āzāt*, which literally mean free, upright, and noble.[3] The closest Arabic word to this ancient word is '*ḥurrīya*'. Both '*āzādī*' and '*ḥurrīyah*' have been widely employed in Persian literature. Dihkhudā, an erudite scholar and political activist in the Constitutional Revolution, defines *āzādī* in his Persian *Lexicon* as:

> emancipation (*ʿitq*); freedom (*ḥurrīyat*); choice (*ikhtiyār*); opposite of servitude (*bandagī*) and slavery (*riqqīyat*) and submission (*ʿubūdīyat*) and captivity (*isārat*) and compulsion (*ijbār*); the ability to act or not to act; the ability to choose.[4]

It can be said that the word *ḥurrīyat* as an equivalent of the modern political term 'freedom' has been employed since the late eighteenth century. In 1798, Napoleon Bonaparte captured Egypt and made a speech in the name of the French Republic, which 'was shaped on the basis of liberty and equality'. Although it had not been widely accepted as an equivalent to the European terms of liberty or freedom, the Arabic word *ḥurrīya* was used as an equivalent to 'liberty' when Bonaparte's speech was translated into Arabic.[5] In Persian, the same word gradually became prevalent and stood for the modern sense of freedom. Riẓā Qulī Mīrzā, a grandson of Fatḥ ʿAlī Shāh, sometimes uses both '*ḥurrīyat*' and '*āzādī*' together in his travelogue, though freedom is a term associated with discourses on slavery and as an antonym of 'slavery and servitude' (*riqqīyat va bandagī*). By the terms 'western freedom', sometimes he means 'the abolition of slavery'. He blames Americans for hiring African slaves; however, he simultaneously uses freedom in another sense as he claims that 'the desirable rule of freedom' is more widely observed in America than in Britain and France.[6]

Overall, it seems that there were no tangible differences between the two words *āzādī* and *ḥurrīyat*. However, in writings whose styles are more Arabized and archaic, the word *ḥurrīyat* is employed more than the word *āzadī*. For instance, Nāʾīnī, a pro-constitutionalism religious leader settled in Najaf, uses '*ḥurrīyat*' and '*āzādī*' 44 and 39 times, respectively, in his *Tanbīh al-ummah wa tanzīh al-milla*, a Persian language book written in archaic prose and full of Arabic phrases and words.

The word '*ikhtiyār*' also was sometimes employed as an equivalent to the modern sense of 'freedom'. For instance, Malkam Khān, the founder of the *farāmush'khānah*, wrote the secret rules of this association in Arabic and used the word '*ikhtiyār*'. The reason why he used the word '*ikhtiyār*' instead of the more common Arabic word '*ḥurrīya*' is worthy of attention here. It seems that the theological indications of the term '*ikhtiyār*' as 'free will' and the whole debate on this issue in the entire history of Muslim thought provided Malkam Khān with a proper background for promoting the idea of freedom. Ādamīyat points out that the nineteenth-century writers used the word '*ikhtiyār*' to mean 'having free will' and 'freedom'. They deliberately avoided the word '*āzādī*' and instead employed a very familiar term from the terminology of Muslim philosophy.[7] In his Persian treatise *Ṣirāṭ al-mustaqīm*, Malkam Khān used the word '*ikhtiyār*' to convey the same sense:

> By *āzādī* we mean nothing but *ikhtiyār*, and by *ikhtiyār* we mean admirable *ikhtiyār*, not deplorable *ikhtiyār*. Because deplorable *ikhtiyār* which results in turmoil in the order of the Prophet's rule is against our purpose, and the foundation of the order of the cosmos is based on the rule of his highness.[8]

As late as 1907/1325, Muḥammad 'Alī Furūghī, who was the most educated writer in Western philosophy at his time, similarly preferred to employ the term *ikhtiyār* in the sense of freedom in his *Ḥuqūq-i asāsī yaʿnī ādāb-i mashrūṭīyat-i duval*.[9] It should be noted that he wrote his work when no standardized terminology for Iranian political thought had yet been developed. In such a logosphere, new ideas were being introduced to the society through terms that were not yet fixed, and therefore different terms have sometimes been inaccurately used to convey similar messages. Thus, besides the three words *āzādī*, *ḥurrīyat*, and *ikhtiyār*, one must trace the idea of freedom by investigating other relevant terms such as constitution (*mashrūṭah*), justice (*ʿadālat*), equality (*barābarī*), and law (*qānūn*). Nonetheless, usages of the words *ḥurrīyat* and *ikhtiyār* as equivalent words to modern 'freedom' did not last long, and gradually the word *āzādī* became the only standard word for this newly emerged concept.

2.2 The expansion of the meaning of freedom

The European sociopolitical freedoms were new phenomena for Iranian observers, and their accounts of these liberties failed to provide deep insight into the theoretical foundations of the idea. However, they could expand the meaning of the word '*āzādī*', which up to the time had often meant freedom from jail and freedom from slavery; it had also meant license. The expansion of the meaning of freedom is equivalent to the expansion of the interpretations of the three variables of freedom. In the rest of the chapter, I first analyze a report on the sociopolitical freedom of the British people as a sample of this expansion of meaning, and then I further illustrate the point through examining four significant themes of the travelogues.

2.2.1 Freedom of the British people

In his travelogue titled *The Ambassadors' Wonder-letter* (*Ḥayrat'namah-'i sufarā*), Mīrzā Abū al-Ḥasan Khān Īlchī revealed what he called 'the harmlessness and freedom of the people of London' through reporting the popular uprising of 1810. Providing supplementary clarifications in the footnotes, I first quote his account, and then show how it can be analyzed using MacCallum's framework.

According to Īlchī:

> A Member of the British Parliament, Sir Francis Burdett, rebelled against the King's decree . . . and rebuked the ministers and the king, and disturbed the parliament's and government's affairs, saying that the king and the story of expenditure (*ikhrājāt*) are not necessary.[10] He disagreed with the *kūsil's*[11] vote, and accordingly, by the verdict of the parliament, he should be imprisoned and kept in jail for three months; after the opening of the parliament, he will be released at the discretion of *kūsil*. However, the people who supported him were preventing (the soldiers) from arresting him.[12]

At night, Burdett's supporters threw stones at the ministers' and *kūsiliyān's* houses. The next day, while the unrest was still going on, Īlchī asked the guards:

> Why has the turmoil not calmed down? They answered that the members of the *kūthil* had not yet finished their deliberations to allow us to enter the house in order to take the culprit to the king's jail. This answer filled me with increasing wonder; for if such a massive crowd [of people] and such incompetence [of the state in its suppression] had occurred in an Iranian city . . . more than ten thousand people would have been killed.[13]

At this point, Īlchī uses the word freedom, stating 'this report aimed to reveal the benevolence, harmlessness, and freedom of the people of this city as nobody would be punished until proven guilty in order to avoid persecution of an innocent person'.[14] One day later, the city was still in turmoil when, in a meeting, Īlchī told a British lord:

> The power of the kingdom is more in the suppression of the revolt than in (giving) this much freedom. . . . Your enemy, Napoleon Bonaparte, is laying in ambush for you, and . . . some ordinary people have been wronged by the event. What kind of freedom is this that causes damages and certainly undermines the pillars of the state of England? Ministers, governors and nobles of the state should find a remedy for this affair. An ounce of prevention is worth a pound of cure.[15]

Īlchī finishes his account by reporting Burdett's arrest and imprisonment. He was also surprised by the way the prisoner was treated: 'He received a three-month prison sentence, and after three months he would be released and reappointed as a representative of the subjects. And while in prison, he would not be in chains and his friends could see him'.[16]

Now, let us translate Īlchī's explanation of the freedoms of Londoners into MacCallum's triadic structure. In this text, Īlchī uses the word freedom three times. At first glance, neither his style of writing nor his pronouncement on freedom is sufficiently clear. Nevertheless, it can be seen that his understanding of freedom is tied to the concept of law. As I understand it, Īlchī explicitly or implicitly makes five points about freedom in London:

(1) Burdett, as a Member of British Parliament, is not free *from* legal restraints (here by the verdict of parliament) *to* rebel against the king's decree, *to* rebuke the ministers and the king, and *to* disturb parliamentary and governmental affairs.
(2) Burdett as a guilty person sentenced to imprisonment is free *from* soldiers' intrusion on his privacy without a legal warrant *to* bar himself in his house; in other words, the soldiers missioned to arrest Burdett are not free *from* the legal restraints *to* intrude on his privacy without a legal warrant.
(3) Londoners are free *from* any legal or arbitrary persecution and punishment until proven guilty *to* protest for supporting their rebel MP.
(4) Burdett as a political prisoner during his stay in prison is free *from* any legal or arbitrary restraint *to* not to be in chains[17] (*ghul va zanjīr*), *to* receive visits, and *to* have contact with the outside world.
(5) After release, Burdett is free *from* any legal or arbitrary restraint *to* return to his MP position.

This analysis shows that Īlchī's report does not express only one sense of freedom, but rather refers to five different interpretations of freedom, though he is probably not aware of the differences. These differences in his usage of freedom are rooted in differing identifications of the three variables of agent, constraints, and purpose of freedom. The distinction is significant not only in conceptual terms but also in the practical sense of realizing or attaining freedoms in society. In any given society, some of these freedoms might be present whereas others might be absent. Furthermore, a given social movement might encourage the realization of some of these freedoms while discouraging others. It will be seen that none of these freedoms existed in Iran when Īlchī wrote his travel accounts.

Nonetheless, in his conversation with the British lord, Īlchī does not refer to all of the five aforementioned freedoms; rather, he is only concerned about the freedom in protesting against the state. His argument against 'giving this much freedom' can be reformulated as follows: (1) Security has priority over freedom. (2) Sometimes certain individual freedoms threaten domestic/national security and lead to chaotic conditions. Therefore, for the sake of domestic/national security or for the safety of the citizens, the government may and must restrict some individual and civil freedoms. Īlchī's opinion indeed provides an answer to the question of the relative importance of several social values when they come into conflict with each other. Such a question, as John Rawls points out, is not concerned with the definition of freedom at all, but rather with a theory of rights and justice.[18] We will return to this issue later.

2.2.2 Freedom of the British king

The limits to the freedom of British kings is one of the noticeable aspects of the European freedom observed by the Persians. This issue has been reported differently in their travel accounts, with the common thread being that the king of England, in contrast to the shah of Iran, does not enjoy absolute freedom, but is rather obligated to observe the law and to respect the nobles and the representatives of the peoples.

Iʿtiṣām al-Dīn, a Persian-speaking resident of India who travelled to England in 1768, wrote a relatively detailed account on the legal power and freedom of the British king. I translate his account into triadic structure as follows: the king is not free *from* the constraint of observing the rules of justice (*āyīn-i ʿadālat*) and *from* the nobles' approbation (*ṣavābdīd-i ruʾasā-yi qawm*) *to* govern arbitrarily and *to* be 'cruel, ill-natured, selfish, unaware and ignorant' (*ẓālim, bad'nafs, khvud'gharaẕ, bī'vuqūf, nādān*). The king is only free *to* declare war and peace.[19] Iʿtiṣām al-Dīn's utterance does not make clear whether the king is free *from* all restraints *to* declare war and peace, or whether he is still constrained to observe the rules of justice and the approbation of nobles.

According to ʿAbd al-Laṭīf Mūsavī Jazāyirī Shūshtarī, another Persian-speaking resident of India who wrote *Tuḥfat al-ʿālam* in 1801, the king, before making his military decisions, summons governors and representatives and asks for their written consultations: 'Considering all opinions, he decrees in conformity with the majority. When the numbers of pro and con votes are equal, the king is free and holds the casting vote. Then nobody may change the decision'.[20]

Shūshtarī also mentions the history of the transformation of 'absolute and arbitrary rule' (*ḥukmrānī-i bil-istiqlāl val-infirād*) to 'limited kingship' (*salṭanat-i maṣlūb al-ikhtiyār*) based on consultation with the House of Parliament (*khānah-ʾi mashvarat*). The aim of this transformation, according to him, is 'the regulation of kingship' (*intiẓām-i salṭanat*) and the prevention of 'corruption and bloodshed'. After such reform, the king is not free *to* 'kill or harm anyone even his servants' but he is free *to* 'reward and prize anyone' and *to* pardon three condemned to death each year.[21]

However, an Iranian resident of India named Mīrzā Abū Ṭālib Khān Iṣfahānī (1752–1806), who travelled to Europe from 1799 till 1803, assumed that the king of England is absolutely free in all governmental affairs and that he has the power to forgive criminals and to overturn a court's capital punishment. Furthermore, the king is potentially free *to* do 'any unconventional and illegal act' (*kār-i ghayr-i mustamar va khalāf-i qānūn*) since he is the only one who commands the armed forces (*qūvah-ʾi qahrīyah*). However, the king prudently looks ahead and knows that if he neglects to consult the Parliament or rejects their advice, turmoil and public unrest (*balvā-yi ʿām*) will follow and the king will lose control.[22] Nevertheless, Mīrzā Abū Ṭālib mentioned that the king had deprived himself of the right to oust judges so that they may judge without fear. Mīrzā Abū Ṭālib realized that the king cannot actually use his potential freedom[23] and that in practice, 'the king and rulers do not take any action without the Parliament's order'.[24]

Along similar lines, Mīrzā Muḥammad Ṣāliḥ Shīrāzī, who studied in England between 1815 and 1819, narrated the story of a London craftsman whose shop was located on the right-of-way but for six months had refused to evacuate. Even the king had no power to coerce him to sell the land. Mīrzā Ṣāliḥ wondered at how this freedom was compatible with a lawful and orderly system. He went on to state that

> A land with such security and freedom which is called 'the land of freedom' (*vilāyat-i āzādī*) . . . has been regulated to such a point that all people, king or street beggar, are constrained by the country's system (*niẓām-i vilāyatī*). Anyone who slightly deviates from and opposes such regulations will be punished. Nobody is able to deviate, and in spite of the freedom (*dar ʿayn-i āzādī*), all people, young or old, are bound by the regulations so that nobody is able to violate them (*mukhālifat*).[25]

A translation of Mīrzā Ṣāliḥ's utterance in MacCallum's formula would be as follows: people of England, king or beggar (in spite of freedom), are not free *from* the constraint of the rules and regulations of the country (*niẓām-i vilāyatī*)[26] *to* commit what would be deviation from, or in disagreement with, the *niẓām-i vilāyatī*.

Mīrzā Ṣāliḥ did not clearly identify the constraint and purpose of the freedom of British agents. He only determined what they were not free to do. His utterance indicated a significant concern: how can one be free and simultaneously be bound by rules and regulations? This concern shows that in the horizon within which Mīrzā Ṣāliḥ's contemporary audience perceived it, there was a prevalent misperception of freedom as chaos and license. In other words, some people tended to think of freedom as freedom *from* all constraints *to* do whatever they wanted.

2.2.3 Freedom of the members of the British parliament

The Iranian observers of freedom in England also perceived the significant role of the parliament in restricting the king's absolute freedom. The members of the parliament were elected by the people without the state's interference.[27] This independence let them exercise freedom of speech and criticism during ordinary parliamentary proceedings.

Mīrzā Ṣāliḥ's report on the MP's freedom of speech can be reformulated as follows: a member of the Parliament is free *from* any preventing constraints (whether legal or arbitrary) *to* 'express whatever comes into his mind about the country's affairs and other issues'.[28] In this utterance, the phrase 'and other issues' not only fails to clarify the third variable of freedom, but actually makes it vaguer.

Mīrzā Abū Ṭālib's observation of the Parliament of England during the last year of William Pitt's Prime Ministry (1783–1801) showed that total freedom could not be exercised in practice. Mīrzā Abū Ṭālib visited the Parliament several times and 'through accurate observation' (*bih naẓar-i im'ān*) saw it as 'fooling the subjects and deceiving the common people' (*maẕḥakah bar ru'āyā va farīb-i 'avām*). To him, MPs 'seemed like parrots whose speeches belonged to someone else behind the curtain, namely Mr. Pitt, . . . but were the Chief Minister not so independent, the Parliament would be powerful and would reap many benefits'.[29]

Mīrzā Mahdī Khān Mumtaḥin al-Dawlah Shaqāqī (1843–1920), a student of the Dār al-Funūn who was dispatched to Paris to study architecture in 1857 and returned to Iran seven years later, mentioned his visit to the British Parliament in his travel accounts. His wistful discussion on the MPs' boldness and freedom of speech (*tajarrī va āzādī-i zabān*) can be formulated as follows: the British MPs are free *to* criticize 'the existence of their king' (*vujūd-i pādishāh-i khvud*). This utterance is extremely brief. It neither refers to the constraint of freedom, nor does it clearly explain the purpose of freedom. As can be grasped from the context, this brevity is deliberate. He was embarrassed to describe the freedoms of Europe since he believed that readers were not ready to listen to such issues due to 'the ethical corruption of governors'. He wished that after 50 or 100 years, his countrymen would become capable of 'understanding the status of civilized people' (*dark-i maqām-i mutamaddinīn*) through the development of knowledge and compulsory education.[30]

2.2.4 Freedom of religion in Russia and England

In both Iranian travellers' observations of European freedom and in the Iranian elite's reflections on such freedom, freedom of religion was given special attention. Although this freedom was not a new issue in the Iranian tradition, this was the first time that it was being discussed as an individual right. In chapter five, I will address the question of freedom of religion in the late Qajar era. For the time being, a brief look at the Iranian reports provides a blueprint of the issue.

In his travelogue, Muṣṭafá Afshār (d. 1829), an official secretary of 'Abbās Mīrzā's court in Tabriz who accompanied the Iranian diplomatic mission to Russia in 1829, described freedom of religion in Russia as follows: different religious sects in Russia are free *from* any obstacle *to* observe 'the rituals of their religion' (*ṭā'āt-i muqarrarah dar maẕhab-i khvud*). Afshār traced this freedom and the prohibition of 'interference in and distortion of [others'] religion and faith' (*dakhl-u-taṣarruf bih maẕhab va dīn*) in an official order by the Russian Emperor which was issued 44 years earlier.[31]

Afshār's discussion on freedom of religion is relatively brief. The agents of this freedom, as he declares, are Armenians, Jews, Muslims, Catholics, Protestants, and 'some other sects'. Based on the context, the obstacle from which they are free may be the interferences of the state or those of other believers (and even unbelievers). Identifying the purpose of freedom, only one aspect of religion, namely 'rituals', is mentioned, while the other two aspects of religion related to beliefs and interactions between believers (in Islam: *i'tiqādāt* and *mu'āmilāt*) remain unspoken. Yet the questions are whether Russian believers are free *to* proselytize and *to* publicize their beliefs and *to* observe the religious precepts regulating their social interactions and *to* enforce religious sanctions (*hudūd va ta'zīrāt*).

I'tiṣām al-Dīn also reports on freedom of religion in England. According to him, Christians were fanatic so that if a Muslim in their city 'loudly called to prayer (*adān*) or exposed the Islamic signs (*shi'ār-i Islām*), they burned him alive'. However, the motto of England was 'total peace' (*ṣulḥ-i kull*) and therefore Muslims in England were free *from* anyone's preventions (*ta'arruẓ*) *to* 'construct mosques and *to* say prayers (*namāz*) and *to* fast'.[32]

2.2.5 Freedom of male-female intimacy

In the religious society of nineteenth-century Iran, women were traditionally prevented from being seen by men. The practice of concealing women from men (*pardah'nishīnī*) was implemented by both the physical segregation of the sexes and women's veils. Iranian travellers accustomed to such a tradition were filled with wonder when encountering public male-female intimacy in Europe. They devoted pages of their travel accounts to describing the spectacle of women's appearance in public parks, parties, playhouse, ballrooms, and coffeehouses.[33] Although it was rare for Iranian travellers to openly demand such freedoms in their reports, religious opponents of freedom always accused them of desiring debauchery and licentiousness. The question of the freedom of women will be addressed in a separate chapter of this book; at present, I only mention two preliminary utterances on this issue.

In a relatively comprehensive observation of freedom in England, Mīrzā Abū Ṭālib Iṣfahānī asserted that the English laws of freedom (*qavānīn-i āzādī*) included spiritual peace and wisdoms. Translated into the triadic relation, his utterance of freedom can be reformulated as follows: the people of England are free *from* fear, violent threat, and the anger of rulers (*ghaẓab-i ḥukkām*) *to* do 'whatever does not harm anyone or violate any laws' (*har kārī kih mūjib-i iẓrār-i kasī yā shikastan-i qānūnī nashavad*).[34] He accurately identified the criteria for determining the purpose of freedom as that which does not harm others or violate the law. He went on to emphasize that 'it is not true that everyone can do whatever he wants'[35] (*nah īn kih har kas har kār khvāstah bāshad, tavānad kard*).

Mīrzā Abū Ṭālib referred to various examples of the purpose of freedom: to go along the alleys and shop whenever one desires, to go to brothels (*khānah-'i zanān-i ubāsh*), to walk hand in hand with one's wife or beloved in a garden, to openly (*'alā ru'ūs al-ashhād*) criticize kings and ministers by means of speech, picture, and book (*bih zabān va taṣvīr va kitāb*).[36] This clearly shows that his perception of freedom not only implies the political sense of the concept but also includes its social aspects, such as the freedom of movement and mobility as well as the freedom of male-female intimacy. Referring to fear (*khawf*), he integrates the concept of security into the notion of freedom; this is why he expresses his admiration for the ability to walk around the city freely, shop, and carry the purchases home in safety.

Likewise, ʿAbd al-Laṭīf Shūshtarī gave graphic descriptions of the public display of European women and male-female intimacy in ballrooms and cabarets (*khānah-ʾi raqṣ va bayt al-surūr*).[37] A translation of his utterance of *farangī* women's freedom into MacCallum's formula would be as such: a *farangī* woman is free *from* the constraints of her husband's prevention *to* socialize (*nishast-u-barkhāst*) and enjoy intimacy with a stranger (*jūshish bā mard-i bīgānah*).[38] According to him, the law guarantees such freedom for women in England, and cultural custom completely tolerates the unveiling of women. Interestingly enough, he mentions that 'this obscenity (*amr-i qabīḥ*) originated from America and spread through France . . . to the rest of *Farangistān*'.[39]

2.3 Concluding remarks

The preceding analyses show that although the Iranian travellers did not investigate the theoretical foundations of freedom, they perceived that freedom was an outstanding characteristic of the Western world. They provided relatively comprehensive accounts of the representations of freedom in European sociopolitical life. Translating their utterances into the triadic structure, I have illustrated the variety of their observations in identifying the three variables of agent, constraint, and purpose of freedom. Tables 2.1 and 2.2 compare these differences.

Table 2.1 Europeans are free to do

reporter (date of account)	*x is free from y to do (become) z*		
	agent (x)	*constraint (y)*	*purpose (z)*
Iʿtiṣām al-Dīn (1768)	the king of England	***	to declare war and peace
ʿAbd al-Laṭīf Shūshtarī (1801)		***	to reward anyone and to pardon three condemned to death yearly
Mīrzā Abū Ṭālib Iṣfahānī (1799–1803)		***	to forgive criminals and to overturn the court's death sentence; to do any unconventional and illegal act (*kār-i ghayr-i mustamar va khalāf-i qānūn*)
Mīrzā Ṣāliḥ Shīrāzī (1815–19)	the members of British Parliament	any preventing constraints (whether legal or arbitrary)	to express whatever comes into his mind regarding the country's affairs and other issues
Mumtaḥin al-Dawlah Shaqāqī (1857–64)		***	to criticize the existence of their king (*vujūd-i pādishāh-i khvud*)

Table 2.1 Continued

reporter (date of account)	*x is free from y to do (become) z*		
	agent (x)	*constraint (y)*	*purpose (z)*
Muṣṭafá Afshār (1829)	different religious sects in Russia (including Armenians, Jews, Muslims, Catholics, Protestants)	any obstacle	to perform the worships assigned in their religion (*ṭāʿāt-i muqarrarah dar maẕhab-i khvud*)
Iʿtiṣām al-Dīn (1768)	Muslims in England	anyone's preventions (*taʿarruẓ*)	to construct mosques and *to* say prayers (*namāz*) and to fast
Mīrzā Abū-Ṭālib Iṣfahānī (1799–1803)	the people of England	fear, violent threat and the anger of the rulers (*ghaẓab-i ḥukkām*)	to do whatever does not cause harm to anyone or violate any law; to go to brothels; to walk hand in hand with his wife or beloved in a garden; to openly criticize kings and ministers by means of speech, picture, and book
ʿAbd al-Laṭīf Shūshtarī (1801)	*farangī* women	the constraints of his husband's prevention	to socialize (*nishast-u-barkhāst*) and enjoy intimacy with a stranger (*jūshish bā mard-i bīgānah*)

Table 2.2 Europeans are not free to do

reporter (date of account)	*x is not free from y to do (become) z*		
	agent (x)	*constraints (y)*	*purpose (z)*
Iʿtiṣām al-Dīn (1768)	the king of England	observing the rules of justice (*āʾīn-i ʿadālat*) and the nobles' approbations (*ṣavābdīd-i ruʾasā-yi qawm*)	to govern arbitrarily and to be cruel, ill-natured, selfish, unaware, and ignorant
Mīrzā Abū Ṭālib Iṣfahānī (1799–1803)		law (the rules limiting the kingship)	to kill or harm anyone, even his servants
Mīrzā Ṣaliḥ Shīrāzī (1815–1819)		the rules and regulations of the country (*niẓām-i vilāyatī*)	to do what would be a deviation from or in disagreement with the *niẓām-i vilāyatī*
Mīrzā Abū-Ṭālib Iṣfahānī (1799–1803)	the members of British Parliament	the Prime Minister William Pitt's influence	to speak freely during ordinary parliamentary proceedings

Notes

1 ʿAbd al-Raḥīm Ṭālibūf Tabrīzī, 'Īẕāḥāt dar khuṣūṣ-i āzādī', in *Āzādī va siyāsat*, ed. by Īraj Afshār (Tehran: Saḥar, 1366), p. 87.
2 Ibid.
3 Paul Horn and Heinrich Hübschmann, *Asās-i ishtiqāq-i fārsī*, trans. by Jalāl Khāliqī'muṭlaq (Tehran: Bunyād-i Farhang-i Īrān, 1356), vol. 1, p. 23.
4 For many examples of the different usages of the word *āzādī* in classic Persian poetry and prose, see 'Alī Akbar Dihkhudā, *Lughat'nāmah* (Tehran: Chāpkhānah-'i Majlis, 1325), s.v. 'āzādī', 'āzādagī' and 'āzādah'.
5 See Bernard Lewis, 'Islam and Liberal Democracy: A Historical Overview', *Journal of Democracy*, 7:2 (1996), 52–63 (pp. 57–8). In 1783, the Ottoman dragomen were faced with the new notion of 'political freedom' or 'independence' in preparing a Turkish text for a treaty between the Russian empire and the Ottoman sultan. They did not use the terms *ḥur* and *ḥurrīyet* as Turkish equivalents for such a term; rather, they employed the Persian word *serbest* (meaning *āzād*), which became the common Turkish term for 'freedom' during nineteenth-century Ottoman reforms (Lewis, *The Political Language of Islam*, pp. 109–11). For instance, the first Ottoman reform decree of 1839, *ḥatt-i sherīf-i gulḥāne*, issued by Sultān Ḥamīd, contained the following clause: 'Everyone shall possess and dispose of his possession and his property in complete freedom [*kemāl-i serbestīyette*], without interference from any quarter' (cited in Bernard Lewis, *Political Words and Ideas in Islam* (Princeton, NJ: Markus Wiener Publishers, 2008), p. 13).
6 See Riẕā Qulī Mīrzā, *Safarnāmah-'i Riẕā Qulī Mīrzā navah-'i Fatḥ 'Alī Shāh*, ed. by Aṣghar Farmānfarmā'ī Qājār (Tehran: Dānishgāh-i Tihrān, 1346), pp. 525–7.
7 Ādamīyat, *Andīshah-i taraqqī va ḥukūmat-i qānūn*, p. 66.
8 Mīrzā Malkam Khān, 'Sirāṭ al-mustaqīm', in *Risālah'hā-yi Mīrzā Malkam Khān Nāẓim al-Dawlah* (Tehran: Nashr-i Nay, 1381), pp. 433–98 (p. 481).
9 See Muḥammad ʿAlī Furūghī, 'Ḥuqūq – i asāsī yaʿnī ādāb – i mashrūṭīyat – i duval', in *Rasāʾil-i mashrūṭīyat: mashrūṭah bih ravāyat-i muvāfiqān va mukhālifān*, ed. by Ghulām Ḥusayn Zargarī'nizhād, 2 vols. (Tehran: Intishārāt-i Muʿassisah-ʾi Taḥqīqāt va Tawsiʿah-ʾi ʿUlūm-i Insānī, 2008), vol. 1, pp. 773–843 (p. 831).
10 This part of the report is not accurate. In fact, Sir Francis Burdett (1770–1844) came into conflict with the House of Commons in 1810 as a strong voice for parliamentary reform. When the House sentenced a radical named John Gale to imprisonment, Burdett tried to release him and denounced a proceeding, 'denying the power of the House of Commons to imprison the people of England'. A revised version of the proceeding was published in a weekly newspaper. See Francis Burdett, *Sir Francis Burdett to His Constituents: Denying the Power of the House of Commons to Imprison the People of England* (London: Printed for R. Bagshaw, and J. Budd, 1810). For more information, see Melville Watson Patterson, *Sir Francis Burdett and His Times (1770–1844)* (London: Macmillan and Co., Limited, 1931).
11 The word '*kūsil*' (كوئل) must be a distorted transliteration of an English word (maybe 'castle' or 'council' or less probably 'consul'). However, none of them is correct in this context. As mentioned in the previous note, the correct word would be 'the House of Commons'.
12 Abū al-Ḥasan Khān Īlchī, *Ḥayrat'nāmah: safar'nāmah-'i Mīrzā abū al-Ḥasan Khān Īlchī bih Landan* (Tehran: Mu'assasah-i Khadamāt-i Farhangī-i Rasā, 1364), p. 254.
13 Ibid., p. 256.
14 Ibid.
15 Ibid., pp. 256–7.
16 Ibid., p. 257.
17 This could also be formulated as freedom *from* being chained.
18 Rawls, pp. 176–8.

19 I'tiṣām al-Dīn, *Shigaf'nāmah-'i vilāyat* quoted in Ḥā'irī, p. 122.
20 'Abd al-Laṭīf ibn Abī Ṭālib Jazā'irī, *Tuḥfat al-'ālam va zayl al-tuḥfah* (Tehran: Kitābkhānah-i Ṭahūrī, 1363), p. 277.
21 Ibid., p. 276.
22 Mīrzā Abū Ṭālib Khān Īṣfahānī, *Masīr-i Ṭālibī* (Tehran: Intishāt-i 'Ilmī va Farhangī, 1363), vol. 2, p. 239.
23 This potential freedom was a thing of his imagination, a reflection of the actual freedom of rulers in the east.
24 Mīrzā Abū Ṭālib Khān Iṣfahānī, vol. 2, p. 242.
25 Mīrzā Muḥammad Ṣāliḥ Shīrāzī, *Guzārish-i safar*, ed. by H. Shahīdī (Tehran: Rāh-i Naw, 1373), p. 205.
26 By '*niẓām-i vilāyatī*', Mīrzā Ṣāliḥ apparently meant the law.
27 Mīrzā Ṣāliḥ's report on the British citizens' freedom to choose is clearly translatable into the triadic structure: the British citizens are free *from* the interference of the state *to* choose the Lord Mayor and the representatives of the House of Commons (Mīrzā Muḥammad Ṣāliḥ Shīrāzī, pp. 281–2, 310–12).
28 Ibid., p. 312.
29 Mīrzā Abū Ṭālib Khān Iṣfahānī, vol. 2, p. 242.
30 Mīrzā Mahdī Khān Mumtaḥin al-Dawlah Mahdī Khān Shaqāqī, *Khāṭirāt-i Mumtaḥin al-Dawlah* (Tehran: Firdawsī, 1362), pp. 212–13.
31 Muṣṭafá Afshār, *Safar'nāmah-'i Khusraw Mīrzā bih Piṭirzbūrgh*, ed. by M. Gulbun (Tehran: Kitābkhānah-'i Mustawfī, 1349), pp. 327–8.
32 I'tiṣām al-Dīn, *Shigraf'nāmah-'i vilāyat* quoted in Ḥā'irī, p. 122.
33 For a study on imagining European women in Iranian travel accounts, see Mohamad Tavakoli-Targhi, *Refashioning Iran: Orientalism, Occidentalism, and Historiography* (Houndmills, Basingstoke, Hampshire; New York: Palgrave, 2001), pp. 54–76.
34 Mīrzā Abū Ṭālib Khān Iṣfahānī, vol. 2, p. 231.
35 Ibid.
36 Ibid.
37 Jazā'irī, pp. 264–7.
38 Ibid., p. 266.
39 Ibid.

3 Freedom *from*

The question of legislation

On 5 August 1906 (14 Jumada II, 1324), in what came to be known as the Constitutional Decree (*farmān-i mashrūṭiyat*),[1] Muẓaffar al-Dīn Shāh enacted to form a National Consultative Assembly (*majlis-i shūrā-yi millī*) for the sake of 'the peace and tranquillity of all the people of Iran' and for the strengthening of 'the foundations of the state'. Two months later, this majlis began its work as the first legislative parliament in Iran and also shouldered the responsibility of the legislation of the constitution. Through the law, the majlis attempted to control the arbitrary rule and absolute power of the shah and the government; and on the other hand, it prevented the people from violating the rights of others. As an institution that intended to determine the limitations of the freedom of the government and that of the people, such a majlis faced a fundamental question from its early days: to what extent and wherefore is the majlis considered a legitimate authority to make the laws which impose limitations on the freedoms of individuals?

The first majlis was illegally shut down after almost 21 months, and arbitrary rule returned for a period of 13 months (known as *istibdād-i ṣaghīr*). Unlike the first one, the second constitutional period was achieved through an armed and bloody uprising, and the second majlis was inaugurated after Muḥammad ʿAlī Shāh was overthrown. This significant alteration in the political arrangement somewhat alleviated the struggle between the monarchy and the majlis, and changed the priorities of legislation.

Assessing the parliamentary proceedings and the laws enacted by the first two Parliaments, in this chapter I compare the first constitutional period (August 1906–June 1908) with the second (July 1909–February 1921), while addressing the question of the legitimacy of the majlis as well as the following questions: What were the criteria based on which the legislators deemed an action to be free? What freedoms were recognized for Iranian people in these parliamentary laws, and which of the government's interferences in the people's freedoms were allowed? Did these legal interferences aim to ensure that an activity would not go beyond certain bounds, or were they intended to ensure that the activity would also result in certain consequences? What legal mechanisms were enacted to protect a person's freedom against the interferences of the state and other people? These questions address different aspects of the issue of the imposition and enforcement of legal obligations on a person's activities. Answering such questions will clarify the Iranian elite's understandings of the second variable of the triadic formula of freedom.

3.1 The Constitutional Decree: an answer to which question?

Along with three other legal documents, the Constitutional Decree was regarded as one of the four pillars of the Iranian Constitutional Revolution.[2] However, the text of this first pillar does not clearly declare what structure it intends to establish. The decree's text is as follows:

> To the Right Honourable His Excellency the Prime Minister,
>
> Whereas God Most High (glorious is His state!) has entrusted to Our hands the direction of the progress and prosperity of the well-protected realms of *Iran*, and has constituted Our Royal Personage the Guardian of the rights of all the people of *Iran* and all Our loyal subjects, therefore on this occasion, Our Royal and Imperial judgement has decided, for the peace and tranquillity of all the people of *Iran*, and for *strengthening the* foundations of the State, that such reforms as are this day required in the different departments of the State and of the Empire shall be effected; and we do enact that *a National* Assembly of delegates elected by *the men of Qajar descent (shāhzādigān), the ʿulamā, the nobles and notables (aʿyān), the men of wealth (ashrāf)*, the landowners (*mallākīn*), the merchants and the guilds (*aṣnāf*), by election of the above mentioned classes shall be formed and constituted, in the capital Tehran; which [*majlis*] shall carry out the requisite *consultation and deliberation* on all necessary subjects connected with important affairs of the State and Empire and the public interest; and shall render the necessary help and assistance to Our Cabinet of Ministers in such reforms as are designed to promote the happiness and well-being of *Iran*; and shall, with complete confidence and security, through the instrumentality of the first Lord of the State, submit *their opinions (ʿaqāʾd-i khvud) on the state's and the nation's happiness and the public interests and demands*, so that these, having been duly ratified by us, may be carried into effect.
>
> It is evident that, in accordance with this blessed rescript, from this moment [the majlis or the Prime Minister?] will determine and prepare the code (*niẓām'nāmah*) and regulations of this majlis and the provisions and necessities for its formation, being enacted and signed by elected delegates and after receiving Royal Approval, by the help of God Most High, the majlis, which is the guardian of the justice, may be inaugurated and may start the necessary reforms in governmental affairs, and the implementation of the holy sharia laws.
>
> We likewise enact that *[they or you?]* should publish and proclaim the text of *this blessed* rescript, so that all the people of *Iran*, being duly informed of Our good intentions, all of which regard the progress of the government and *nation of Iran*, may, with tranquil minds, engage in prayer for *the government and this indestructible majlis (majlis – i bī'zavāl)*.

Given [under our hand] in the *Ṣāḥib'qirānīyah* Palace, on 14th of Jumada II in the 11th year of Our Reign.[3]

Making no mention of the constitutionalism of the Iranian monarchy, the *farmān* only promised to establish an institution named '*majlis-i shūrā-yi millī*'. It is evident from the text that the aims of this majlis are 'the peace and tranquillity and progress', and that its members are delegates whom classes and guilds have elected by themselves.[4] However, the responsibilities of the majlis are still not clear. In the text, the majlis is requested to conduct the following tasks: (a) consult and deliberate on all necessary subjects pertaining to important governmental affairs and public interest, (b) assist and help the cabinet in the reforms, (c) submit their opinions to the Shah, (d) enact and sign the standing order (*niẓām'nāmah*) and regulations of this majlis, (e) start the necessary reforms in governmental affairs and the implementation of the holy sharia laws, and (f) also in a relative clause, the majlis is introduced as the guardian of the justice.

Each of these explanations, however, may lead to confusion over the definition and functions of the majlis: (a) is the consultation an act between the members of the majlis to reach an agreement or an act between the majlis and the government? In other words, is the majlis merely a consulting institution? (b) How does the majlis assist the government in reforms? Are these assistances administrative or advisory? Or are they regarded as interactions between the independent legislative power and the executive power? (c) What does the *farmān* mean by 'representatives' opinion (*ʿaqāyid*)'? Does it refer to the parliamentary enactments that should receive the Royal Approval to be implemented, or does it merely refer to comments which are allowed to be submitted to the Shah as constructive advice? (d) By the word '*niẓām'nāmah*', which is followed by the phrase '*va tartībāt-i īn majlis* (and the regulations of this majlis)', does the writer mean '*niẓām'nāmah-ʾi īn majlis* (the code of this majlis)' or '*niẓām'nāmah-ʾi* [*asāsī*] (the constitution)'? (e) Is the phrase 'the implementation of the holy sharia laws' a prepositional phrase (whose preposition 'in' is omitted) used as a modifier of 'the necessary reforms', or is it a noun phrase conjunct to the phrase 'the governmental affairs'? In other words, is the majlis supposed to start the implementation of the sharia or to start the necessary reforms for its implementation? That is to say, which one of the following affairs is the responsibility of the majlis: the implementation of the sharia or preparations for its implementation? (f) Does the relative clause 'the majlis, which is the guardian of justice' mean that it functions as an independent judicial court (*ʿadālat'khānah*) and takes the responsibility of judicial proceeding and judgment?

The legal and political indications of the decree cannot be grasped through merely analyzing its text. It should be noted that the shah's decree was indeed a sort of caving in to a public demand. Surprisingly, the popular uprising was not very widespread; neither did the government's resistance meet the level of expectations. This public demand is the very question to which, according to the logic of question and answer, the text of the decree should be understood as an answer. According to varying interpretations, the '*majlis-i shūrā-yi millī*' promised in this decree could be a mere *consulting institution* (a favourable interpretation for monarchists), or a *supervisory majlis* for promoting justice and implementing the sharia laws (an interpretation suggested by proponents of *mashrūʿah*), or a *consultative legislative majlis* for enacting the constitution and parliamentary laws, namely, a combination of a constituent assembly and a parliament (an interpretation supported by the constitutionalist). It is possible that this vagueness in the decree's text was intentional since it would enable the monarchy to give a restrictive interpretation of the privilege at the earliest possible opportunity. To shed light on the context of the decree, we should take at least two steps back.

On 15 December 1905, following a series of events (including the discovery of a fancy- dress party photograph which showed Joseph Naus, the Belgian director of customs, in clerical attire, the imposition of heavy custom tariffs, the beating of the soles of the feet of a few sugar merchants on the order of ʿAlāʾ al-Dawlah, the governor of Teheran, and the struggle between Sayyid Abū al-Qāsim Imām Jumʿah and Sayyid Jamāl Vāʿiẓ at the Central Royal Mosque), led by two chief religious leaders, Sayyid Muḥammad Ṭabāṭabāʾī[5] and Sayyid ʿAbd Allāh Bihbahānī, a group of clerics, merchants, and shopkeepers of Tehran staged a *bast* or sit-in inside the ʿAbd al-ʿAẓīm Shrine, south of Tehran, to demonstrate their anger at the government. The number of the *bastis* did not exceed 3,000 as estimated in a diary kept by Shaykh Muḥammad Mahdī Sharīf Kāshānī, a close friend of Bihbahānī and a well-respected mediator for a settlement between the *ʿulamā* and the court during the Constitutional Movement. The most significant demands voiced by the protesters were the establishment of *ʿadālat'khānah* and the implementation of Islamic law. At this stage of the uprising, known as Lesser Migration (*muhājirat-i sughrá*), Muẓaffar al-Dīn Shāh issued a decree promising to 'organise and establish governmental justice (*tartīb va tàsīs-i ʿadālat-i dawlatī*)'. A day before the decree was issued, a night-letter (*shab'nāmah*) entitled 'the voice of the human angel' passed on from hand to hand between the *bastis*, and its content, according to Sharīf Kāshānī, affected all the people. Giving a report on the injustice of rulers, the misrule of governors, and foreigners' encroachment on the country, the anonymous writer suggested three remedies for overcoming the crisis:

> (1) our land must be protected from foreign powers; (2) we must be free in our personal measures so that nobody has the right to interfere in our affairs; (3) we must not be wronged by anyone . . . and the unjust sultans must never do their subjects any harm without the due process of law.[6]

The content of this night-letter indicates that the rule of law and freedom were also among the protesters' demands and they were probably summarized in the demand for an *ʿadālat'khānah*. Nevertheless, the shah's decree was never executed; independent judicial courts were not instituted, and Joseph Naus and Atābak ʿAbd al-Majīd Mīrzā ʿAyn al-Dawlah were not dismissed. Complaining about the shah's breach of promise, the people released several petitions and night-letters asking the *ʿulamā* to follow up on the demands. In response to one of these letters, a writer in another letter released on 5 April 1906 stated that all Iranians should feel guilty about this situation. Because, he says, for the lack of 'public awareness and dutifulness', people did not identify 'disciplining the system of government' as their 'top priority' and 'the point of departure'.[7] There are echoes of Mīrzā Malkam Khān in the following questions posed by the writer:

> Suppose that they do codify the law; firstly, who must determine the conditions of [legislating] the law? Who is in charge of the department of legislation? Where are the law-enforcement representatives? Is the master of judgment (*mīr-i qaẓā*) to be eaten or worn? What is the meaning of the word justice? Does the *ʿulamā's* interference in the people's affairs take place in their home or in the assembly of justice (*Majlis-i ʿadālat*)? Where is the limitation of the authorities of the Excellencies? . . . Where are the boundaries of heinous freedom (*āzādī-i maẕmūm*) and rebelliousness?[8]

Although such questions did not receive enough attention at that time, they eventually challenged Iranian thinkers.

The main theoretical barrier to the establishment of laws limiting the absolute power of the shah was the myth of Divine Grace (*farr-i īzadī*). This point can be grasped from a discussion on 4 Rabi I 1324 (28 April 1906) in which the chief minister Atābak ʿAyn al-Dawlah called on the ministers and a number of the nobles and notables to consult about instituting the *ʿadālat'khānah*. During the meeting, there was a confrontation between three views which could arguably be called monarchist, reformist, and conservative. The majority, as Amīr Bahādur declared, were the proponents of absolute monarchy and believed that

> whatever would be ordained by the *ʿadālat'khānah* and the law, the shah's will must be put above it, so that whenever the shah desires to do something, his command would be considered as God's command (*chih farmān-i yazdān, chih farmān-i shāh*).[9]

The counterargument presented by Iḥtishām al-Salṭanah was that 'the law restrains all people's authorities, although the limitations that the law imposes on the shah's authority must be first endorsed [by the shah]'. Surprisingly, the conservative position was represented by Nāṣir al-Mulk, who was educated in England and was familiar with modern political regimes. In response to Iḥtishām al-Salṭanah, he rejected the very necessity of legislating the law, saying that 'at the moment, Iran does not need a consultative parliament; the *ʿadālat'khānah* would suffice'. Similarly, the minister of the court addressed Iḥtishām al-Salṭanah, telling him that 'You, as a member of the Qajar clan must not consent to the elimination of the Qajar monarchy'.[10] As an unaccompanied voice, Iḥtishām al- Salṭanah replied that 'I swear to God that the power of the government and the progress of monarchy will only be achieved through assisting the nation. Take the opportunity to accompany the people! Appease the nation and don't disappoint them!' It was here that Amīr Bahādur ardently claimed that 'as long as I am alive, I won't allow the *ʿadālat'khānah* or the consultative majlis to be established'.[11] According to Kāshānī, their discussion finally ended with bad feelings, and the report of the meeting annoyed the shah so much so that he ordered Iḥtishām al-Salṭanah to be sent on a mission far away from Tehran to the Ottoman border.[12] This was the tolerance and capacity of the Iranian court for the establishment of the law and the legislative majlis. Meanwhile, ʿAyn al-Dawlah attempted to fuel the shah's concern and induce him to believe that 'the people are using me as a pretext when in fact all they demand is the elimination of the monarchy'.[13]

A few days later (in Rabi' I 1324/April 1906), Sayyid Muḥammad Ṭabāṭabā'ī, one of the two main cleric leaders of constitutionalism, took the second step in writing a letter to Atābak ʿAyn al-Dawlah and warning him that, sooner or later, these reforms would be carried out. Therefore, it would be better if these reforms were put in place by him and the shah, rather than by Russia, Britain, and the Ottoman Empire, and at the price of the fall of the Qajar dynasty and the decline of Shiite Iran. Pushing the demand further, he reminded ʿAyn al-Dawlah that

> From the very beginning, our promised goal was not the establishment of the *ʿadālat'khānah*. It has not been our demand to govern and direct the Tribunal of Justice (*dīvān'khānah-'i ʿadlīyah*) which, like other governmental departments, is not to be administrated by the people. Our request is that a national majlis deserving to the country's potentials and in accordance with the exigencies of the time be established.[14]

After this letter, the chief minister Atābak ʿAyn al-Dawlah increased the pressure on the protesters, and Nayyir al-Dawlah, the Governor of Tehran, imposed a kind of martial rule. The suppression soared in late July and resulted in the departure of the leading clerics of Tehran to Qum (known as the Greater Migration or *muhājirat-i kubrá*, led by Bihbahānī and Ṭabāṭabā'ī and a few other clerics, whom Shaykh Faẓl Allāh Nūrī reluctantly joined a couple of days later) and the staging of the *bast* by the merchants and the guilds in the garden of the British embassy in Tehran.

In a meeting held by the migrant clerics in Qum, traces of their disagreement over the issues of legislation and freedom were revealed. These disagreements would later lead to a schism between the two religious approaches. Ṭabāṭabā'ī made a speech about constitutionalism (using the word *mashrūṭah*) 'in which the people would feel the taste of liberty and freedom (*ḥurrīyat va āzādī*)'. When he defined this 'divine freedom' as liberation from 'the chains of slavery' and deliverance from 'the several thousand year oppression',[15] Nūrī warned him: 'do not be in a hurry for I worry that you might fail and not be able to control the movement'. Emphasizing that 'total freedom and absolute liberty are in principle wrong . . . and this word is totally a blasphemy in Islam'. He added that

> I earnestly request of you all not to say anything breaching Islam. Then foreigners will mock us . . . if you want my opinion, you should eliminate the word freedom, as in the end this word will disgrace us.[16]

It should be noted that Ṭabāṭabā'ī had mentioned the limits of freedom imposed by the law, stating that

> Constitutionalism means that laws will be enacted for the shah, the majlis, the ministers, the gentlefolk, the deputies, etc. that would restrict them. In short, constitutionalism is something that puts a limit on all governmental and public affairs as well as the *shar*ʿ and the *ʿurf* and cultivators and farmers, etc., so that no one can say or do something without permission of the law.[17]

Nevertheless, Nūrī also rejected the legislation of law. He argued that

> Firstly, our law was written and given to us about 1300 years ago; even if they intend to codify a law today, it must be in accordance with the Qur'an and the sharia . . . and [secondly,] you said that there would also be limits on the sharia. You should be advised that there is no limit on the sharia.[18]

The Sayyid and the Shaykh did not reach an agreement in this debate. We will return to their disagreement later.

Let us go back to the public protest that this time involved the British embassy and came to fruition very quickly; first, Atābak ʿAyn al-Dawlah was dismissed on 29 July 1906 and then, in an address to Mīrzā Naṣr Allah Khān Mushīr al-Dawlah, the new chief minister, the royal prescription of August 5 was issued. The shah's decree must be understood as an answer to these demands.

3.2 The first majlis and the question of the legitimacy of legislation

To avoid being deceived again by the government's breach of promise, the first majlis hastily started work on 7 October 1906, before completion of the election and as soon as 61 deputies from Tehran were elected. In an opening speech, the shah's decree of August 1906 was interpreted and the role of the majlis was explained by the majlis deputies. This speech emphasized that if the nation requested the 'right to vote and a consultative assembly', it was 'for the sake of preserving the egg of Islam (*bayẕah-ʾi Islām*) and the power of monarchy'. It further emphasized that if the state granted them the demand, it was in support of the nation and their absolute freedom to develop the country . . . it was the great aptitude of the nation that caused the state to confirm their personal and national rights'.[19] As the speech indicates, the writers believed that the rights of the nation are natural rather than legal bestowed by the king that can be taken back whenever he wishes. The capability of achieving these personal and national rights, however, is not initially actual, but rather subject to 'waking from the sleep of ignorance', so the majlis has the duty 'to awaken the nation and inform them of their legitimate rights'.[20] The word *mashrūṭah* was not mentioned in this speech, and the place of the majlis in the new political system remained unclear.

When the first majlis started work, a fundamental question was still to be adequately answered: What does parliamentary legislation mean? And what is the source of legitimacy for parliamentary law which allows it to determine the king's and the nation's rights and duties? A simplified answer to this question had been provided by Yūsuf Khān Mustashār al-Dawlah (1823–95) in his book *Yik kalamah*

(*One Word*) (published in 1278/1861). Supporting all nineteen-fold rights of the French constitution with Qur'anic teachings, he referred to the origin of judgment (*ḥukm*) as 'the root of the principles of European governance':

> No individual person in the world, whether king or beggar, civilian or soldier has the right to rule (*ḥukm*). That is, they are not rulers, but are delegates with responsibilities. If they are called 'rulers', it is in a metaphorical sense, and not in reality. Who, then, is a ruler? In other words, who is the mainspring of rulership? Islamic religious law and the opinions of the learned men of Europe are in agreement on this point: the ruler is God Himself.[21]

Mustashār al-Dawlah himself did certainly reflect on the differences between secular and divine law. Using a literary technique, he introduced an author surrogate who had vast knowledge of Islamic heritage to explain the five main differences between the French code and the Muslim sharia books as follows:

[1] The code is written with the approval of the government and the people, and not according to one opinion.

[2] The French code combines and orders all the applicable law codes. It is free of uncommon expressions, unsupported opinions and contradictions, whereas the books of Islamic jurisprudence preserve weak opinions too. And there are many contradictions in each of these rulings in such a way that it is difficult to distinguish sound rulings from weak ones.

[3] The French code is written in the language of the common people. Its meanings and purposes are easily understood and they do not require any explanation or marginal gloss.

[4] The most important difference is that the *code* considers only worldly matters, so that it is suitable for the condition of every person, irrespective of their ethnicity and religion. There is a different book for religious matters. In contrast, in the books of Islamic law, worldly matters are tempered and mixed with other-worldly affairs such as obligatory prayers, fasting and pilgrimage. This causes great harm in administering the affairs of the common people because non-Muslim peoples living in Islamic lands have no desire to read your code of law. . . . Thus, if the foremost *ʿulamā*, wherever they may be, were to write Islamic codes in separate books such as the book of the acts of worship, the afterlife, the books of civil and commercial matters, this would not be detrimental to the sharia.

[5] [French] codes include the *ʿurf* and common regulations too.[22]

Considering the fivefold difference, he then suggested that Iranians must provide comprehensive and comprehensible books comprising all the codes 'acceptable to the people'. According to his suggestion, the source of this book would be 'all the most respected books of Islam . . . and all the *codes* of civilized governments', and it should be written in 'an assembly whose members include men of learning and understanding, and men of wisdom and policy'. Receiving 'the endorsement of his majesty the king', the preservation of this book of codes has been delegated to 'a special independent assembly', and unquestioning obedience to it would be 'the duty of the government and the people'. He considers this method of legislation of the code not without precedence and based on the principle of 'discussion and consultation' (*muzākirah va mushāvirah*).[23]

Mustashār al-Dawlah's work had a great impact on the constitutionalist and law-seeking élite. They also supported the legitimacy of the majlis by using the Qur'anic terms of 'consultation (*mashvirat*)' (Q, 3:159), 'following the best word (*mutābiʿat az qawl-i aḥsan*)' (Q, 39:18), 'and commending the right and forbidding the wrong (*amr bih maʿrūf va nahy az munkar*) (Q, 3:104:)'.[24] They benefited greatly from strong religious supporters. Besides the two Sayyids (Bihbahānī and Ṭabāṭabāʾī) who were cleric leaders of constitutionalism and whose informal attendance at the majlis was considered a religious endorsement of the parliamentary proceedings, three *marjaʿs* in Najaf (Ākhūnd Mullā Muḥammad Kāẓim Khurāsānī, Shaykh ʿAbd Allāh Māzandarānī, and Ḥāj Mirzā Ḥusayn Khalīlī Tihrānī) frequently and explicitly considered the establishment of the majlis – for the sake of 'removing injustice, protecting the wronged, strengthening the nation and the state, promoting the welfare of the people, and preserving the egg of Islam' – 'rationally, religiously and commonly (*ʿaql-an va sharʿ-an va ʿurf-an*), not only a preference but also an obligation', so that opposition to the majlis was equated with opposition to Islam and the prophet.[25]

Despite emphasizing the obligation to obey the majlis, all constitutionalist *ʿulamā* distinguished parliamentary law from religious law. A group of them believed that the task of the majlis was not the legislation of law, because Islamic laws are complete both in acts of worship (*ʿibādāt*) and in worldly matters (*muʿāmilāt*), so that there is no need for any 'new establishment' (*taʾsīsāt-i jadīdah*).[26] According to this group, parliamentary laws were not religiously legislated (*qānūn-i tashrīʿī*), but were either 'determining subjects' (*taʿyīn-i mawẓūʿ*) or 'legislating rules for the implementation of Islamic laws'.[27] Another group of the constitutionalist *ʿulamā* accepted that the duty of the majlis was the legislation of law. Referring to the differences between secular and religious law, however, they confined the right of parliamentary legislation to 'general political matters (*kullīyāt-i umūr-i siyāsīyah*)' and worldly and supervisory affairs that are 'consultable, adaptable and changeable (*qābil-i mashvarat va jarḥ va taʿdīl va taghyīr va tabdīl*)'.[28]

These arguments failed to convince the proponents of *mashrūʿah* (religious constitutionalism). Soon after the majlis was bombarded and closed on Muḥammad ʿAlī Shāh's order in June 1908, they took advantage of the opportunity to publicly express their opposition to the legitimacy of parliamentary legislation. In October 1908, Muḥammad Ḥusayn Tabrīzī, a leading clerical upholder of *mashrūʿah*, came into conflict with the majlis, claiming that some parliamentary laws, such as the imposition of taxes and customs duties, as well as pricing (*tasʿyīr*), were against Islamic law.[29] He asserted that it was wrong to rely on the opinions of *ʿulamā* in Najaf to obey the majlis in Tehran, because they were neither infallible nor residing in Tehran to witness what happened in the majlis. These *ʿulamā*, he claimed, trusted the words of a few people and mistakenly supposed that the majlis was for the reform of the country and promotion of the sharia.[30]

Equally important was Shaykh Faẕl Allāh Nūrī, who had started to criticize constitutionalism and the majlis in June 1907. In a treatise published in 1909, he explained his disagreement and argued against the election of deputies and the reliance on the majority vote. He believed that the majlis was heresy and that deputation was senseless, because

> in worldly matters there is no need for such religious orders (*tartībāt-i dīnīyah*) . . . and in religious matters one should refer to the guardianship rather the deputation (*rājiʿ bih vilāyat ast nah vikālat*); and in the Major Occultation, the guardianship must be held by the *faqīhs* and *mujtahids* not by such and such grocer and draper.[31]

He went on to issue the *fatvā* that

> *Mashrūṭah* is forbidden (*ḥarām*), because the foundation of this system and the constitution and the legislation on the basis of the majority vote, even in religiously neutral matters (*umūr-i mubāḥ*), are forbidden and heresy in religion (*bidʿat dar dīn*).[32]

Nūrī believed that if secular legislators enforce people to do religiously neutral acts as legal obligations, this act would afterwards be religiously forbidden. On this presentation of secular rule as religious law, he wrote:

> Governmental matters and its rules have always existed, but all people saw how the ridiculous laws and poor opinions of the majlis (*muzakhrafāt-i qānūnī va ārāʾ-i sakhīfah-ʾi majlisī*) seemed to all Muslims as being the most obligatory (*awjab-i vājibāt*) so that opposing these [worldly rules] was understood as apostasy. What heresy is worse than this?

Explicitly arguing against legislative power, he added:

> In Islam, nobody has the right to legislate or enact the *ḥukm*. Islam is not incomplete for someone to intend to complete it. As for events that may occur (Arabic: *al-waqāyiʿ al-ḥādithah*), people must refer to the gates of the *aḥkām* who are the Imam's deputies (*nuvvāb-i Imām*). They will then deduce the *ḥukm* from the Qur'an and the *Sunna* (prophetic traditions) instead of legislation and enactment.[33]

In these same days, the writer of *Tadhkirat al-ghāfil wa irshād al-jāhil* developed Nūrī's opinion, arguing that (1) if the purpose of the majlis was to enact the new law, it went against the belief in the Prophet Muḥammad as the last prophet of God and in Islam as the complete religion; and (2) if its purpose was to enact rules in accordance with Islamic law, firstly such lay folk could not succeed in undertaking such a task, and secondly [even if they could do so], it was acting on the basis of 'rational preference (*istiḥsān-i ʿaqlī*)' and therefore was forbidden [according to the Shia]; and (3) if their task was not related to religious public affairs at all and was only the code of conduct of government officials, why did they refer to the sharia and the Qur'an and resort to the endorsements of religious excellencies (*ḥujaj-i Islām*) and call the opponents of the code the enemy of the Imam of the time? and (4) if the purpose of the majlis was the implementation and strengthening of Islamic law, why did the majlis deputies not turn to religious reason instead of ordinary people's votes, and why did they pass laws on the basis of freedom and equality which were ruining the constructive pillar of the divine law?[34]

As arbitrary rule had returned, there was no opportunity for the constitutionalists to respond to these criticisms in Iran. However, the *ʿulamā* of Najaf were not only issuing ardent *fatvās* inviting people to *jihad* against arbitrary rule and to reclaim the *mashrūṭah* and the majlis, but they were also writing treatises in response to the demands of the proponents of *mashrūʿah*. In his *Al-lȧālī al-marbūṭah fī wujūb al-mashrūṭah*, written in late 1908 and early 1909, Shaykh Muḥammad Ismāʿīl Gharavī Maḥallātī answered 18 objections, mostly pointed out in two treatises *Kashf al-murād* and *Hurmat-i mashrūṭah*, including the false claim that the majlis determines religious law.[35] He argued that 'freedom from all kinds of forced domination, unaccountability and coercion' is 'independently inferred from reason (*mustaqillāt-i ʿaqlīyah*)', since the meaning of freedom is nothing but 'removal of injustice and cruelty imposed by the powerful people on the weak (*rafʿ-i ẓulm va taʿaddī-i aqviyā bar ẕuʿafā*)'. This means that Maḥallātī, like most *uṣūlīs*, believes that human intellect does not need any other sources of knowledge or even any directive precept of religion (*ḥukm-i irshādī*) in order to recognize 'the praiseworthiness of justice and the blameworthiness of oppression' (*ḥusn-i ʿadl va qubḥ-i ẓulm*) and to judge the necessity of the removal of injustices.[36] Those *uṣūlī* thinkers who accepted the principle of cohesion between rational precept and religious precept (*mulāzimah-ʾi bayn-i ḥukm-i ʿaqlī va ḥukm-i sharʿī*) could infer from the rational obligation of 'freedom from arbitrary rule' (*wujūb-i ʿaqlī*) that this freedom was also religiously obligatory (*wujūb-i sharʿī*).[37]

Reflecting on the foundations of constitutionalism and in the same line of analysis, Mīrzā Muḥammad Ḥusayn Gharavī Nāʾīnī argued that to be bound by parliamentary law is not an obligation imposed with the intention of and in the name of religious legislation, but that it rather belongs to the category of obligations arising from contracts. He further added that these laws, as the introductory measures toward putting limitations on the dominance of injustice (*taḥdīd-i istīlāʾ-ī ẓulm*), which is religiously obligatory, would be rationally enforceable and therefore accidentally obligatory (*vājib-i bil-ʿaraẓ*), even though introduction to *vājib* would not be regarded as *vājib* by nature (*vājib-i bi-zzāt*).[38]

After the defeat of Muḥammad ʿAlī Shāh and the establishment of the second constitutional period, the dispute over the question of the legitimacy of parliamentary legislation settled. As the works written in this era demonstrate, the question was no longer addressed. The right of the majlis in legislation was accepted, although questions of whether certain laws passed by the majlis were in accordance with Islamic law were sometimes asked.

3.3 The first majlis and restraining arbitrary rule

It would not be an overstatement to say that the most important task of the first Parliament (October 1906–June 1908) was to determine the boundaries of freedom and the rights of the nation, or in the words of Mīrzā Muḥammad Ḥusayn Nā'īnī, 'the degree of the King's dominance and the nation's freedom'.[39] Members of the first majlis also considered the constitution as 'the marker of the boundaries between the monarchy and the nation'.[40] In the words of Ṭālibuf, the deputies should distribute 'the public wealth of freedom', which had belonged solely in the hands of the shah during arbitrary rule and prior to constitutionalism, among the nation equally. Such a task was pointed out by Ṭālibuf in January 1907, almost 100 days after the inauguration of the majlis, in his *Īẕāḥāt dar khuṣūṣ-i āzādī* (*Clarifications of Freedom*). This treatise was in fact a deliberation on the duties of the parliament as well as those of the nation on how to protect the wealth of freedom.[41] He wrote in the first line of the chapter 'On the Parliament' that 'in order to safeguard its wealth, the Iranian nation has elected 162 guardians from among itself and has delegated them to the heart of the country as the deputies of the National Consultative Assembly (*majlis-i shūrā-yi millī*)'.[42] Then, at the beginning of the chapter 'On the Duties of the Nation', he wrote:

> Now all the people of Iran know that this wealth of glory has been bequeathed to us from our forefathers and has been in the custody of a pious and religious person in a secure treasury such that whenever we reach the age of maturity we could claim it. Since the threshold of the coming of age of the people is manifested by their desire to sacrifice their life, property and children for the sake of freedom, the religious excellencies [*ḥujaj-i Islām*] in general and the venerable Ḥājī Mīrzā Muḥammad Āqā [Ṭabāṭabā'ī] in particular, endorsed the maturity to Muẓaffar al-Dīn Shāh, God bless his soul, who was naturally willing to implement this sacred wish of the nation. It was then placed under the supervision of 162 representatives in the treasury of the nation.[43]

To Ṭālibūf, the first task of this majlis as the guardian of freedom was the preparation and approval of the constitution or 'the document of the rights of the Shah and the subjects'.[44] Choosing a commercial (but also judicial) language comprehensible for the people of his time, he went on to add:

> [The legislation of law] is to establish justice. The notion of justice is moderation. This means that the law will keep balanced the pointer of the scale that weighs the *rights* and *boundaries* of the nation.[45]

The members of the majlis knew what was unbalancing the equilibrium: lack of balance in rights and duties. When a discussion on the freedom of press occurred for the first time during one of the early days of the parliament, Mīrzā Javād Khān Saʿd al-Dawlah, who was a representative of the notables from Tehran, said:

> It is required that the printing offices and newspapers be free. However, alongside such freedom, it is required that a department of justice be established and certain *rules* and *conditions* be determined so that no one would be free to write or print whatever he/she wishes; and in the case of the publishing and distributing of anything defaming or dishonoring someone, the defamed person should have the *right*, according to these rules, to call to account and to sue the author and the publisher.[46]

After being approved by the majlis, the constitution received royal assent from Muẓaffar al-Dīn Shāh on 30 December 1906, a few days before he died. As mentioned in the shah's assent, the constitution was in fact mostly about 'the tasks and obligations of the majlis and its boundaries in relation with the government'. In his assent, the shah acknowledged that the reason behind the establishment of the majlis was the 'noble principle' (*aṣl-i aṣīl*) that 'every individual member of the country (*har yik az afrād-i ahālī-ʾi mamlikat*), depending on his rank, has a right and a share in approving and supervising public affairs'.[47] Such a right and share was acquired through the election of representatives. The explicit acknowledgment of popular sovereignty was much more significant than what was vaguely stated in the Constitutional Decree.[48] The head of the country had now also acknowledged that the nation was free from any undemocratic and arbitrary interference in the legislation of law as well as in the supervision of the implementation of law.

This brief constitution dealt more with approving certain freedoms rather than with permitting legal interferences in public freedom. Article 12 endorsed parliamentary immunity of the representatives, and Articles 15 and 38 endorsed freedom of speech for the members of the majlis and majority rights in legislating laws. The right of the parliament in legislating laws for various affairs and its authority in supervising the proper implementation of law were also stipulated in a set of articles.

Among the nation's rights, however, only a few related to the parliament's activities were mentioned in some articles. In Article 13, which was on the publicity of parliamentary proceedings, the freedom of press was pointed out, stipulating that members of the press are free as far as 'their contents do not violate any fundamental principles of the government and nation'. It went on to add that any animus, libel, and defamation 'will be liable to interrogation, prosecution and punishment'. Also, Article 32 left the hands of the people free in writing their 'petition or criticisms or complaints' to 'the Parliamentary Office of Petitions' (*daftar-i ʿarāʾiẓ-i majlis*), and obliged the majlis to be accountable or follow up on the ministries' responses.[49]

Again, the constitution made no reference to the word *mashrūṭah* and the fact that the monarchy was constitutional. In the last article added by the shah, he stipulated that his successors should consider 'preservation of these boundaries and principles' as 'their royal task', but did not specify any name for this system of ruling.

The Supplementary Fundamental Laws of October 1907 rectified such a shortcoming. In Article 7, a reference was made to constitutionalism stating that 'the basis of constitutionalism (*asās-i mashrūṭiyat*) is unstoppable either partially or generally', and 18 articles (from Article 8 to 25) were allocated to stipulating the rights of the Iranian nation. If we divide possible interferences in individual freedom into legal and illegal ones, the subjects of ten of the aforementioned 18 articles concern prohibiting illegal interference, while four other articles prohibit both legal and illegal interferences.[50] Illegal interferences that are prohibited according to this law are illegal trespassing on a person's life, property, home, and honor (Article 9); illegal arrests (Article 10); illegally issuing a verdict and executing punishment (Article 12); illegally entering a person's house (Article 13); illegal banishment (Article 14); religiously unlawful occupation of a property without paying its fair price (Article 15); illegal confiscation of assets and properties (Article 16); illegal dispossession of properties and lands possessed by owners or occupiers (Article 17); illegal seizure and disclosure of postal correspondence (Article 22); and illegal seizure and disclosure of telegrams without permission of the telegraphers. In all aforementioned articles, prohibition of any interference is initially pointed out and then a rendition of the phrase 'except in accordance with the law' (*magar bih ḥukm-i qānūn*) is added. There are four cases, however, where this phrase is not mentioned and where interferences are absolutely prohibited: (a) referring an individual from a court in which the individual is expected to be judged by another court (Article 11); (b) prevention of learning any religiously permissible sciences, knowledge, and industries (Article 18); (c) prior censorship (*mumayyizī*) of the press and books that are not heretical or harmful to religion (Article 20); and (d) banning communities and associations that do not cause religious or social sedition (*fitnah-'i dīnī va dunyavī*), are not disruptive of order, and are established based on observation of the law (Article 21).[51]

The recurrent usage of the phrase 'except in accordance with the law' indicates that, at the time, legislators were mainly concerned with protecting people's freedoms against the infringement of those agents who considered themselves above the law. These legislators considered law as a shield that protected people's freedom and were oblivious to the fact that future legislators might employ the same justification, use the same phrase of 'except in accordance with the law', and legislate rules that were inherently tyrannical. Incidentally, in the very first and second majlis, laws were legislated that permitted the government to legally but unjustly interfere in the individual's freedom. Surprisingly, these laws even authorized encroachment on freedoms that, based on the constitution, were absolutely immune from such interferences. Here we mention several examples of such laws.

3.3.1 The first Iranian Press Law

The first Iranian Press Law (passed in February 1908) was susceptible to restrictive interpretations imposing legal censorship. To what extent the majlis was responsible in enacting this law is not known, since this law was regulated based on a bill offered by Mīrzā ʿAlī Aṣghar Khān Atābak's government in July 1907.

At the beginning of this law, Article 20 of the constitution was quoted to claim that the Press Law was enacted in consonance with this article and that it aimed to 'protect public rights and prevent the trespasses of men of the pen and the press'. However, while Article 20 asserted that 'the press in general were free and prior restraint on them was forbidden, except for heretical books and materials harmful to the true religion', in Article 1 of the Press Law, publishers were forbidden to publish materials 'whose authors and their reputations' were unknown to the publishers, and Article 4 specified that 'before being published, new religious books must be scrutinized and approved by a body named the Assembly of Religious Sciences that is going to be set up in the Ministry of Culture'.[52] Disregarding such examples of blatant violation of the constitution, the crimes mentioned in some articles of the Press Law are so vague and interpretable that the state could invoke them to execute the harshest punishments against authors and newspapers and deprive them of freedom by seemingly 'legal' interferences.

For example, Article 31 ordained a fine of 10 to 30 *Tūmāns* in cash, an imprisonment term of three months to one year, and the temporary or permanent confiscation of the newspaper whose author or director insulted 'His Majesty the King'. However, it is not clear what is meant by 'insult', nor is it clear which body gets to confirm the insulting nature of printed phrases. Using three more vague expressions ('seditious' (*fitnah'angīz*), 'harmful to religion and Islamic beliefs', and 'disrespecting, defaming and discrediting individuals or bodies'), Articles 32, 33, and 34 determine some other boundaries of freedom of the press. Article 49 is the most unfair and in itself is capable of establishing a system of 'legal' censorship muzzling the free press. According to this article, the penalty for the publication of material that contains any of the following points would be the banning of the newspaper:

(1) Harming the foundations of Islam.
(2) Disrespecting the throne.
(3) Disclosing military secrets.
(4) Creating general anxiety (*hayajān-i kullī*) and disturbing public tranquility.
(5) Inviting opposition to the official powers of the country.
(6) Distributing obscene images which go against chastity and modesty.

It should be noted here that, according to Article 79 of the Supplementary Fundamental Laws regarding political and press offenses, the court must convene in the presence of a jury. However, such a technique of supervising the proper implementation of the Press Law and safeguarding political freedoms and free press was not implemented until 1931.[53]

The imposition of such legal obligations and the permission for such interferences in an individual's freedom of speech agitated even pro-majlis newspapers. The liberal newspaper *Musāvāt* allocated a special issue to opposition to this law. The headline, 'The Feast of Manifestation of the Press Law (*ʿĪd-i ẓuhūr-i qānūn-i maṭbūʿāt*)', was written sarcastically in red. Throughout its eight pages, the newspaper had employed mocking and exaggeratory language to discuss scientific and historical subjects instead of exploring political affairs in order to show that under such a law, only topics related to 'spiritual revelations' (*mukāshifāt-i hāhūtī*) and 'celestial insights (*ishraqāt-i ʿarshī*)' can be published. Addressing those readers 'who were distracted and astonished by the change of *Musāvāt's* policy and style', this issue ended by saying that 'if they knew the reason for such a good policy, they certainly would not be surprised but would rather praise *Musāvāt* for its total compliance with the law, and for its wise and peaceful adoption of such a policy. Because the advent of the splendid and blessed letter of the Press Law, a thousand times greetings to its legislator, does not allow more than what was published in this blessed issue'.[54]

Maʿārif newspaper also published, in its second year's twelfth issue, a reader's criticism of the publication of the Press Law in a previous issue:

> [T]he Press Law that you have published in your newspaper is a remnant of the autocratic era and a reminiscence of the time of the Iranian nation's ignorance, but God-given freedom cleansed such opacity and impurity. The constitution that has been written on the pages of history and the folios of time by the pure blood of the awakened Iranian people will wipe out and efface such writings.[55]

Under this letter, the newspaper's director replied in a sarcastic tone:

> Your criticisms are in no way justifiable and we do not consider ourselves eligible to be criticized . . . shouldn't we remind ourselves of the miseries of the autocratic era and be grateful for the freedom we have today? Do you consider that writing history causes you humiliation? . . . one should safeguard the reminiscence of the autocratic era so as to determine the value of today's freedom.[56]

Even prior to the ratification of the Press Law, the first majlis had shown impatience toward freedom of the pen. Initially, a few majlis deputies disapproved of certain topics published by newspapers, particularly criticizing 'intrusions (*fuẕūlī'hā*)' by the two radical newspapers *Ḥabl al-matīn* of Tehran and *Ṣūr-i Isrāfīl*, and pronounced the word 'ban' (*tawqīf*) in their cases. *Ḥabl al-matīn* unhesitatingly replied that constitutionalism without freedom of speech and pen is as paradoxical as a thin-bearded man growing a thick beard. It argued that

> During the time when you could not imagine anything but oppression and arbitrary rule . . . *Ḥabl al-matīn* [of Calcutta] was writing about constitutionalism . . . publishing booklets on law [and] writing about the need to have a legislative body. Is it now an intruder?[57]

However, the majlis did not budge. *Ṣūr-i Isrāfīl* was banned on the order of the majlis and was accused of opposing religion because it had published an article censuring fundamentalism, superstition, and prejudice in its twelfth issue (5 September 1907) and had expounded it in its fourteenth issue (19 September 1907).[58]

Despite all this, the first majlis's opinion on freedom cannot be grasped only from the Press Law or its proceedings about freedom of newspapers. The fact is that, in this regard, the majlis was under pressure from two sides. On the one hand, pro-freedom and constitutionalist newspapers and night-letters did not recognize any boundaries, so much so that they were even threatening to assassinate the shah, government members, and majlis deputies.[59] On the other hand, the opponents of constitutionalism, in particular the clerical upholders of *mashrūʿah* who were agitated by the freedom of the press, accused the majlis that

> Since the establishment of this majlis, all freedom-seeking and materialist individuals as well as Babis in Tehran have come out from behind the curtains and have started factionalism, licentiousness, and banditry; tell me what kind of relation and kinship exists between this layer of people and this majlis in *Bahāristān*.[60]

Since June 1907, when the opponents of constitutionalism, led by Shaykh Faẕl Allāh Nūrī, took *bast* or sit-in in the ʿAbd al-ʿAẕīm Shrine to protest to the procedure of legislating Supplementary Fundamental Laws, majlis deputies were increasingly accused of opposing religion. During their *bast*, Nūrī and his followers put out leaflets called *Lavāyiḥ* that repeatedly warned the majlis that

> Here is the Supreme Islamic Consultative House (*Dar al-Shūrā-yi Kūbrā-yi Islāmī*) . . . it is impossible for the majlis to be influenced by the Parisian or British Parliaments and to derive the laws of freedom of speech and pen from them, to change the sharia and religious law, or to permit taverns, prostitution, the unveiling of women, and toleration of religiously-forbidden acts.[61]

The writers of the *Lavāyiḥ* considered that all corruptions were hatched by 'several atheist freedom-seekers for whom the sharia law is a hindrance; they intend to stop the majlis from abiding by Islamic laws'.[62] In one of these leaflets, Ākhūnd Mullā Muḥammad ʿAlī Mujtahid Rustam'ābādī explained to the *ʿulamā* of Najaf that the reason for his 'non-cooperation with the majlis is the freedom of press that has influenced religion' and 'is about to break the 1300-year-old cord of true religion using gentle, calm, and deceiving words and attractive writings'.[63] In such a battlefield, the majlis had to avoid being accused of secularism and latitudinarianism at the expense of negating freedom of the press. In the following chapter, we will have more opportunities to examine various aspects of freedom of expression.

3.3.2 Other legal liberties

The first majlis could more comfortably defend freedom when it was not under accusations of failing to be properly religious. Instances of majlis deputies vehemently defending the legitimate freedoms of the nation against autocratic and unjustified interferences of the government can be seen in their efforts to protect the rights of individuals to assemble,[64] to send telegraphs,[65] and to enjoy judicial security. The majlis particularly refused to cave in when the issue concerned the right of judicial security. For instance, after the unsuccessful assassination attempt on the life of Muḥammad ʿAlī Shāh on 28 February 1908, several suspects were arrested and then were set free after being interrogated, while several others were still held in custody in the palace of the shah. The minister of war presented a report on the investigation to the majlis on 9 March. Then, Sayyid Ḥasan Taqī'zādah, the representative of the guilds form Azerbaijan, called for attention and caution to be paid in the investigations, and Sayyid Naṣr Allāh Taqavī, the representative for the clerics from Tehran, stressed that the interrogations must be open.[66] A month later, it was revealed that despite insistence by the majlis, two of the accused men had been interrogated in the *Gulistān* Palace and not in a public court. The people were agitated and asked the majlis to prosecute the interrogators and torturers. The concern was that the illegal interrogation of the accused was a return to the era of arbitrary rule. However, ill-intending individuals had made the shah believe that these groups of people intended to stop the suspects from being 'arrested, interrogated or punished'. A group of deputies went to see the shah and warily informed him that 'the constitution has been written to mark the boundaries between the monarchy and the nation'. They added that since certain articles 'like the right of prosecution in public courts applies to all, the nation has become agitated and is demanding that the law be observed and implemented'. Otherwise, they explained, the people are serious in the belief that the culprits be arrested and punished, since 'they are aware that in conditions in which attempts can be made on the life of the country's king, there would be no security for other individuals'.[67] Despite all these precautions, the majlis was unable to allay Muḥammad ʿAlī Shāh's concerns and convince him to heed the law. Instead, the majlis was targeted by cannons on 23 June 1908, an incident that ended in bloodshed. The 13-month period of the Lesser Arbitrary Rule (*istibdād-i ṣaghīr*) began at this point.

3.4 The second majlis and restraining license and chaos

If the first majlis was constantly struggling with the two forces of arbitrary rule and religious fanaticism, the second majlis – inaugurated four months after Tehran was taken over by the constitutionalist *mujāhidīn* (combatants) and Muḥammad ʿAlī Shāh was dethroned – was, through to the very end, faced with domestic chaos, a weak central government, and foreign threats. The conquerors of Tehran, *mujāhidīn* and *Bakhtiyārīs* in particular, went beyond limits and 'disturbed the public peace of mind'. Their commanders did not reprimand them, and they did not fear their commanders. They were busy, day and night, committing theft, plundering, and living in pleasure. This is the picture that Sharīf Kāshānī, a constitutionalist chronographer, has depicted of the turmoil in Tehran on the eve of the inauguration of the second majlis.[68] In the following year, the situation became even worse; Aḥmad Shāh was still under age and Nāṣir al-Mulk, who had been selected as the Regent in October 1910 after the death of the first

Regent ʿAlī Riẕā Khān ʿAẓud al-Mulk, was procrastinating on his return from London. Sharīf Kāshānī writes in remorse:

> May God help us secure our future, because we believe our country has turned constitutionalist, but in fact the country's affairs are in the hands of a bunch of ignorant self-interested people, be it deputies or ministers or constitutionalists . . . unaccountability, unlawfulness, and disorder are one hundred degrees worse than the era of arbitrary rule.[69]

Chaos can be defined as a situation where there is an absence of all obstacles to freedom, in such a way that the person who has more power enjoys more freedom. Understanding freedom as being unrestrained or as absolute license was certainly not a new concept, but formerly the hierarchy of those who were unrestrained was in better order: the arbitrary ruler, at the apex of the pyramid, enjoyed absolute freedom, and others were busy exerting the law of coercion upon their subordinates at some level of the pyramid, depending on how close they were to the shah (this, of course, followed no rule but the autocratic will of the shah). Now, however, that system of arbitrary rule had collapsed and had not been replaced by a new order or law.

The situation was, of course, the continuation and aggravation of the disorder that had begun throughout the first constitutional period. During the early months of the first constitutionalism, telegrams were being received from Rasht explaining that farmers of Gīlān imagine that 'constitutionalism means absolute freedom (*bilmarrah āzād būdan*) and evasion of taxes'.[70] Letters arrived from Kirmānshāhān stating that

> The people of this ruined city try to interpret the meaning of freedom and liberty in materializing their aims, expressing their old grudges, hatred and jealousy, . . ., and are shameless, unrestrained, unbridled and make attempts to waste, destroy and excommunicate each other.[71]

Constitutionalists made efforts to rectify such misunderstandings. Sayyid Jamāl al-Dīn Vāʿiẓ Iṣfahānī, the famous constitutionalist preacher, delivered sermons on the pulpit saying that 'freedom . . . without equality is mere oppression, absolute unrestraint (*muṭlaq al-ʿinānī*) and violation of the rights of others by certain individuals'.[72] At the same time, an author in the majlis newspaper complained about the disorder, saying that it had not only left the government's hands open in interfering in the affairs of people (*ahālī*), but that it had also converted every person into an arbitrary ruler in his own sphere of power:

> In the absence of law, you and I can establish our arbitrary and personal government (*ḥukūmat-i mustaqillah*). In the absence of law, a country faces chaos because of the pursuit of personal interests, and we, the wretched people, become cast away and offended.[73]

Similarly, another author in the *Rūḥ al-Qudus* newspaper bemoans the fact that whereas yesterday we had only one arbitrary sultan, today 'we have neither constitutionalism, nor republic, nor autocracy (*nah mashrūṭah, nah jumhūrī, nah mustaqillah*)' but rather 'chaos and the rule of khans (*harj-u-mraj va mulūk al-ṭavāyifī*)' and are under the oppression and cruelty of 'thousands of shahs with the hat or the turban'.[74]

On the other hand, the upholders of the *mashrūʿah* government were arguing that freedom and constitutionalism are nothing but such arbitrary behavior and chaos. At the time when the majlis had been bombarded and shut down, and Muḥammad ʿAlī Shāh was hesitant about how to react to the people's request while occasionally considering the reopening of the majlis, the *Ṣubḥ'namah-ʾi Daʿvat al-Islām* quoted Shaykh Faẕl Allāh Nūrī as saying that

> We do not want the law of Mustashār al-Dawlah, Taqī'zādah or Bāqir the grocer; the law of Islam and a shah who deserved to be obeyed would suffice. For God's sake be fair: one Iran, 15 million kings?[75]

Such description of Iran's constitutionalism perhaps reflected the surface of the reality. However, the existing chaos was not the result of parliamentary legislation, but had emerged because of disregard for the law and misunderstandings of freedom as anarchy. This fact was mentioned two years later, in June 1911, by the authors of the treatise *Taʿāvun-i māsūnī*,[76] who said that one of the obstacles to the full materialization of constitutionalism in Iran was the inattention of the movement to the decision of the majority, when in fact the majority's decision 'is the spirit and basis of social order and the main element of constitutionalism'.[77] Explaining the causes of the chaos that was indeed the greatest calamity of the newly emerged concept of freedom during the era of constitutionalism, the authors added that

> Iran has been trapped under the pressure of arbitrary rule principles exerted by the absolute power of an individual throughout centuries. It is not surprising for this nation, out of love and excitement for freedom and as a consequence of all the previous restrictions that it has experienced, to expect something which no nation under any circumstances may obtain where the affairs of the nation would be ruled by a group of people collectively or by every single one of its individuals. . . . The result of such a notion, which is unfortunately common among many people, cannot mean anything but chaos and the absolute negation of government, namely an order or disorder that requires entrusting authority to all individuals, which is in turn to deny all individuals of their powers.[78]

Such an extreme conception of freedom worried the majlis to such an extent that, on several occasions, they found the only remedy for the chaos in giving carte blanche to the government to interfere in individuals' freedoms. In other words, the situation began to turn from chaos into arbitrary rule. This will be further discussed later on.

Another characteristic that made the horizon of the question of freedom in the second majlis different from that of the first majlis was its politico-intellectual currents. In the second majlis, which included only 20 deputies from the first majlis, the various groups of representatives became more clearly distinguishable from each other and gradually formed political parties. Initially, the radicals who had set up a small and secret association called '*ijtimāʿīyūn-i ʿāmīyūn*' during the first majlis now declared their existence under the name 'Democrat Party'. Its parliamentary leadership was first entrusted to Sayyid Ḥasan Taqī'zādah and later to Suliymān Mīrzā. Influenced by the Russian Social Democratic Party, they pursued revolutionary ideas such as the distribution of land and limitations on clerical influence in politics. In opposition to this group, there was the *ijtimāʿīyūn-i iʿtidālīyūn* party that, after its coalition with the two small parties *ittifāq va tarqqī* and *jamāʿat-i taraqqī'khvāāhān*, was no longer a minority.[79]

Compared to a few years earlier, the elite and the sociopolitical statesmen had come to a better understanding of political views and actions in the new world, and also of constitutional exigencies; not only were the ideals and goals more thoroughly deliberated, but policies and procedures were also better examined. Political parties now had their own manifestos, though sometimes their being translations distanced them from the sociopolitical realities of Iran. Having an open program for political parties, particularly for parliamentary parties, was considered a necessity that would prevent the parties from founding their ideologies on the basis of 'devotion or hatred towards individuals' and demoting the parties into 'the old factionalisms (*dastah'bandī'hā-yi ayyām-i qadīm*)'. In a note to the majlis deputies, the Regent, Nāṣir al-Mulk, noted that the demotion of parties into factions would result in the 'uprooting of the freedom and prosperity of the country', 'making it impossible to prevent anything', and consequently causing the emergence of 'disputes and civil wars' followed by 'chaos' which would turn into 'arbitrary rule'. Because when political parties, rather than rely on the political manifesto, use 'favouring or hating individuals' as their criterion in making decisions, 'they sacrifice public interests for personal interests and will eventually produce an oligarchy (*īlqārshī*), namely arbitrary rule by a few individuals in the country, which would definitely be worse and more lethal than a single person's arbitrary rule'.[80] Nāṣir al-Mulk considered an appropriate party manifesto, one that, instead of dealing with generalities, would encompass all the objectives that for the 'modernization of a nation are among indispensable aspirations (*āmāl-i ḥatmīyah*)'. Such a manifesto should also illustrate 'the best and the most possible path toward achieving these goals'.[81]

Among all those 'indispensable aspirations', he refers to the great gift of freedom as an example. He explains that its 'extremity', on the one hand, would be 'captivity under a despotic government (*ḥukūmat-i jābirah*)', and on the other hand, would be 'confusing freedom with arbitrary behaviour (*khvud'sarī*)'. Therefore, a person's freedom 'is allowable as long as it does not interfere with another person's freedom'.[82] This being said, Nāṣir al-Mulk points out the task of the majlis deputies as follows:

> Observing the exigencies of the time as well as the customs and traditions of the country . . . they must examine all paths to achieving this goal

> [i.e. freedom] and choose the most possible and expedient one as their manifesto . . . through which they can safely and moderately depart toward the goal.[83]

Prior to Nāṣir al-Mulk's parliamentary note on the need for paying attention to the ways of achieving freedom, most of the key majlis parties had made general references to freedom. In the civil rights section of its manifesto, the Democrat Party, which had been accused of being revolutionary, idealist, and unorthodox, had only mentioned the term 'freedom of expression and the press, freedom of assembly and associations along with the freedom to hold strikes'. It had not, however, provided a definition for freedom and its limits.[84] In the treatise on the principles of democracy, however, the Democrats defined the limits of freedom as that which 'would not disturb the freedoms of others'. On freedom of the press, they said that observation of the Press Law would be beneficial.[85]

The *iʿtidālīyūn* (Moderates), who had been accused by the Democrats of taking sides with the landlords and the men of wealth and of trying to regulate laws that would benefit these classes,[86] offered a list of freedoms in their second manifesto: 'freedom of assembly, the press, speech, correspondence, telecommunication, contract, travel, residence, job, nationality, etc.'. They recognized all individuals as 'entitled to absolute freedom (*ṣāḥib-i āzādī-i muṭlaq*)'. Though what they meant by 'absolute freedom' was not clear, they immediately added the provision that 'the freedom of every individual is continuous and expandable as far as it does not trespass upon the freedoms of other individuals, does not disturb order in social places, and is not contrary to social principles'.[87]

Though both key parties had apparently introduced freedom of others as the border of an individual's freedom, during numerous proceedings of the majlis, their representatives did not abide by this principle and did not consider the limits of legal interferences in an individual's freedoms as only that which prevented an individual's infringement on another individual's sphere of freedom.

In practice, the second majlis deputies had three criteria in determining the borders of the freedom of every individual:

(1) Occasionally, they referred to the freedoms guaranteed by the constitution, arguing that the validity of the law is conditional upon upholding such freedoms. In discussions about 'freedom in the educational programmes of private schools' and 'giving carte blanche to the government to eliminate terrorism', the issue of observing the freedoms stipulated in the constitution and its non-infringement by the parliamentary laws was raised, though in both cases the limits of the people's freedoms became more confined than what had been guaranteed for them in the constitution.
(2) The second criterion was that laws must not limit freedoms recognized by religion. This rule was specifically referred to in discussions about ownership while invoking the religious principle which states that 'people have command of their properties and their lives'. We should also remember that those in favour of religious laws usually invoked the same religious principle in their opposition to the first majlis and some of its laws, such as the imposition

of tax and customs tariffs as well as the pricing of products. The second majlis probed the issue during debates on transacting opium – sap (*shīrah-ʾi taryāk*) and the right to excavate private properties in search of antique objects.

(3) The third criterion was usually discussed whenever no particular article of the constitution or any sharia law was invoked. In such cases, majlis deputies would consider compatibility with the 'spirit of constitutionalism' or 'the principles of natural right of freedom' as the criteria for the correctness of law. An example of such reasoning emerged in discussions about the monopolization of the soap industry during four sessions held in March and May 1910, and during discussions on the right of resigned representatives to be employed in government departments. Let us pay a closer look at examples of the application of these criteria.

3.4.1 Constitution, the scale of limits to freedom

Earlier, we saw how the constitution and its supplement, as the greatest achievement of the first constitutionalism, were written with the intention to restrain arbitrary rule, with legislators refusing to compromise the rights of the nation as much as possible. However, the provision 'except in accordance with law' was the Achilles' heel of the rights of the people in the constitution in that it legally permitted future lawmakers to make exceptions and to withdraw certain freedoms. Despite all this, the spirit of the constitution was loyal to freedom and did not easily acquiesce to arbitrary interpretations. It was such steadfastness that made it possible for the constitutionalists who were critical of the Press Law to oppose the first majlis by referring to the constitution and to condemn its act of passing a law that violated certain freedoms stipulated in the constitution. Several times during the second majlis, disputes broke out between the deputies who, by resorting to the pretext of 'except in accordance with the law', wanted to authorize interference in people's freedoms, and those who found the spirit of the law inconsistent with allowing such interferences.

3.4.1.1 The issue of freedom of education in private schools

The freedom of education in private schools once came up in connection to the following question: are private schools free from the interferences of the Ministry of Science and Education to choose their curriculums? Representatives disputed over this issue. Eventually, the following two articles of the bill proposed by the minister of education were approved by a majority of the votes: Article 9, 'private schools must continue to follow the official curriculum and regulate their programs by pursuing government order step by step'; and Article 59, 'any school that acts contrary to the official curriculum or that is not capable of carrying out that curriculum will be reprimanded and the Ministry of Science has the right to shut the school down'. They then voted on another article according to which the Ministry of Education's curriculum had to be pursued in home-schooling cases, otherwise parents would be made responsible. This article was not approved.[88]

After the voting, Taqī'zādah pointed to a fundamental issue, saying that the bills approved by the majlis were contrary to the freedom of education and learning stipulated in Article 18 of the constitution; he explained that the majority vote in this regard was therefore invalid, and that no voting should have even taken place. Freedom of education and learning, he believed, was the distinguishing point between an arbitrary government and a constitutional one without which 'the country could not tread the path of development. . . . The greatest benefit of constitutionalism is this very freedom'. The only restriction on freedom of teaching and learning that Taqī'zādah recognized was the provision 'except what is religiously forbidden', which was stipulated in Article 18. However, Shāh'zādah Asad Allāh Mīrzā, a deputy for Tehran and a member of the *i'tidālīyūn* party, believed that Taqī'zādah's objection was baseless since 'in Articles 18 and 19 of the constitution, . . . whatever is stipulated about freedom of education refers to individuals, whereas whatever is stated about coercion refers to institutions, including both public and private schools'.[89] According to his interpretation, the constitution made a distinction between the agents of freedom of teaching and learning, and attributed freedom to individuals and not to institutions. Accordingly, absolute freedom would be considered for education at home while school education would be bound by government curriculum. The debate on the majlis floor did not come to fruition and was referred to the Education Commission for its consistency with the constitution to be re-examined.[90]

3.4.1.2 The issue of giving carte blanche to the government

The most challenging question concerning freedom which was posed in the second majlis was as follows: can the law delegate absolute authority to the government to interfere in individuals' freedom in order to preserve security and put an end to chaos? This question first arose following the assassination of several leading constitutionalists, including Sayyid 'Abd Allāh Bihbahānī in July 1911, an incident that made the majlis deputies furious. Addressing the cabinet, Asad Allāh Khān, a deputy for Kurdistan and a member of the *i'tidālīyūn* party, asserted that they must wield their power to blind the eyes of those who had opened fire in favour of arbitrary rule. He went on to aggressively add

> Blinding eyes, in this situation, is the first step of freedom-seeking. Blinding the eyes [of these terrorists] for the sake of the peace of a hundred thousand people is nothing but freedom-seeking.[91]

Following up on his speech in the next session, he warned the majlis that 'at present, the country's enemy is the Mauser; if yesterday the two monsters of arbitrary rule and reaction (*istibdād va irtijā'*) were the enemy, today a third one appears that provokes conflict, fuels sedition and uses weapons'.[92] He then noted that, even though the constitution has guaranteed freedom of association, it has made this freedom subject to the condition of not being disruptive of order and security, and therefore planned methods for how they can be controlled. Thus, it would not be contrary to the constitution if carte blanche were given to the government to limit corrupt associations. However, regarding freedom of the press, he pointed to a condition in the constitution that imposed limitations on executors' authorities. This condition stipulated that once a newspaper was banned on grounds of being disruptive of order and security, its offense must be announced within 24 hours after the banning. Accordingly, Asad Allāh Khān concluded, even entrusting carte blanche to the government would not be sufficient to rectify the situation. Thus, he requested that the majlis declare martial law for three months so that the government may disarm and disperse such associations.[93]

In the same session, the chief minister Mīrzā Ḥasan Mustawfī al-Mamālik, the minister of war Aḥmad Qavām al-Salṭanah, and the minister of foreign affairs Ḥusayn Qulī Khān Navvāb, demanded the delegation of carte blanche to the cabinet for a certain period of time. Ḥāj Āqā Shīrāzī, a deputy for Fars and a member of the *iʿtidālīyūn* party, objected by saying that the purpose of such carte blanche must be made clear, 'so that the deputies become aware of what they are voting for'.[94] He preferred martial law to carte blanche. In his response, the minister of the interior ʿAbd al-Ḥusayn Mīrzā Farmān'farmā said 'the city is still not in such state of disorder to require martial law'. The chief minister added that the ministers cannot guarantee to provide security for the city 'within the legal limitations (*dar ḥudūd-i qānūnī*)', and that they demanded 'to be given carte blanche for a limited period'. [95]The minister of war then interpreted carte blanche in four articles, three of which concerned disarmament, and the last one which stated the following: 'Article 4 – Those associations and newspapers that cause corruption and disorder will be constrained by force'.

The majlis was ready to vote on this proposal when it became ʿAbd al-Ḥamīd Khān Matīn al-Salṭanah's[96] turn to speak. Expressing his satisfaction with the rejection of the vague proposal of carte blanche, he described that day as a historic day in which 'Iranians were an inch away from losing all the freedoms that had been achieved during these four years'.[97] Accepting the four explanatory articles proposed by the minister of war, he then ambiguously opposed a part of Article 4 that entrusted the government with absolute authority to limit the press. Indeed, he endeavored to interpret this authority as that which implemented the rules and laws of the majlis. His attempt was rejected by the minister of the post Asad Allāh Mīrzā, who argued that 'even the legal authorities of the government are gradually being denied'.[98] Without responding to Matīn al – Salṭanah's concern about freedom of the press, Asad Allāh Mīrzā diverted the debate to focus on the difference between 'the ban on weapons (*manʿ-i aslaḥah*)' and 'disarmament (*nazʿ-i aslaḥah*)' to prove that previous parliamentary laws referring to 'the ban on weapons' and were not sufficient to account for the issue of disarmament.

The last attempt to impose some limitations on the government's demand for absolute authority was made by Muʿazziz al-Mulk,[99] who insisted on determining when and where carte blanche applied. He argued that

> if these authorities are within the boundaries of the law, they do not require parliamentary approval; if they are beyond the law, they are exigencies of the situation and therefore it must be written: in Tehran and for a certain period of time.[100]

In response to this request, the minister of war added the two conditions 'in Tehran' and 'for three months' to the government's proposal. After these changes and limitations, the majority of the majlis voted in favour of granting carte blanche to the government.

Eight months later, the majlis once again faced the freedom-versus-security dilemma. The new government, in its security program, had demanded having 'carte blanche in order to remove corruption (*ikhtiyārāt-i tāmmah dar rafʿ-i mavādd-i fisād*)', once more under the pretext of fighting terrorism and providing security. The advocates of carte blanche considered terrorism the greatest threat to freedom. Noting that the constitution is an agreement determining the nation's and the government's boundaries, one of the opposing representatives said that if the extent of authority stipulated in the constitution is not sufficient for the government to fulfil its duties and carte blanche is required, it should be put to a referendum. To give carte blanche to the government is beyond the authority of the majlis and against the constitution.[101] In response to opponents, the minister of interior Mīrzā Ṣādiq Khān Mustashār al-Dawlah, who once was the second majlis deputy for Tabriz before being appointed minister, distinguished between arbitrary rule and carte blanche, stating that 'arbitrary rule is the personal decision made either by one person or by a group, whereas carte blanche is demanded by the government from the representatives of the people and therefore reinforces the will of the nation'.[102] He then warned the deputies that they should not let fear of the return of arbitrary rule prevent them from doing what they should do, otherwise they would regret this negligence. In his opinion, the majlis debates over this issue were unrealistic, since outside the Parliament building, as he pictured it, the situation was 'so appalling and chaotic that the deputies should give the government not only carte blanche, but also whatever stronger authority imaginable in order to stabilize such a situation'.[103]

Finally, Vaḥīd al-Mulk, as the last opponent, noted that demanding absolute authority to interfere in the freedom of the press and proceeding press offenses in the administrative courts (*maḥākim-i idārī*) rather than courts of justice (*maḥākim-i ʿadlīyah*) violated three articles of the constitution:

> Firstly, Article 71 of the Supplementary Fundamental Laws that introduces the Supreme Ministry of justice (*dīvān-i ʿadālat-i ʿuẓmá*) as the place officially destined for the redress of public grievances; secondly, Article 77 that says that the proceedings of political and press offences must be open, and that where it is desirable that the proceedings be private, this must be agreed to by all members of the tribunal; thirdly, Article 79 . . . ordering that in case of political and press offences, a jury must be present in the tribunals.[104]

Despite the protests of deputies who tended to vote for freedom in the challenging freedom-security dilemma, security triumphed once again. Without further clarification, the government proposal for carte blanche was passed with 47 votes in favour, 17 against, and 9 abstentions.

The ratification of carte blanche resulted in several objections throughout the country. The Regent received protests from Hamadan and Khorasan asking him to fulfil his duties in preserving people's freedom and putting an end to 'the violation of the constitution, the deprivation of freedom, and reactionary return (*'awdat-i irtijā'ī*)'.[105] After these telegrams were read in a session on 29 June 1911, it was decided that the majlis should respond to them. Āqā Mīrzā Murtaẕá Qulī Khān Ṣamṣām, a deputy for Isfahan and a member of the *i'tidālīyūn* party, prepared the following response:

> Relying on the philosophy of law, whereas there is no article in the constitution stipulating the impermissibility of giving carte blanche, we have to refer to the indication and the spirit of the constitution and its interpretation in order to discern the compatibility or incompatibility of carte blanche with the constitution. Furthermore, according to the very constitution which is the foundation of the new system of governance, the majlis has the right to interpret the law . . . [and] the majority of the majlis must always be obeyed as long as the country is under constitutional monarchy. Nobody should dare to disobey the majlis, unless he himself is against the foundation of Constitutionalism and intends to misuse the constitution to achieve his own illegitimate goals. Since the majority means the majlis itself . . . to deny the majority is to deny the majlis, which is to deny Constitutionalism.[106]

So once again, the deputies in this session violated the minority's rights under the pretext of the right of the majority. Thus, they not only gave the government absolute authority to interfere with the freedom of individuals, but also refused to recognize the minority's right to protest.

3.4.2 Is parliamentary law legitimate to put a limit on freedoms guaranteed by religious law?

A few months before the triumph of the Constitutional Movement, when Nāẓim al-Islām Kirmānī met Shaykh Faẕl Allāh Nūrī to gain his support for the movement, Nūrī criticized constitutionalism, asking Kirmānī, 'do you have any idea that, in a constitutional government, I have to pay taxes if I wish to multiply the windows of this room or to make two holes instead of one?'[107] Nūrī's opinion is rooted in his traditional understanding of the *fiqh*. Relying on the Islamic principle which states that 'people have absolute command over their properties', this view emphasizes the right of individual ownership and insists on minimizing the government's interferences in the freedom of the possessor to use the possessor's personal properties. However, public interest, the exigencies of production and business in the modern world, and the transformation of state function often forced constitutionalist legislators to restrict some religiously legitimate freedoms which had been common in the old order. In the same way, it was possible that the implications of a parliamentary law indicated the permission of something forbidden by the sharia.

3.4.2.1 The issue of giving exclusive rights of the opium-sap trade to the government

An example of the contradictions between parliamentary and sharia laws appeared when the majlis deputies were addressing the following question: to what extent is it morally and religiously allowed to give exclusive rights of trading opium-sap to the government in order to gradually reduce its production and finally prohibit it and treat the addicts? The deputies agreed that opium was harmful and that opium-sap was even worse; therefore, they were not against the restriction or even the prohibition of opium-sap consumption. However, some of them found it humiliating for the government to have monopoly of the opium-sap trade. Shāh'zādah Abu al-Ḥasan Mīrzā Shaykh al-Ràīs, a deputy for Māzandarān and a member of the *hay'at-i mu'talifah* party, believed that

> Tax could be levied on opium but not on burnt-opium, since burnt-opium, from which opium-sap is produced, is evil (*khabā'is*) and according to the Qur'anic principle of '[God] makes *al-khabā'is* unlawful to them',[108] its trade is forbidden even for the government. But if we consider burnt-opium as valuable and sellable, according to the sharia, the possessor is free to sell it at any price and to anyone that he wishes; no one can force him to sell it to the government or at a specified price.[109]

Another deputy added that 'there is no point in discussing and voting on an issue whose permissibility has been determined by the sharia as the majority cannot make any changes in Islamic laws'.[110] This indicates that, for them, the legislation is only allowed within the discretionary sphere of Islamic law (*manṭaqat al-firāgh-i shar'ī*) and religiously neutral affairs (*mubāḥ*).

3.4.2.2 The issue of possession of personal property

Another example of the contradictions between parliamentary and sharia laws arose when the majlis was discussing a proposal stipulating that 'excavation in quest of antique objects in the lands of the country is absolutely prohibited except after receipt of official permission from the ministry of education'.[111] The question was whether such a limitation was also imposable on private properties. Ḥāj Shaykh 'Alī Khurāsānī, a deputy for Sabzivār and a member of the *hay'at-i mu'talifah* party, said that 'although this is a good article, it negates a freedom, so a proviso must be added to exempt personal properties'.[112] Another member of the *hay'at-i mu'talifah* party and a deputy for Khuzistān, Shaykh Muḥammad 'Alī Bahjat Dizfūlī, answered to this objection by arguing that all laws restrict a level of freedom: 'The law is always incompatible with freedom. Certainly, absolute freedom does not exist . . . the law always puts a limitation on freedom'.[113]

While accepting the general principle that 'all laws restrain freedom', Shaykh al-Ràīs added that 'the law only prevents the freedom which is religiously illegal or harmful to another person's freedom, whereas it is stated in Islam that people have absolute command over their properties'. He then asked Bahjat, 'why do you adduce such assertions about political affairs which are common in non-Islamic countries? Islam has its own rules of ownership that differ from those of European countries where only the possession of the land's surface is transferrable to the consumer'.[114]

This debate did not reach a conclusion and was finally sent to the commission of education for further deliberation.

3.4.3 The linkage between law and natural right of freedom

To what extent may the law restrain a person's natural right of freedom? It was previously noted that during the first constitutional period, the law was found as the preserver and distributor of the public wealth of freedom; therefore, the utmost concern of lawmakers was the legislation of such laws that placed limitations on the government's authority to interfere in an individual's freedom. They certainly knew that, in the distribution of freedom between people, everyone should have an equal share and no one should violate another person's freedom. Nevertheless, the central issue for lawmakers was how they could reclaim a larger share of the freedom of the nation from the rulers and return it to the people. Yet it was during the first constitutional era that Muḥammad ʿAlī Furūghī, in his discussion about the national monarchy (*salṭanat-i millī*), emphasized that 'since a hundred years ago, everyone has been convinced that the nation must be autonomous and that the state as the representative of the nation has a mandate to administrate on behalf of the people and to preserve their rights'.[115] Therefore, the state, Furūghī added, must take on the two separate responsibilities of legislation and implementation of the law.[116] Considering the fact that the law as a national contract must be in accordance with the nation's will and vote,[117] 'the state must not be free to legislate whatever it wants, but must be bound to observe some obligations and limitations'.[118] Insisting on the necessity of the preservation of the public rights held naturally and inherently by all the people, Furūghī wrote that 'the legislation and implementation of the law must not be incompatible with these rights, as the state has been established for the sake of preserving these very rights', namely, freedom and equality.[119] He went on to emphasize that 'a law is not legitimate and just unless it is compatible with the rights of the nation'.[120] Nonetheless, for him, an individual's rights were limited by two boundaries: the rights of others and public interest, which is sometimes given priority over personal interests.[121]

This idea received more attention during the second constitutional era, when the chaotic exercise of personal freedom violated both the rights of others and public interest. For instance, Sayyid Muṣṭafá ʿAdl (Manṣūr al-Salṭanah), a leading scholar of law and a future minister of justice under Riẕā Shāh Pahlavī, in his 1909 book *Ḥuqūq-i asāsī yā uṣūl-i mashrūṭīyat*, determined violation of the rights of others and public interest as two cases in which the person's right could restricted.[122] In a chapter devoted to explaining the freedom of the nation, he listed the main cases in which the law could limit an individual's freedom for the sake of public interest and security. According to him, such legal restrictions could be imposed on a variety of freedoms: personal freedom, freedom of property, freedom of housing, freedom of trade, commerce and industry, freedom of conscience, freedom of assembly and association, freedom of education, and freedom of expression and of the press.[123] He also added to the list some other cases in which the law allowed the government to entirely and absolutely prevent a part of people's rights and freedoms in order to establish public order and security.[124] Muṣṭafá ʿAdl's providing such a long list of legal restrictions imposable on the people's freedom, in a book entitled *The Fundamental Rights or the Principles of Constitutionalism*, indicated that the central question of the thinkers of the second constitutional era had turned from the question of restricting arbitrary rule into the question of restricting license and chaos. Studying an example of the second parliamentary debates sheds light on this point.

3.4.3.1 The issue of the right of the majlis to elect a deputy for a region whose deputy has died or resigned

The debate arose in response to the following question: 'in the case that a majlis deputy dies or resigns, may the majlis elect another representative for that region?' Many deputies believed that the election of parliamentary members is a nontransferable right of the nation. It should be noted that the second parliament had already elected 19 representatives on behalf of the people, and yet the number of attendees at this session (the 303rd session) was 66, which was slightly more than half.[125] To prevent such disorder, some deputies proposed an article saying that a deputy who fails to come to the majlis for more than two months after his election must resign. Others believed that this was incompatible with the freedom of the deputies.[126]

Similarly, in a session which took place in June 1911, a discussion ensued about a proposal stating that a resigned member of the majlis cannot apply for any government job before the end of the period of delegation.[127] During this discussion, Āqā Sayyid Ḥusayn Ardibīlī, a deputy for Khorasan who was a member of the Democrat Party, insisted that all Iranians had the right to be elected, to elect, and to apply for any government departments. He introduced these three rights as 'the natural rights of all Iranians' which no one must be deprived of.[128] However, this hope was not fulfiled; in November 1911 and following the Russian ultimatum, the second majlis was unexpectedly forced to close down by the government, and Iranians were for three years deprived of the right of national sovereignty and the natural right of electing and being elected.

3.5 Concluding remarks

By analyzing a number of significant legal texts such as the Constitutional Decree, the first Constitution and its Supplement, the first Press Law, and the Proceedings of the first two majlises, this chapter has aimed to examine the Iranian legislators' interpretations of the second variable of the triadic concept of freedom, namely the restraint on freedom. The research method, as explained in the introduction, is grounded in a hermeneutical interpretation of Collingwood's logic of question and answer. The questions, to which the above-mentioned texts must be understood as the answers, have been reconstructed, and the horizon in which such questions arose have been analyzed. In conclusion, the results of this study can be summarized as follows:

(1) The first legislative majlis in Iran faced two theoretical barriers: (a) the myth of Divine Grace (*farr-i īzadī*), according to which the shah's will must be put above all laws; and (b) the idea of sufficiency of the sharia, according to which only the divine law has legitimacy. The constitutionalists gradually overcame both barriers. Encountering the former, they interpreted the majlis, which was promised in the Constitutional Decree of August 1906, as neither an independent judicial court (*ʿadālat'khānah*) nor a consulting majlis (*majlis-i mashvaratī*), but rather as a consultative legislative majlis (*majlis-i shūrā-yi qānūn'guzārī*). Encountering the latter barrier, they made a distinction between worldly matters and religious matters, stating that the majlis had the right to legislate only worldly matters and to enforce the law within the discretionary sphere of Islamic law (*manṭaqat al-firāgh-i sharʿī*) and religiously neutral affairs (*mubāḥ*).

(2) Despite some resistance and objections, the majlis held the authority to determine the limits of freedom or, as Nāʾīnī said, 'the degree of the King's authority and the nation's freedom'. In such a horizon, the constitution was considered as 'the marker of the boundaries between the monarchy and the nation' and the majlis deputies were regarded as the guardians and distributors of 'the public wealth of freedom'.

(3) During the first constitutional period (August 1906–June 1908), the concern of the first majlis was to establish the rule of law. In legislating the constitution and its supplement, the majority of the majlis believed that the main obstacle to freedom was arbitrary rule. Therefore, they endeavoured to restrain the government's illegal and arbitrary interferences in the people's freedom. However, they did not develop a rational criterion for identifying legitimate and justifiable legal interferences. Using the ambiguous phrase 'except in accordance with the law' (*magar bih ḥukm-i qānūn*) in ten articles of the Supplementary Fundamental Laws, the legislators provided the state with the opportunity to limit the legitimate freedoms of the people under the pretext of 'legal interferences'.

(4) During the second constitutional period (July 1909–February 1921), the main concern of the second majlis was to restrain the chaos and to strengthen the central government in order to put an end to domestic insecurity and foreign threats. Chaos is a situation where there is an absence of all obstacles to freedom, in such a way that the one who has more power enjoys more freedom. To rectify such a situation, the majlis gave carte blanche to the government and empowered it to interfere even in the freedoms guaranteed by the constitution. As a result, the situation began to turn from chaos towards arbitrary rule.

(5) During the second constitutional era, the notion that a person's freedom should be limited by the freedom of others or by the public interests became more acceptable. However, in practice, most of the legal limitations on a person's freedom were legislated by virtue of the priority of public interests over personal interests.

In both constitutional periods, by imposing and enforcing legal obligations on a person's activities, legislators attempted not only to ensure that the person's freedom would not violate the freedom of others, but also to guarantee the public interest of the society. It is worth mentioning that legislators had a religious understanding of the notion of public interest. This point will be further discussed in the next chapter through examination of their interpretations of the purpose of freedom.

Notes

1 The decree written by Qavām al-Salṭanah and signed by the shah has no title. The shah himself referred to it as 'Our previous Rescript dated 14th of Jumada II (*dastkhaṭ-i sābiq-i khvudimān*)' (see Aḥmad Kasravī, *Tārīkh-i mashrūṭah-ʾi Īrān* (Tehran: Hermes Publishers, 2010), p. 160).

2 According to Browne, these four pillars are as follows: '(1) The Royal Proclamation of August 5, 1906, (2) The Electoral Law of September 9, 1906, (3) The Fundamental Laws of December 30, 1906, and (4) The Supplementary Fundamental Laws of October 7, 1907'. For an English translation of these documents, see Edward Granville Browne, *A Brief Narrative of Recent Events in Persia: Followed by a Translation of 'The Four Pillars of the Persian Constitution'* (London: Luzac and Co., 1909), pp. 65–101.

3 Muẓaffar al-Dīn Shāh, '[*farmān-i mashrūṭīyat*]', quoted in Muḥammad Mahdī Sharīf Kāshānī, *Vāqiʿāt-i ittifāqīyah dar rūzgār* (Tehran: Nashr-i Tārīkh-i Īrān, 1362), pp. 85–6); Nāẓim al-Islām Kirmānī, *Tārīkh-i bīdārī-i īrāniyān*, ed. by Saʿīdī Sirjānī (Tehran: Piykān, 1376), vol. 3, p. 564; translated to English by Browne (pp. 65–6). To make it more accurate, I revised the translated text. The revised parts are underlined.

4 As the *farmān* had not named some of the classes and guilds, the shah was forced by the objections of the public to reissue another proclamation 'in order to complete Our previous Rescript of 14 Jumada II 1324', emphasizing the phrase 'the delegates elected by the nation (*muntakhabīn-i millat*)'. In this supplementary proclamation, the majlis was referred to as *majlis-i shūrā-yi Islāmī* instead of *majlis-i shūrā-yi millī* (for the text of this proclamation, see Kasravī, p. 160.)

5 For more information about Ṭabāṭabāʾī's endeavours for reform, see Vanessa Martin, *Islam and Modernism: The Iranian Revolution of 1906* (Syracuse, NY: Syracuse University Press, 1989), pp. 65–85.

6 For the text of this night-letter, see Sharīf Kāshānī, pp. 40–5.

7 Ibid.

8 For the text of the night-letter, see Sharīf Kāshānī, pp. 55–8.

9 Sharīf Kāshānī, p. 60.

10 Ibid.; Nāẓim al-Islām Kirmānī, vol. 2, pp. 384–5.

11 Sharīf Kāshānī, p. 60; Nāẓim al-Islām Kirmānī, vol. 2, pp. 385–6.

12 Sharīf Kāshānī, p. 61; Nāẓim al-Islām Kirmānī, vol. 2, p. 386.

13 Sharīf Kāshānī, p. 61.

14 For the text of Ṭabāṭabāʾī's letter to ʿAyn al-Dawlah, see Sharīf Kāshānī, pp. 61–3.

15 Ibn Mīrzā Naṣr Allāh Mustawfī Tafrishī, *Tārīkh-i inqilāb-i mashrūṭah-ʾi Īrān* (Malik Library, MS 3819, Sha'ban 1325 / September 1907), pp. 27–8.

16 Ibid.
17 Mustawfī Tafrishī, p. 28.
18 Ibid., p. 28–9.
19 For the text of the speech, see Sharīf Kāshānī, pp. 105–6.
20 Sharīf Kāshānī, p. 106.
21 Mīrzā Yūsuf Khān Mustashār al-Dawlah Tabrīzī, *The Essence of Modernity: Mirza Yusof Khan Mustashar ad-Dowla Tabrizi's Treatise on Codified Law (Yak Kalima)*, trans. by A.A. Seyed-Gohrab (Amsterdam: West Lafayette, Ind: Rozenberg Publishers; Purdue University Press, 2007), p. 82.
22 Mustashār al-Dawlah Tabrīzī, *The Essence of Modernity*, pp. 12–16.
23 Ibid., p. 20.
24 Sayyid Naṣr Allāh Taqavī, 'Maqālah-ʾi suʾāl va javāb dar favāyid-i majlis', in *Rasāʾil-i mashrūṭīyat: mashrūṭah bih ravāyat-i muvāfiqān va mukhālifān*, ed. by Ghulām Ḥusayn Zargarī'nizhād, 2 vols. (Tehran: Intishārāt-i Muʿassisah-ʾi Taḥqīqāt va Tawsiʿah-ʾi ʿUlūm-i Insānī, 1387), vol. 1, pp. 547–62 (p. 557); Shaykh Mahdī Tabrīzī, 'Suʾāl'hāʾī dāyir bih mashrūṭīyat', in *Rasāʾil-i mashrūṭīyat: mashrūṭah bih ravāyat-i muvāfiqān va mukhālifān*, ed. by Ghulām Ḥusayn Zargarī'nizhād, 2 vols. (Tehran: Intishārāt-i Muʿassisah-ʾi Taḥqīqāt va Tawsiʿah-ʾi ʿUlūm-i Insānī, 1387), vol. 2, pp. 59–76 (p. 65); Nūr Allāh Najafī Iṣfahānī, 'Muklimāt-i Ḥājī-i Musāfir va Muqīm dar bayān-i ḥaqīqat-i maʿnā-yi mashrūṭh va muṭlaqah', in *Rasāʾil-i mashrūṭīyat: mashrūṭah bih ravāyat-i muvāfiqān va mukhālifān*, ed. by Ghulām Ḥusayn Zargarī'nizhād (Tehran: Intishārāt-i Muʿassisah-ʾi Taḥqīqāt va Tawsiʿah-ʾi ʿUlūm-i Insānī, 1387), vol. 2, pp. 297–364 (pp. 315–17); Mīrzā 'Alī S̱iqat al-Islām Tabrīzī, 'Risalah-ʾi lālān', in *Rasāʾil-i mashrūṭīyat: mashrūṭah bih ravāyat-i muvāfiqān va mukhālifān* (Tehran: Intishārāt-i Muʿassisah-ʾi Taḥqīqāt va Tawsiʿah-ʾi ʿUlūm-i Insānī, 1387), vol. 2, pp. 365–401 (p. 399); and Muḥammad Ḥusayn Nāʾīnī, 'Tanbīh al-ummah va tanzīh al-millah', in *Rasāʾil-i mashrūṭīyat: mashrūṭah bih ravāyat-i muvāfiqān va mukhālifān*, ed. by Ghulām Ḥusayn Zargarī'nizhād (Tehran: Intishārāt-i Muʿassisah-ʾi Taḥqīqāt va Tawsiʿah-ʾi ʿUlūm-i Insānī, 1387), vol. 2, pp. 403–90 (pp. 440, 458).
25 See, for instance, the telegram from the *marājiʿ* of Najaf cited in 'Mashrūḥ-i muzākirāt-i majlis-i avval (Proceeding of the 1st Majlis)', *Lawḥ-i mashrūḥ-i muzākirāt-i majālis shūrā-yi millī va Islāmī* (Tehran: Kitābkhānah, Mūzih va Markaz-i Asnād-i Majlis-i Shūrā-yi Isāmī, 2015) [on DVD], Sessions 3 Jumada II 1324, 13 Dhu'l Hijja 1324/ [25 July 1906, 28 January 1907].
26 ʿImād al-ʿUlamāʾ Khalkhālī, 'Bayān-i maʿnī-i salṭanat va fawāyid'ihā', in *Rasāʾil-i mashrūṭīyat: mashrūṭah bih ravāyat-i muvāfiqān va mukhālifān*, ed. by Ghulām Ḥusayn Zargarī'nizhād, 2 vols. (Tehran: Intishārāt-i Muʿassisih-i Taḥqīqāt va Tuvsiʿih-i ʿUlūm-i Insānī, 1387), vol. 2, 9–57 (pp. 31–2).
27 Shaykh Mahdī Tabrīzī, vol. 2, p. 74.
28 The answer was issued on 11 September 1907 by the majlis to the proponents of the *mashruʿah* who had migrated to the ʿAbd al-ʿAẓīm Shrine. See majlis-i shūrā-yi millī-i Irān, 'Javāb-i ṣādir az majlis-i muqaddas va muḥtaram-i shūrā-yi millī-i Irān- 3 Shaʿbān 1325', in *Lavāyiḥ-i Āqā Shaykh Faẕl Allāh Nūrī* (Tehran: Nashr-i Tārīkh-i Īrān, 1362), p. 68.; see also Shaykh Muḥammad Ismāʿīl Maḥallātī Gharavī, 'Al-lāālī al-marbūṭah fī wujūb al-mashrūṭah', in *Rasāʾil-i mashrūṭīyat: mashrūṭah bih ravāyat-i muvāfiqān va mukhālifān*, ed. by Zargarī'nizhād, Ghulām Ḥusayn, 2 vols. (Tehran: Intishārāt-i Muʿassisah-ʾi Taḥqīqāt va Tawsiʿah-ʾi ʿUlūm-i Insānī, 1387), vol. 2, pp. 199–276 (pp. 235–6); Najafī Iṣfahānī, vol. 2, pp. 314–15; and Nāʾīnī, vol. 2, pp. 453, 467, 469.
29 Muḥammad Ḥusayn ibn ʿAlī Akbar Tabrīzī, 'Kashf al-murād min al-mashrūṭah wa al-istibdād', in *Rasāʾil-i mashrūṭīyat: mashrūṭah bih ravāyat-i muvāfiqān va mukhālifān*, ed. by Zargarī'nizhād, Ghulām Ḥusayn, 2 vols. (Tehran: Intishārāt-i Muʿassisah-ʾi Taḥqīqāt va Tawsiʿah-ʾi ʿUlūm-i Insānī, 1387), vol. 1, pp. 173–230 (pp. 214–15).

30 Tabrīzī, vol. 1, p. 198.
31 Shaykh Fażl Allāh Nūrī, 'Risālah-ʾi ḥurmat-i mashrūṭah, yā pāsukh bih suʾāl az ʿillat-i muvāfiqat-i avvalīyah bā mashrūṭīyat va mukhālifat-i s̱ānavīyah bā ān', in *Rasāʾil-i mashrūṭīyat: mashrūṭah bih ravāyat-i muvāfiqān va mukhālifān*, 2 vols. (Tehran: Intishārāt-i Muʿassisah-ʾi Taḥqīqāt va Tawsiʿah-ʾi ʿUlūm-i Insānī, 1387), vol. 1, pp. 253–73 (p. 260).
32 Nūrī, 'Risālah-ʾi ḥurmat-i mashrūṭah', vol. 1, p. 264.
33 Ibid., pp. 272–3; see also Shaykh Fażl Allāh Nūrī [?], 'Tazkirah al-ghāfil wa irshād al-jāhil', in *Rasāʾil-i mashrūṭīyat: mashrūṭah bih ravāyat-i muvāfiqān va mukhālifān*, ed. by Ghulām Ḥusayn Zargarī'nizhād, 2 vols. (Tehran: Intishārāt-i Muʿassisah-ʾi Taḥqīqāt va Tawsiʿah-ʾi ʿUlūm-i Insānī, 1387), vol. 1, 275–303 (p. 285); and Tabrīzī, vol. 1, pp. 214–17.
34 Nūrī [?], 'Tazkirah al-ghāfil', vol. 1, p. 286.
35 See Maḥallātī Gharavī, vol. 2, p. 235.
36 Likewise, another solution was suggested for those new freedoms that seemed to be incompatible with the sharia. In an important unsigned article published in *Ṣūr-i Isrāfīl*, the writer clearly argued that 'changes in circumstances require the interpretation, contraction and expansion of laws'. The writer claimed that the method of this revision of religious law is based on the very principles employed by the *ʿulamā* in justifying variations in commandments due to the alteration of circumstances, and accidental attributes (*ʿunvānāt-i ṭārīyah*). In other words, since the circumstances of the Prophet's time have been changed, a primarily obligatory (*wājib*) or optional action (*mubāḥ*) may enter under accidental attributes such as hardship (*ḥaraj*), difficulty (*ʿusr*), lack of alternative (*iżṭirār*), or social disorder (*ikhtilāl-i niẓām*), and therefore become temporarily prohibited (*ḥarām*) and vice versa. Here, the role of human intellect is to recognize the differences between circumstances and to find a remedy in the public interest of the Muslim society (for more details, see section 4.2.).
37 For more information about the opinions of *akhbārī* and *uṣūlī faqīhs* on the ability of human intellect to understand praiseworthiness and blameworthiness of arbitrary human actions (*ḥusn va qubḥ*) and the principle of cohesion (*mulāzimah*), see Muḥammad Rizā Muẓaffar, *Uṣūl al-fiqh*, trans. by Muḥsin Gharaviyān (Qum: Intishārāt-i Dār al-Fikr, 1385), vol. 1, pp. 370–420.
38 Nāʾīnī, vol. 2, p. 453.
39 Ibid., p. 421.
40 This point was 'warily mentioned to Muḥammad ʿAlī Shāh' by a group of them during investigations into the illegal treatment of those who were accused of assassinating Muḥammad ʿAlī Shāh ('1st Majlis', Session 12 Rabi I, 1326 / [14 April 1908]). Interpreting his parliamentary oath as not committing treason against either the throne or the nation, Āqā Shaykh Ḥusayn told to Muḥammad ʿAlī Shāh, '[I have sworn] to let neither a morsel of the king's rights go in favour of the nation nor a bit of those of the nation go in the king's favour' ('1st Majlis', Session 9 Rabi I, 1326 / [11 April 1908]; three deputies of the first majlis are called Shaykh Ḥusayn, so it cannot be found out to whom this name refers).
41 Ṭālibūf was elected to the first Parliament for Tabriz, but he hesitated to attend the majlis (for the probable reason behind his hesitation, see Īraj Afshār (ed.), *Āzādī va siyāsat* (Tehran: Saḥar, 1366), pp. 16–17.
42 Ṭālibūf Tabrīzī, 'Īżāḥāt dar khuṣūṣ-i āzādī', p. 94.
43 Ibid., p. 110.
44 Ibid., pp. 120–21.
45 Ibid., p. 122, emphasis added.
46 '1st Majlis', Session 14 Shawwal 1324 / [1 December 1906]. For information about the context of this speech, see Gūʾil Kuhan, *Tārīkh-i sānsūr dar maṭbūʿāt-i Īrān* (Tehran: Āgāh, 1360), vol. 2, p. 72.

47 See Muẓaffar al-Dīn Shāh's introduction in 'Qānūn-i asāsī-i mashrūṭah, (The Fundamental Laws of December 1906)', *Lawḥ-i qānūn: Majmūʿah-i qavāmīn va muqarrāt-i kishvar* (Tehran: Markaz-i Pazhūhishha-yi Majlis-i Shūrā-yi Islamī, n.d.) [on DVD].

48 For a discussion on the role of popular sovereignty within Islamic constitutional thought, see Amirhassan Boozari, *Shi'i Jurisprudence and Constitution: Revolution in Iran* (New York: Palgrave Macmillan, 2011), pp. 62–5.

49 *Qānūn-i asāsī-i mashrūṭah*, Articles 13, 32.

50 See 'Mutamim-i qānūn-i asāsī (The Supplementary Fundamental Laws of October 1907)', *Lawḥ-i qānūn: Majmūʿah-i qavāmīn va muqarrāt-i kishvar* (Tehran: Markaz-i Pazhūhishha-yi Majlis-i Shūrā-yi Islamī, n.d.) [on DVD].

51 See 'Mutamim-i qānūn-i asāsī', Articles 9–22.

52 See 'Qānūn-i maṭbūʿāt, muṣavvab-i 5 Muharram 1326 (The Press Law of February 1908)', *Lawḥ-i qānūn: Majmūʿah-i qavāmīn va muqarrāt-i kishvar* (Tehran: Markaz-i Pazhūhishha-yi Majlis-i Shūrā-yi Islamī, n.d.) [on DVD].

53 Kuhan, p. 216.

54 See *Musāvāt*, no. 19 (5 April 1908).

55 *Maʿārif*, yrs. 2, no. 12 (20 April 1908).

56 Ibid.

57 *Ḥabl al-matīn* (Tehran), no. 59 (5 January 1907).

58 See below, section 4.3.2.

59 For instance, see the night-letter entitled '*Fadāʾiyān-i vaṭan*' cited in Sharīf Kāshānī, pp. 131–2.

60 Shaykh Faẕl Allāh Nūrī and Muhājirīn, '[Mā munkir-i majlis nīstīm]', in *Lavāyiḥ-i Āqā Shaykh Faẕl Allāh Nūrī* (Tehran: Nashr-i Tārīkh-i Īrān, 1362), pp. 44–5 (p. 45).

61 Shaykh Faẕl Allāh Nūrī, *Lavāyiḥ-i Āqā Shaykh Faẕl Allāh Nūrī* (Tehran: Nashr-i Tārīkh-i Īrān, 1362), p. 43.

62 Muhājirīn-i Zāvīyah-ʾi Muqaddasah, 'Rāfiʿ Al-Shubahāt', in *Lavāyiḥ-i Āqā Shaykh Faẕl Allāh Nūrī* (Tehran: Nashr-i Tārīkh-i Īrān, 1362), pp. 51–3 (p. 52).

63 Mullā Muḥammad ʿAlī Mujtahid Rustam'ābādī, '[Ṣūrat-i javāb-i taqāẕā-yi tashrīḥ-i ḥaq va bāṭil]', in *Lavāyiḥ-I Āqā Shaykh Faẕl Allah Nūrī* (Tehran: Nashr-i Tārīkh-i Īrān, 1362), pp. 35–7 (p. 35).

64 For instance, see '1st Majlis', Session 21 Shawwal 1325 / [27 November 1907].

65 For instance, see '1st Majlis', Session 18 Jumada I 1326 / [18 June 1908].

66 '1st Majlis', Session 5 Safar 1326 / [9 March 1908].

67 '1st Majlis', Session 12 Rabi I, 1326 / [14 April 1908].

68 Sharīf Kāshānī, p. 421.

69 Ibid., p. 573.

70 See '1st Majlis', Session 11 Safar 1325 / [26 March 1907].

71 'Maktūb az Kirmānshāhān', *Majlis* (Tehran, 23 Rabi I 1325 / [7 May 1907]), no. 86, pp. 1–2 (p. 1).

72 Sayyid Jamāl al-Dīn Vāʿiẓ Iṣfahānī, 'Dar mȧnī-i āzādī', *al-Jamāl* (Tehran, 11 Rabi I 1325 / [24 April 1907]), no. 7, pp. 1–3 (p. 1).

73 Q.Ḥ.T., 'Qābil tavajjuh-i ʿumūm-i aʿẕā-ʾi anjuman'hā-yi ukhuvvat-i īmānīyah va himmat', *Majlis* (Tehran, 24 Rabi I 1325 / [8 May 1907]), no. 87, pp. 2–3 (p. 2).

74 'Taqsīm-i istibdād yā tajziyah-ʾi salṭanat', *Rūḥ al-Qudus* (Tehran, 13 Safar 1326 / [17 March 1908]), no. 20, pp. 1–4 (p. 3).

75 Attributed to Shaykh Faẕl Allāh Nūrī, *Subḥ'nāmah-ʾi daʿvat al-Islām*, no. 1 (7 Rabi I 1327), cited in Nāẓim al-Islām Kirmānī, *Tārīkh-i bīdārī-i Īrāniyān*, ed. by Saʿīdī Sirjānī (Tehran: Piykān, 1376), vol. 5, p. 343.

76 'Taʿāvun-i māsūnī', in *Farāmāsūnrī dar Īrān: az āghāz tā tashkīl-i luzh-i bīdārī-i Īrān*, ed. by Maḥmūd Katīrā'ī (Tehran: Iqbāl, 1361), pp. 194–5. This treatise is originally a speech delivered by two French freemasons (Lātis and Lūbān?) in an Iranian

masonic lodge, *luzh-i bīdārī-i Īrān*, and was translated into Persian by Vuṡūq al-Dawlah and published by Dabīr al-Mamālik in 1911.

77 Katīrā'ī, 'Ta'āvun-i māsūnī', p. 206.

78 Ibid.

79 *Marām'nāmah'ha va niẓām'nāmah'hā-yi aḥzāb-i siyāsī-i Īrān dar duvumīn majlis-i shūrā-yi millī*, ed. by Manṣūrah Ittiḥādīyah (Tehran: Nashr-i Tārīkh-i Īrān, 1361), pp. XIV–XV.

80 Nāṣir al-Mulk's letter cited in 'Mashrūḥ-i muzākirāt-i majlis-i duvum (Proceeding of the 2nd Majlis)', *Lawḥ-i mashrūḥ-i muzākirāt-i majālis shūrā-yi millī va Islāmī* (Tehran: Kitābkhānah, Mūzih va Markaz-i Asnād-i Majlis-i Shūrā-yi Isāmī, 2015) [on DVD], Session 23 Safar 1329 / [23 February 1911].

81 Ibid.

82 Ibid.

83 Ibid.

84 Firqah-'i siyāsī-i dimukrāt-i Īrān, 'Marām'nāmah-'i firqah-'i siyāsī-i dimukrāt-i Īrān ('āmīyūn) [1329/1911]', in *Marām'nāmah'ha va niẓām'nāmah'hā-yi aḥzāb-i siyāsī-i Īrān dar duvumīn majlis-i shūrā-yi millī*, ed. by Manṣūrah Ittiḥādīyah (Tehran: Nashr-i Tārīkh-i Īrān, 1361), pp. 1–8.

85 Yik nafar dimūkrāt, 'Uṣūl-i dimūkrāsī bih qalam-i yik nafar dimūkrāt', in *Marām'nāmah'ha va niẓām'nāmah'hā-yi aḥzāb-i siyāsī-i Īrān dar duvumīn majlis-i shūrā-yi millī*, ed. by Manṣūrah Ittiḥādīyah (Tehran: Nashr-i Tārīkh-i Īrān, 1361), p. 41.

86 See Ibid., p. 33.

87 Ḥizb-i ijtimā'īyūn-i 'itidālīyūn, 'Dastūr-i mashrūḥ-i maslakī yā marām'nāmah-'i ḥizb-i ijtimā'īyūn-i 'itidālīyūn', in *Marām'nāmah'ha va niẓām'nāmah'hā-yi aḥzāb-i siyāsī-i Īrān dar duvumīn majlis-i shūrā-yi millī*, ed. by Manṣūrah Ittiḥādīyah (Tehran: Nashr-i Tārīkh-i Īrān, 1361), p. 101.

88 '2nd Majlis', Session 12 Rabi II 1328 / [23 April 1910].

89 Ibid.

90 Ibid.

91 '2nd Majlis', Session 23 Rajab 1328 / [31 July 1910].

92 Ibid.

93 '2nd Majlis', Session 26 Rajab 1328 / [3 August 1910].

94 Ibid.

95 Ibid.

96 He was a deputy for Khorasan and a member of the *Hay'at-i mu'talifah* party.

97 '2nd Majlis', Session 26 Rajab 1328 / [3 August 1910].

98 Ibid.

99 He was also a deputy for Khorasan and a member of the *hay'at-i mu'talifah* party, but tended towards the *I'tidālīyūun* party.

100 2nd Majlis', Session 26 Rajab 1328 / [3 August 1910].

101 '2nd Majlis', Session 14 Rabi I 1329 / [15 March 1911].

102 Ibid.

103 Ibid.

104 Ibid.

105 2nd Majlis', Session 2 Rajab 1329 / [29 June 1911].

106 '2nd Majlis', Session 2 Rajab 1329 / [29 June 1911].

107 Nāẓim al-Islām Kirmānī, vol. 1, p. 322.

108 *The Qur'an* (7:157).

109 '2nd Majlis', Session 19 Muharram 1329 / [20 January 1911].

110 Muḥammad Hāshim Mīrzā, see '2nd Majlis', Session 19 Muharram 1329 / [20 January 1911].

111 '2nd Majlis', Session 24 Muharram 1329 / [25 January 1911].
112 '2nd Majlis', Session 24 Muharram 1329 / [25 January 1911].
113 Ibid.
114 Ibid.
115 Furūghī, vol. 1, pp. 785–6.
116 Ibid.
117 Ibid., p. 790.
118 Ibid., p. 830.
119 Ibid.
120 Ibid.
121 Ibid., p. 831.
122 Sayyid Muṣṭafá ʿAdl (Manṣūr al -Salṭanah), *Huqūq-i asāsī yā uṣūl-i mashrūṭīyat* (Tehran: Nashr-i Chashmah, 1389), p. 84.
123 See ʿAdl (Manṣūr al-Salṭanah), pp. 97–115.
124 ʿAdl (Manṣūr al-Salṭanah), p. 108.
125 '2nd Majlis', Session 4 Shawwal 1329 / [28 September 1911]. A large number of the elected deputies never came to the majlis, and a group of them left the majlis before the end of the period of delegation. Only 39 persons completed the period of delegation (see Manṣūrah Ittiḥādīyah, *Majlis va intikhābāt az mashrūṭah ta pāyān-i Qājār* (Tehran: Nashr-i Tārīkh-i Īrān, 1375), p. 130).
126 Opposing their view, Mūrtaẕá Qūlī Khān, a deputy for Isfahan and a member of *iʿtidālīyūn*, argued that 'a deputy who has been absent with no acceptable excuse is preventing the freedom of other deputies' (see '2nd Majlis', Session 4 Shawwal 1329 / [28 September 1911]).
127 '2nd Majlis', Session 24 Jumada II 1329 / [22 June 1911].
128 Ibid.

4 Freedom *to*

The question of permissibility

4.1 Is freedom intrinsically valuable or only instrumentally valuable?

The Iranian constitutionalists' principal demand was freedom *from* arbitrary rule and lawlessness, but did they also have a specific purpose of freedom in mind? The analysis of this question leads us to a more general and fundamental question: to what extent should freedom have a specified purpose? In other words, is it sufficient to know that we are/would like to be 'negatively' free 'from' **Y**? Or should we, in addition to this, know that we are/would like to be 'positively' free 'to' do/become **Z**? It was previously mentioned that to some theorists, freedom is a dual relationship between an agent and a constraint with there being no need to suppose a certain aim for freedom. If this question were asked from Isaiah Berlin, he would reply

> A man struggling against his chains or a people against enslavement need not consciously aim at any definite further state. A man need not know how he will use his freedom; he just wants to remove the yoke. So do classes and nations.[1]

Berlin and other proponents of 'negative liberty' hold that the concept of freedom can be distorted by questioning the aim of freedom, because when one answers this question by saying that he or she aims to do/to become **Z**, a number of value-questions would often arise: Is **Z** worth doing? Is it an authentic, virtuous, and rational action or state? Does this action/state help the agent to take control of his or her own destiny in his or her own best interest? And more importantly, is the agent at all able to recognize his or her own best interest by himself or herself? In response to such questions, some theorists of 'positive liberty' cast doubt on a person's eligibility to determine the 'true aim' of freedom, delegating the responsibility of the determination of such aim to authorities outside of the agent of freedom. Going one step further, some theorists believe that such a 'true aim' should be imposed on the individual's behavior as a reasonable restraint or restriction upon which the happiness of the individual and the society depends. For this group of theorists, this restraint is the very reasonable freedom of a person. Thus, coercion appears in the guise of freedom.

Although this concern of negative-freedom theorists is worthy of consideration, it cannot logically result in the conclusion that freedom does not need to be understood as a relation between an agent and a purpose (whether specific or non-specific), since freedom-seekers doubtlessly know that as soon as they break free of the chain of arbitrary rule and lawlessness, there will be many new things they will be free to do, even though they may not yet have decided which of them they will do. That is to say, not having a specified aim is not the same as having no aim. Iranian constitutionalists were in such a situation. They demanded a political regime in which they would have more freedom overall. Such freedom without a specific aim can be called 'overall freedom' which, according to Ian Carter's definition, is 'the amount of freedom one has in either absolute or relative terms, and represents some kind of an aggregation over one's specific freedoms'.[2]

This is why, contrary to 'the period of arbitrary rule (*dawrah-ʾi istibdād*)', the constitutional period is frequently referred to as 'the period of freedom (*dawrah-ʾi āzādī*)' in the literature of the period.[3] This chapter reconstructs the questions and answers which addressed the aim of freedom during the first constitutional period as well as the second one.

4.2 Disputes over the interpretation of the aim of freedom

The constitutionalists, whether clerics or laity, in explaining their understanding of freedom both as the absence of certain constraints and as the presence of the opportunity to do certain actions, repeatedly emphasized that they accepted neither freedom *from* the constraints of obeying God and the law, nor freedom *to* commit religiously prohibited acts and *to* violate other people's rights. However, their critics apparently believed that freedom would not remain within these boundaries and that it could not be made compatible with Islam. Suffice it to say that in the first months of the Lesser Arbitrary Rule (*istibdād-i ṣaghīr*), several leading clerical figures of constitutionalism separately highlighted such distortions in various ways. Interpreting the constraints on freedom, Nāʾīnī wrote in April 1909 (Rabi I 1327) that 'by freedom we mean freedom from enslavement by tyrants (*riqqīyat-i ṭavāghīt*) and not withdrawal of the obedience to God'.[4] Two months earlier, Ṣiqat al-Islām Tabrīzī had similarly emphasized that 'Iranian Constitutionalism (*mashrūṭah-ʿi īrānī*) does not intend to establish heresy and to consider customary law as the indispensable religious divine law', and then argued that

> Tyrants distort the meaning of constitutionalism for the sake of their own advantage and call freedom . . . irreligiousness and a violation of the sharia. What all nations want is freedom from arbitrary rule, and this is the reason behind the conflict. Religion and the state are separated; every believer has accepted the precepts of his own religion and that is his provision for the hereafter. Good God! How can all this effort by both clerics and the laity . . . be for the sake of apostasy?[5]

Similarly clear was the constitutionalists' emphasis on sharia and law in their explanation of the aim of freedom. For instance, in the inaugural speech of the first majlis on 18 August 1906 (27 Jumada II 1324), Malik al-Mutakallimīn presented the nation's aim of freedom as follows: 'to say and to do whatever they find necessary for their interests', 'to restore the past failures of the homeland' and 'to preserve the egg of Islam and the power of the Monarchy'.[6] Nā'īnī likewise pointed out that freedom of the press and freedom of speech aimed to pave the way for the people's awareness and to help them perceive the country's grounds of progress as well as the honor of independence and ethnology (*qumīyat'shināsī*). He added that 'such freedoms would [encourage] the people to preserve the great honor of religion and their solidarity for reclaiming the divine gift of freedom and lost religious rights, while also helping them receive education, edification, as well as individual and national progress'.[7]

Constitutionalists clearly explained what they meant by freedom and insisted that people ignore the distorted facts presented by others.[8] Nonetheless, their opponents adamantly claimed that the aim of the constitutionalists was nothing but the violation of moral and religious values and public order through freedom. Why did the opponents not endeavor to define a realm of liberty, albeit a very limited one, rather than totally denying freedom? Why did they not try to give an interpretation of the constraints and aims of freedom that would be compatible with Islam? Is it not true that, according to the sharia, the only limitations on people's freedom concern the abandonment of *vājib* (obligatory acts) and the committing of *ḥarām* (forbidden acts), with absolute freedom to do/not to do *mustaḥabb, makrūh*, and *mubāḥ* (recommended, detestable, and religiously neutral acts)? Thus, *pro-mashrū'ah* jurists could also accept freedom *from* every restraint except the constraint of the sharia, *to* do everything except religiously prohibited acts; such an interpretation could be considered a positive theory of liberty. Why did they not do this? Why did those people who could present themselves as advocates of positive freedom by endorsing an interpretation of 'true freedom' and by disapproving other interpretations, prefer to oppose freedom in principle?

This is not an easy question to answer. Perhaps they were not aware of such a possibility of interpretation and considered freedom a value belonging to a certain system of values within a particular political structure incompatible with Islam. It is worth noting that, according to some reformists of the time, religious authorities were considered eligible to interpret neither the constraints nor the aims of liberty. This attitude further fuelled the scepticism of the opponents of freedom. For instance, when addressing the question of whether there is any limit to human perfection and progress, on 5 September 1907 (26 Rajab 1395), the editorial writer of the *Ṣūr-i Isrāfīl* emphasized that freedom is the only necessary and sufficient condition for achieving progress. He then went on to enthusiastically write:

> The assistance and support of no generous king, the guidance and supervision of no religious leader, and the endeavour and advice of no master of the path would be useful for paving the way of human progress and perfection at all. It

> would be sufficient for a man to be left alone to find his own way of progress and his own path to the perfection of the soul.[9]

Addressing 'the temporal as well as the spiritual authorities' (*ruʾasāʾ-i rūḥānī va jismānī*), the author went on to add:

> The meaning of the new word freedom . . . is that those who claim custodianship of the graveyard of Iran should not limit human perfection to their own 'scholarly' interpretations, but must let humankind endeavour to recognize and pursue perfection using the very tools given by creation.[10]

According to the author, freedom means nothing but possession of the absolutely personal right to define humanity's own perfection. Certainly, the boundaries of such freedom can be expanded only to the extent that it does not harm others. The author also briefly points out that the Qur'an and all jurisprudential treatises written by the *ʿulamā* must be taken into consideration in determining the limits of freedom.

This point was further discussed in an essay on the linkage between 'the seal of prophecy' (*khātamīyat*) and the principle of progress, published in the subsequent issue of the *Ṣūr-i Isrāfīl*.[11] The author of this essay, who is probably the same person as the author of the previous essay, comes to a new definition of the seal of prophecy through a set of premises. His conclusions can be reformulated as follows:

(1) 'Humanity has not yet reached perfection'.
(2) 'Changes in circumstances require the interpretation, contraction, and expansion of laws'.
(3) 'According to the principle of *luṭf* (kindness), God, as the generous origin of munificence (*mabdaʾ-i fayyāẕ*), has to contentiously grant grace and benefit'.

Conclusion: The seal of prophecy means that, through Islam and the principle of progress, man has been placed in 'the path of his mission', and has been given the trace of 'the divine commandments and his natural responsibility'. Thus, man was entrusted with 'all the requirements of his perfection and his life' and it was made incumbent upon him 'to meditate on the Qur'an and infer the rules proper for each time and era from that worthy treasure and infinite ocean'. This Qur'an 'has provided Muslims with the principles of all desires of every time through precise and allegorical verses'.

The methods of such meditation, interpretation, contraction, and expansion of laws, according to the author, are the very principles that the *ʿulamā* employ in order to justify variation in commandments due to the alteration of circumstances, and accidental attributes (*ʿunvānāt-i ṭārīyah*). This statement does not imply that, for him, the people can define the aim of freedom by themselves whereas the restraints on freedom must be defined by the *ʿulamā*. On the contrary, this group of constitutionalists held that the legitimate legislator of freedom was no one but the majlis. This point was clearly pointed out in what one such constitutionalist wrote in the *Ṣūr-i Isrāfīl*:

> A nation is indeed free, when no one is able to govern and dictate them arbitrarily. Such a nation does need a guide, a leader, and a legislator, because the freedom of each person must be to the degree that does not violate the freedom of others or do them harm. Even so, no one is allowed to determine the degree of freedom; no king or minister, no representative or judge, no one but the legislature. It is thus the law which has no animosity towards anyone and no close friendship with anyone, and which rewards and punishes based on merit, which is the true leader of fifteen million people.[12]

From this perspective, the shah, governors, or clerics were no longer considered the higher authority in the interpretation of freedom and the determination of its restraints and aims. This was the major reason behind their opposition to freedom and the new political structure necessitating it. The most effective way of justifying this disagreement was to misrepresent freedom as incompatible with the commandments of Islam. However, in the opinion of the freedom-seekers, these objections were not for the sake of Islam, but rather stemmed from the opponents' personal intentions. This point was explicitly mentioned by not only extremist constitutionalists such as the *Ṣūr-i Isrāfīl's* and *Rūḥ al-Qudus's* writers, but also constitutionalist clergy like Nā'īnī, who, addressing proponents of the *mashrū'ah* in the Lesser Arbitrary Rule period, sarcastically wrote that

> From now on, we, the followers of the oppressor, can only dream of the time when we could misrepresent freedom from the bondage [of the oppressor] as irreligiousness or the demand of Zindiqs, heretics and Babists (may Allāh curse them all). At that time, we distorted the constitutionalism which imposed limits on the cruel government by introducing it as a religion against the true faith. We forced Muslims to obey this unblessed bondage and in return received lands, properties, awards, and rewards.[13]

Yet it should be noted that the opposition to the freedom voiced by the proponents of *mashrū'ah* was reflected not only in public positioning (such as *Lavāyiḥ*), but also in their private letters written to their like-minded fellows. This fact casts doubt on the view that this opposition was merely a populist political action to defeat the constitutionalists, behind which there is no true religion-based reason. For instance, in an unpublicized objection in the form of a letter to Sayyid Aḥmad Yazdī (who had accompanied Shaykh Faẓl Allāh Nūrī in taking the *bast* at the 'Abd al-'Aẓīm Shrine), a follower of his father, Sayyid Kāẓim Yazdī (the leading anti-constitutionalist cleric in Najaf) wrote that, notwithstanding the threats and intimidations, Sayyid Kāẓim did not endorse constitutionalists, because he believed that *mashrūṭah* would result in the emergence of corruption, blasphemy, heresy, and *Westophilia* (*farangī'mȧābī*) as well as the propagation of profanity and impertinence towards the prophets and the Imams, particularly the Prophet Muḥammad and Imam Mahdī.[14] In light of such evidence, I tend to suspend judgment on the motive behind the *pro-mashrū'ah's* opposition, attempting to reconstruct their arguments instead.

In order to precisely understand the *pro-mashrūʿah's* opposition to freedom, one must compare it with Muḥammad ʿAlī Shāh's opposition to freedom. It is hard to believe that his opposition was driven by his piety and religiosity; the shah himself rarely had such a claim. On the contrary, he often justified his objections under the pretext of the fulfilment of his personal duty of ensuring people's tranquility and security, a task for which God had made him responsible. Overall, Muḥammad ʿAlī Shāh had two approaches in dealing with freedom and the *mashrūṭah* during his reign. From the time of his ascendency until 7 November 1908 (12 Shawwal 1326), when he issued a script abrogating the constitutional decree, he claimed to be a supporter of the *mashrūṭah*. During this period, unlike Nūrī and his followers, not only did the shah not condemn the principle of freedom, but he also regarded it as a gift given to the people by him and his father, and therefore, he claimed responsibility for preventing 'the misuse' of this blessing. However, bombardment of the majlis and the gory suppression of the constitutionalists were regarded by the shah as his devotion to duty. The shah's second approach to the *mashrūṭah* came to light when the shah, having promised to reopen the majlis and renew constitutionalism, was seeking a way to break his promise. This was the time when he, along with some anti-constitutionalist clerics, began to create a tide of religious opposition to the *mashrūṭah* and 'the law of freedom and equality'. Using this opposition as a pretext for suspending the election, he then wrote in a royal script addressing the *ʿulamā*:

> Now that you have discovered the incompatibility of the foundation of the majlis with Islam and have issued decrees on its prohibition. . . . We will also totally abandon and promise never to mention such majlis again.[15]

In the first approach, the shah's criticism of freedom was nothing more than the imposition of restrictions on the aim of freedom. Even though he seemed to agree with proponents of the *mashrūʿah* that 'the corrupters' (*mufsidīn*) were employing freedom to weaken the religion and the government, his objection targeted not the principle of freedom, but only the misuse of liberty. A clear example of such approach can be seen in the shah's telegram to the *ʿulamā* of Najaf, sent during the Lesser Arbitrary Rule. Emphasizing his role in the establishment of 'the constitutionalism of the government which is the freedom of the nation' and on his attempt to persuade Muẓaffar al-Dīn Shāh to approve the *mashrūṭah*, Muḥammad ʿAlī Shāh wrote:

> Unfortunately, freedom, which is a foundation of the establishment of constitutionalism, has been misused by a group of corrupters in pursuing their incorrect purposes and corrupt ideas which go against the holy sharia, so that freedom has been misrepresented to the common people. . . . Even the leading clerics of Islam were incapable of preventing them from such measures that were the purpose of freedom and revolt (*gharẕ-i āzadī va shūrish'ṭalabī-i ān'hā*), to the point where they were about to put the government and the [Muslim] faith (*millat*) in great peril and destabilize Iran's six thousand year-old monarchy. We have therefore recognized it as our personal duty to no

> longer continue our tolerance and silence, firstly, for the sake of the religion and then for the preservation of the monarchy.[16]

In the second approach, the shah enjoyed the fruit of the *pro-mashrū'ah* discourse which had been formed since the *bast* of Nūrī and his companions at the 'Abd al-'Aīẕm Shrine (20 June–16 September 1907/9 Jumada I – 8 Sha'ban 1325) and which had been expanded during the Lesser Arbitrary Rule. Almost all their criticism of the *mashrūṭah* was discussed in three important treatises written during this period: *Ḥurmat-i mashrūṭah* (*On the prohibition of Constitutionalism*) by Shaykh Faẕl Allāh Nūrī (1907 or 1908); *Tazkirah al-ghāfil wa irshād al-jāhil* (*To Advise the Negligent and to Guide the Ignorant*) by an anonymous author (late 1908); and *Kashf al-murād min al-mashrūṭah wa al-istibdād* (*To Discover the Meaning of Constitutionalism and Arbitrary Rule*) by Muḥammad Ḥusayn Tabrīzī (1907). In addition to these treatises, some clerics and nobles of the major cities and provinces sent several letters and telegrams in response to a request for a fatwa in order to emphasize the contradiction between the *mashrūṭah* and Islam. This was political propaganda planned by the court to pave the way for abrogating the *mashrūṭah*. On 7 November 1908 (12 Shawwal 1326), in a show of power performed at *Bāgh'shāh* in the presence of the shah and a number of merchants and clerics, about 200 of these telegrams were recited to show that a general consensus on opposition to the majlis and the *mashrūṭah* was beginning to emerge, and that the shah therefore had no option but to abrogate the Constitutional Decree.

The request for fatwa (*istiftā'*) to which the *'ulamā* responded was professionally written. Referring to a *tawqī'* or rescript attributed to the twelfth Imam (*wa'ammā al-ḥawadith al-wāqi'a fa'arji'ū fīhā ilā ruwāt akhbārinā*, 'As to the occurring events, refer to the narrators of our hadiths'), the *istiftā'* considered *mashrūṭah* an event stemming from Europe and named freedom and equality the two foundations for such a political structure. It then proposed three major questions: (1) Is constitutionalism compatible with Islam? (2) Is the law of equality and liberty consistent with Islam? (3) How should Muslims react to the emergence of constitutionalism in their countries? Malik'zādah has cited about 90 responses to this request of fatwa, almost all of which have the same theme. Among these responses, two telegrams put forth a new point; they emphasize not only the illegitimacy of *mashrūṭah*, but also the futility of religious constitutionalism (*mashrūṭah-i mashrū'ah*).

> Constitutionalism, as understood by the Europeans and other foreign nations, is based on the law of equality between Muslims and infidels as well as freedom from religious restriction and tolerance towards sinners. . . . Moreover, even religious constitutionalism, as suggested by some leading *'ulamā*, is impossible because it must accept the law of equality and freedom in order to be endorsed and recognized by other governments and to be applicable to their citizens in Iran.[17]

Considering such diversity, the opposition to freedom voiced by proponents of *mashrū'ah* cannot be reduced from their opposition to legislation into their opposition to the misuse of freedom by corruptors. Legislation could be discussed both as the right to determine a *restraint* on freedom and as an *aim* of freedom. In the previous chapter, we learned how the proponents of *mashrūʿah* opposed the legitimacy of the majlis as an institution determining the restraints on freedom. This issue can be considered from another standpoint and reformulated in the triadic relation of freedom as follows: in a constitutional political system, people are free *from* arbitrary rule *to* legislate by themselves. Facing such a proposition, the proponents of *mashrūʿah* would say that even if people are free from arbitrary rule, religion would not grant them freedom of legislation.

4.3 Types of freedom

Any statement about the types of freedom can be considered as a categorization of the aims of freedom. Such categories do not precisely determine the aim of freedom. However, descriptively speaking, they can always be considered as a list of priorities that a person might pursue when free from restraints, and, normatively speaking, they can be considered as a network of binding human rights. In order to provide a comprehensive categorization of freedom, it is necessary to have knowledge of individual and social human needs. Several Iranian thinkers of the late Qajar era attempted to distinguish different types of freedoms.

The first classification was presented by Ākhūnd'zādah.[18] He divided perfect liberty into the two types of 'spiritual liberty' and 'physical liberty' which had been confiscated from Iranians, the former by 'authorities of Islam' (*ʾuliyāʾ-i dīn-i Islām*) and the latter by 'despotic rulers' (*farmān'ravāyān-i dīsputī*). For further explanation of the various subtypes of freedom, he referred to 'the comprehensive European books'.[19]

Soon afterwards, Mīrzā Malkam Khān named six kinds of 'essential liberties' (*ikhtiyārāt-i sittah-ʾi ẕarūrīyah*) as part of the fundamental teachings of the *farāmūsh'khānah*,[20] and later justified the necessity of these liberties in his treatise *Ṣirāt al-mustaqīm* (*The Straight Path*) by citing verses of the Qur'an and the prophetic Hadith. The order of these liberties in *Ṣirāt al-mustaqīm* is as follows: freedom of body, freedom of speech, freedom of press, freedom of thought, freedom of commerce, and freedom of assembly.[21] Ṭālibuf Tabrīzī added freedom of choice to this list. Similarly important, in a chapter on the rights of people in his *Ḥuqūq-i asāsī* (*The Treatise of Fundamental Rights*), Muḥammad ʿAlī Furūghī presented the most complete classification of freedom by adding 'freedom of property', 'freedom of domicile', 'freedom of education', and 'freedom of petition' to the list. Freedom of education, for him, was a part of 'freedom of self' and 'freedom of beliefs and thought'. Considering the freedom to establish private schools as a subset of this freedom, he regarded the prohibition on private education as both injustice and contrary to prudence. To him, the freedom to submit petitions and requests to legislative and executive powers was indeed the means of protecting other freedoms and rights. Some major classifications of this period are compared in Table 4.1:

Table 4.1 Classification of freedom in the late Qajar literature

Thinker:	*Mīrzā Malkam Khān*	*Mīrzā Abū Ṭālib Bihbahānī*	*Ṭālibuf Tabrīzī*	*Sayyid Naṣr Allāh Taqavī*	*Muḥammad ʿAlī Furūghī*	*Mullā ʿAbd al-Rasūl Kāshānī*
Classification of freedom	Freedom of body[22]	Personal freedom (security of life, property, reputa-tion, honor, and commerce)[23]	Freedom of identity[24]	Freedom in deeds[25]	Freedom of self[26]	
					Freedom of property[27]	
					Freedom of domicile[28]	Freedom in other means of life[29]
	Freedom of commerce[30]				Freedom of business[31]	Freedom in craft and commerce[32]
	Freedom of thought[33]		Freedom of opinion[34]	Freedom of thought[35]	Freedom of opinion[36]	
	Freedom of writing[37]	Freedom of press[38]	Freedom of press[39]		Freedom of press and expression[40]	Freedom in writing a nd the press[41]
	Freedom of assembly[42]				Freedom of assembly[43]	Freedom of assembly[44]
					Freedom of education[45]	
					Freedom of petition[46]	
		Political Freedom[47]				Freedom of choice[48]
	Freedom of speech[49]		Freedom of expression[50]	Freedom of expression[51]		

Some of the aims of freedom are not included in these classifications though they were well discussed during the constitutional period. Among them, one can name 'freedom of religion', which the aforementioned writers might prefer to place under the more general category of freedom of thought and opinion. Overall, freedom of assembly, freedom of speech, freedom of commerce and freedom of opinion were the most important freedoms for the thinkers of the time. All of these freedoms received particular legal consideration in the first two legislative parliaments. The rest of this chapter examines the important debates that surrounded these aims of freedom.

4.3.1 Freedom of assembly

Attempting to attract audiences to share their concerns and thoughts, Iranian reformists realized the significance of the freedom of assembly very early on. In their meetings, they spoke of the crises and decline of Iran, and of the necessity to awaken people and rectify affairs. Such discussions were often not tolerated by either government or some clerics. This was why Malkam Khān, the founder of the *farāmūsh'khānah* (founded sometime between 1857 and 1860) considered the freedom of assembly the cornerstone of social order and all kinds of freedom.[52] Similarly, two years after the closure of the *farāmūsh'khānah* by Nāṣir al-Dīn Shāh's decree in 1863, Ākhūnd'zādah wrote:

> O ye Iranians! If you were aware of the pleasure of freedom and human rights, you would not be in the throes of such servitude and such humiliation. Rather, you would seek knowledge, you would open several *farāmūsh'khānahs* and assemblies, and find means of solidarity.[53]

The lack of freedom of assembly in the pre-constitutional era left no choice but to set up secret societies. After the unsuccessful experience of the *farāmūsh'khānah*, in his newspaper, the *Qānūn* (published in London, 1307–15/1890–98), Malkam Khān promoted a new association called the 'Assembly of Humanity' (*majmaʿ-i ādamīyat*) throughout Iran. Soon after the assassination of Nāṣir al-Dīn Shah (May 1896), new associations came into existence. They were involved in various activities such as establishing schools, publishing enlightening night-letters, writing, and printing revelatory treatises as well as anonymously writing useful articles for newspapers published outside Iran.[54] On the threshold of the triumph of the Constitutional Movement, some of those associations, such as the *anjuman-i maʿārif*, *anjuman-i aḥrār*, and *anjuman-i makhfī-i bīdārī*, played a crucial role in mobilizing revolutionaries and developing public awareness.

During the first constitutional period, the freedom of assembly was stipulated in Article 21 of the Supplementary Fundamental Laws (signed by Muḥammad ʿAlī Shāh in October 1907/Shaʿbān 1325) as follows:

> Societies (*anjumans*) and associations (*ijtimāʿāt*) which do not pose mischief to religion or the state, and which are not injurious to good order, are free

> throughout the whole Empire. However, members of such associations must not carry arms, and must obey the regulations laid down by the Law on this matter. Assemblies in the public thoroughfares and open spaces must likewise obey police regulations.[55]

The content of this article reflects the constitutionalists' opinion on freedom of assembly. As was discussed in the previous chapter, freedom of assembly was one of the four freedoms in which the Supplementary Fundamental Laws prohibited all interferences, without adding the proviso of 'except in accordance with the law' (*magar bih hukm-i qānūn*). Nonetheless, the conditions determined in the article itself could provide a pretext for interference because, although 'not to carry arms' has a clear and objective sense, other parts of the article (such as 'not pose mischief to religion or the state' and 'not injurious to good order') are so ambiguous that the article could lead to the suppression of the freedom of religiously or politically dissident associations.

In fact, both constitutionalists and anti-constitutionalists took advantage of such ambiguous terms in confiscating their opponents' freedom. For instance, when Shaykh Faẕl Allāh Nūrī and his followers began to separate themselves from the constitutionalists and wanted to commemorate the death of the prophet's daughter in the masjid jumʿa mosque on 24 June 1907 (13 Jumada I 1325), the constitutionalists claimed that this assembly was a conspiracy to incite people against *mashrūṭah*. They therefore prevented it from happening and asked Sayyid Muḥammad Ṭabāṭabāʾī to exile (*ikhrāj*) Shaykh Faẕl Allah, Mullā Muḥammad Āmulī, and Mīrzā Luṭf Allāh. Ṭabāṭabāʾī said that Nūrī had recently promised him that he would not oppose *mashrūṭah*; Ṭabāṭabāʾī added that, should Nūrī break this promise, he would be the first to cast him out. The Sayyid was referring to the Shaykh's promise, given following the people's objections against his behavior on 20 June 1907, 'not to commit any acts in disagreement with the holy national majlis', 'to support the majlis everywhere', and 'not to set up any gatherings'.[56] Such a commitment clearly deprived some opponents of *mashrūṭah* of freedom of speech and freedom of assembly.

On the other hand, the constitutionalists' freedom of assembly was also constrained on several occasions. For example, even though Articles 90 to 92 of the Supplementary Fundamental Laws, as well as the State and Provincial Associations Bill of May 1907 (Rabi II 1325), granted provincial associations the freedom to observe the implementation of parliamentary laws, despotic local governors and opposing clerics suppressed such assemblies whenever they could. The reason behind this was that the provincial association, as the symbol of the *mashrūṭah*, was the most significant place for constitutionalists' gatherings in cities.[57]

In these two examples, assemblies were not tolerated, although they were apparently peaceful and harmless. Obviously, whenever a group of people gathered to express their opposition, the freedom of assembly was further restricted. The proponents of arbitrary rule as well as most constitutionalists failed to acknowledge such a freedom. Sometimes, even the *bast* or the sit-in was not tolerated. This was despite the fact that it had been a common and respected tradition which had provided an opportunity for freedom of assembly even in the arbitrary rule era. In its latest examples during the Constitutional Movement, the *bast* had paved the way for the free assembly of protesters in the ʿAbd al-ʿAẓīm Shrine and Maʿṣūmah Shrine in Qum, as well as in the British Embassy in Tehran. When Nūrī and his companions took *bast* at the ʿAbd al-ʿAẓīm Shrine, the *Rūḥ al-Qudus* newspaper published an epistle which portrayed the shrine as speaking and complaining of those who had gathered there:

> They have fled to me in order to gain worldly wealth and destroy the basis of the *mashrūṭah*; they have converted this sacred place of angels to the profane place of evils and demons. . . . Was it not possible to restrain these tyrannical pedants in the chain of the constitutionalism in Tehran . . . or to eradicate them and clean up Iran?[58]

It should be noted that in this period, the right of assembly, even according to most supporters of the freedom of assembly, was not considered intrinsically valuable. Rather, the value of assembly was evaluated by the value of its aim. For instance, Nāʾīnī attempts to define 'true' freedom of assembly by emphasizing that associations must sacrifice personal interests for the sake of exalting the name of Islam and for preserving the human society and the progress of mankind (*ḥifẓ-i jāmiʿah-ʾi nawʿīyah va taraqqī dādan-i nawʿ*).[59] In a similar approach, in an article in the *Rūḥ al-Qudus* newspaper titled 'To Assemblies or the Asleep Community', a writer appreciates the role of European secret societies in the development of Europe, the rebellion against tyrannical kings and priests, and the establishment of constitutionalism and republics in Western countries. He then criticizes Iranian associations and enthusiastically expands an idealistic list of duties that associations must abide by. This list includes publishing newspapers, establishing national schools and hospitals, supporting orphans and street children, as well as encouraging agriculture and domestic industry.[60]

4.3.2 Freedom of expression

Freedom of expression and freedom of opinion were the most controversial and provocative freedoms among all types of liberties discussed in late Qajar political literature. Seeking a remedy for Iran's decline, many writers introduced freedom of expression as a necessary condition for any reform to come. It was perhaps Mustashār al-Dawlah who insisted on the significance of freedom of expression for the first time. Regarding it as the result of the right of defense against cruelty (the fifth article of the French Constitution), he made a linkage between the freedom of expression and the religious principle of 'commanding right and forbidding wrong'. The idea of linking these two doctrines afterwards became a frequent recurrence. According to this understanding, freedom of speech and writing is necessary for the expression of public interests and expedience at the same time as it is limited within such a boundary. In Mustashār al-Dawlah's words,

> Everyone from superior and inferior ranks is absolutely free to write and publish whatever comes to his mind about the good and welfare of the country and the people. If his thought and ideas are accepted by the nation, they will be praised, otherwise they will be banned and deprecated.[61]

In this point of view, freedom of expression has no value per se; rather, it is valuable due to the benefits achieved from expressing the public interests, criticizing shortcomings, and seeking remedies to improve public affairs. That is why Malkam Khān identified this freedom as the 'point of departure for all human progress':

> Since the soul of the world's regulations depends on this point, hoping for acknowledgement by the men of knowledge, we state that the point of departure for all human progress among Iranians would be the primordial right of freedom to express one's own thoughts and opinions freely. Freedom of speech and writing in our age has become the king of the earth.[62]

Another Iranian reformist of the nineteenth century named Navvāb ʿAlī Bakhsh Mīrzā said that the merit of freedom of expression is that issues would be discussed by 'men of wisdom' who

> would certainly find the disadvantages and advantages of affairs and decide to eliminate or implement them . . . [therefore] in political affairs and issues related to the progress of the state and the nation, the freedom of all people [to express their] thoughts is a vital issue.[63]

This approach to freedom of expression continued to be used throughout the constitutional period. After the Lesser Arbitrary Rule put an end to the controversial experience of freedom of press, Nāʾīnī still considered freedom of expression to be a type of the God-given freedom whose true meaning was 'freedom *from* the dominance of tyrants' *to* remove the obstacles that prevent the awakening of the nation, *to* help people become aware of the path to progress and national independence, *to* unify and mobilize people to preserve the religion and regain the God-given gift of freedom and the usurped national rights, and *to* benefit from education, edification, and human and national developments (*istikmālāt-i nawʿīyah va vaṭanīyah*). Nāʾīnī went on to write about the ethics of freedom of expression, emphasizing that this freedom should not be marred by the commitment of immoralities such as defamation, blackmail, remonstrance, or vengeance.[64]

The actual degree of freedom of expression in its written form (i.e. freedom of press) can be assessed better than any other realm of liberty in Qajar Iran, since there are numerous newspapers and articles showing the degree of freedom they had and how they used it. Not surprisingly, the main theme of the newspapers of this period concerns the question of Iran's decline and backwardness and criticizes the external and internal factors behind this crisis. These criticisms can be categorized into the following six subjects: (1) the performance of state administration (including that of statesmen, courtiers, and the shah himself); (2) the structure and nature of the monarchy in comparison with other political systems; (3) the performance of clerics as religious leaders and authorities; (4) traditions and religious culture; (5) people's sociocultural behaviors and customs; and (6) colonial and foreign powers' interference in Iran's internal affairs (especially the interferences by Russia, Britain, and the Ottoman Empire). An assessment of the contents of these criticisms is beyond the purpose of this inquiry. Here, I only aim to examine the extent to which these writings exceeded the boundaries of freedom with regard to the legal and conventional norms of Qajar society. As discussed in the previous chapter, according to the Press Law of February 1908, no one was free to publish anything which was insulting to 'His Majesty the King' (Article 31), 'seditious' (Article 32), 'harmful to religion and Islamic beliefs' (Article 33), or 'disrespecting, defaming and discrediting to individuals or bodies' (Article 34). Likewise, they could not publish anything which disclosed military secrets, created general anxiety, disturbed public tranquillity, invited opposition to the official powers of the country, or distributed obscene images contrary to chastity and modesty (Article 49). There are several examples of the violation of such stringent regulations by even well-known newspapers of the constitutional period. Accusing them of favouring arbitrary rule, the newspapers sometimes harshly challenged some statesmen and clerics, and even some representatives of the majlis and the constitutionalist leaders.[65]

Through examining the reasons for the temporary or permanent ban on some important newspapers of the first constitutional period, one can find examples of extremism which tested the tolerance of the government or the majlis. The first newspaper to officially be banned was the *Ṣūr-i Isrāfīl*. This ban occurred in June 1907 (Jumada I, 1325) after the 6th issue came out, because of an article titled '*Ẓuhūr-i jadīd*' (The New Advent) published in 4th issue. The article led to widespread objections by both proponents and opponents of constitutionalism. They particularly had issue with the following sentence:

> Throughout 1300 years of lust for superiority and greed for closeness to the king, the *ʿulamā* have not managed to separate nonsenses from Islamic philosophy and publish a brief treatise based on the wisdom of their own rightful path and in language suitable for ordinary people.[66]

Accused of heresy and lack of faith, the author of the article attempted to respond to the accusation in a long article titled '*Difāʿ*' (defence), published in the 7th and 8th issues after the removal of the temporary ban. He asserted that by *ʿulamā*, he never meant 'Imams, the saint (*ʾuliyā-i muqarrabīn*) or the special representative [of the hidden Imam Mahdī] (*nuvvāb-i khāṣṣah*). Rather, his criticism was aimed at Muslim scholars who, confident about the power of Islam, have not written the truths of Islam in ordinary language'. Emphasizing that the newspaper aimed to equally criticize both political authorities and spiritual leaders, the author wondered why even friends of this newspaper had bitterly resented this approach.[67] Sayyid Jamal al-Dīn Vāʿiẓ Iṣfahānī was one such friend who, feeling resentful toward the article, wrote a letter to the newspaper's chief editor. While maintaining that the writers of *Ṣūr-i Isrāfīl* were 'noble Muslims, spirits of fairness and the essence of civilization', Vāʿiẓ Iṣfahānī asked why they had violated their limits, and wondered at how 'their pens were fierce like a flame and they berated both the good and the bad, while Shiite clerics have written many books for both common and educated people'.[68]

A month later, the second temporary ban was imposed on the *Ḥabl al-matīn* newspaper which, in the 73rd issue, had complained of Malik al-Tujjār's refuge in the Russian embassy. The ban was in fact due to the Russian ambassador's protest, but was carried out under the nominal pretext of the lottery advertisement in the newspaper being considered against the sharia. The general strike of all Tehran's newspapers caused the ban to last no longer than four days.[69] On 18 September 1907 (10 Shàban 1325), the third official ban was issued by majlis. The *Ṣūr-i Isrāfīl* was closed once again due to the clerics' discontent with an article published in issue 12, on 4 September 1907 (26 Rajab 1325). This article was written in response to a simple question: 'Are there any limits to human perfection and progress?'[70] On 7 November 1907 (1 Shawwal 1325), the *Rūḥ al-Qudus* was banned on charge of 'directly insulting His Majesty the Shah', according to the new minister of education, Murtaẕá Qulī Khān Hidāyat Ṣanīʿ al-Dawlah.[71]

Less than a week later, the *Nayyir-i aʿẓam* newspaper was also closed down and all copies of its 5th issue were collected. The reason for this ban, as Parvīn has inferred,[72] was the political editorial note that criticized the Anglo-Russian Treaty of 1907, the Shah's reliance on Russia, and British foreign policies in Iran. Perhaps in an effort to prevent such criticisms, the minister of education wrote the official decree of 13 November 1907 (4 Shawwal 1325) commanding journalists to stop transgressing 'journalism's boundaries' (*ḥudūd-i rūznāmah'nigārī*) and compelling them 'firstly, to show nothing but respect toward the holy monarchy; secondly, to write nothing about religion; thirdly, to avoid complaining unless it is timely and provable'.[73] This command was too premature and ill-conceived to be carried out.

The Press Law passed in February 1908 (Muharram 1326) did not alter the revolutionary attitude of extremist newspapers. For instance, in late April 1908 (24 Rabi I 1326), an invective against Muḥammad ʿAlī Shāh was published in the *Musāvāt* newspaper, causing the shah himself to complain against the newspaper to the court. The article described the shah as an unqualified ruler who, according to religion, lacked eligibility, and accused him of breaking his oath of loyalty to the constitution, inciting thugs to murder constitutionalists, depredation, and attempting to dismantle the constitutionalism. It even accused him of drinking wine, getting drunk, and kissing young men during the nights and doing whatever he wished to do during the days instead of thinking about the security of borders and the reform and development of the country.[74] Following the shah's complaint, the chief editor of the newspaper, Sayyid Muḥammad Riẕā Shīrāzī (known as Musāvāt), was summoned to court. However, he rejected the legal validity of the sudden subpoena in a written response and refused to attend the court. Making no reference to Musāvāt's correspondence with the court, Kasravī considered his refusal to attend the court a 'rebellion' (*gardan'kashī*) and reported that instead of attending the court, 'he [Musāvāt] wrote a list of evil deeds attributed to Muḥammad ʿAlī Mīrzā and his mother, Um-i Khāqān, on a large cambric and sent it to the bazar, asking people to sign and write their testimony on it'.[75]

Two months later, the shah initiated the Lesser Arbitrary Rule and abolished the freedom of the press. The Lesser Arbitrary Rule should not just be summed up in the suspension of the majlis. Rather, the greatest sign of tyranny was that in this period, among all the newspapers published in the first constitutional period, only one monarchist newspaper was published in Tehran and 19 or 20 newspapers (either pro-shah or pro-*mashrūṭah*) were published in other cities; while during the five-month period between issuing the Constitutional Decree and the death of Muẓaffar al-Dīn Shah, 13 to 15 new newspapers were published. Despite Muḥammad ʿAlī Shah's hostility toward the majlis and free press, about 150 new newspapers (mostly constitutionalist) were published during the 17 months following his coronation.[76] No doubt, the radical newspapers' insults to the shah, opponent statesmen, and *pro-mashrūʿah* clerics gave the shah pretext to prevent the mashrūṭah and to overthrow the majlis. Despite all his cruelty, the shah found the opportunity to pretend to be innocent. Thus, when Shaykh Fażl Allāh wanted to explain the reason behind his refusal to support the *mashrūṭah*, he mentioned the newspapers' 'unspeakable disrespect' (*ʾisāʾah-ʾi adab-i ghayr-i qābil-i bāz'gūʾī*) to 'the sultan of Islam' and mentioned 'the sultan's extraordinary patience with this disrespect'.[77] The shah was indeed not patient; however, it took a while for him to find the opportunity to retaliate. At first, he wanted to exile certain writers, such as Sayyid Jamal al-Dīn Vāʿiẓ, Muḥammad Riżā Shīrāzī (the chief editor of *Musāvāt*), Jahāngīr Khān (the chief editor of *Ṣūr-i Isrāfīl*), and Sulṭān al-ʿUlamā (the chief editor of *Rūḥ al-Qudus*). Finally, after bombarding the majlis, he brutally murdered all the named writers except the chief editor of *Musāvāt*. Among the three revolutionary newspapers, *Musāvāt* (whose editor managed to escape) was the most sharp-tongued and radical. About the editor of *Musāvāt*, Kasravī wrote that 'this man, among all the freedom-seekers, would be the first to deserve the death sentence'.[78]

Several months before the start of the Lesser Arbitrary Rule, another group of the opponents of freedom of speech, namely the *pro-mashrūʿah* clerics, began their opposition. Taking sanctuary at the ʿAbd al-ʿAẓīm Shrine in June 1907, they issued a list of demands; these included the addition of *ʿulamā* supervision to legislation in the Supplementary Fundamental Laws, and the altering of some articles in order 'to restrain, for instance, the press and newspapers from blasphemy and affronting the sharia and the men of sharia and so on'.[79] Providing a detailed list of blasphemy committed by newspapers up to that time – most of which have not yet been verified by researchers – they presented the results of freedom of speech in a distorted way. Nonetheless, here I shall cite some of these imputations in order to shed light on the opponents' pretexts for their opposition to freedom of speech:

> In their entirely sinful newspapers, they sometimes wrote that the holy verses of the Seal of the Prophets . . . stemmed from hallucination caused by drink-

ing camel's milk and eating lizard's meat and sometimes considered the Valī-i ʿAṣr (The Guardian of the Time), the Imam of the Age (may our souls be sacrificed to him) a chimerical matter.[80]

They sometimes interpreted the holy verse of hijab in a suggestive and lascivious way. They sometimes persuaded weak-faith and ignorant people that taverns and whorehouses have merits and benefits.[81]

And if you ask me about the blasphemy of those newspapers, I will say, for example . . . in the 183rd issue of this *Ḥabl al-matīn* it is written that, in retaliation for the murders committed by Ottomans in Urūmīyah, Iranians must have stopped travelling to Ottoman lands and making pilgrimage to the Imam Ḥusayn Shrine and Mecca. Another example is the proclamation of Caucasus's mujāhidīn, sent to Tehran and then to Najaf, . . . in which they wrote that the Prophet's religion is archaic and that the Prophet [Muḥammad] and Jesus are pupils compared to contemporary European politicians and political scholars, and they threatened anyone who mentioned the Prophet's and Imams' hadiths with death, captivity, or plunder. . . . And in the *Ṣūr-i Isrāfīl* newspaper, they called the prophet's religion an amusement; and in the *Kawkab-i durrī* newspaper, they refer to their forefathers as idiots and fools for having such beliefs and practices; and in the 13th issue of the *ʿIrāq-i ʿajam* newspaper, they considered the majlis an alternative Kaaba and in some terms even more significant than Kaaba, as people must turn their face toward the majlis at the moment of death;. . . and in his book, Ṭālibuf regarded sacrifice and *zakat* as foolishness. Similarly, Fakhr al-Islām wrote in his newspaper that the *zakat* which is obligatory for Muslims to pay at the end of the Ramadan (*Zhakāt-i fiṭrah*) and the candles that are vowed for Ashura night as well as other benefactions are not enacted by the law; and it is written in the *Kawkab-i durrī* that man should not waste his life by acquisition of *fiqh* and religious studies, but rather he must endeavour to improve politics and increase his wealth. The idiot writer does not know that the affairs of livelihood and death are in the hand of God.[82]

4.3.3 Freedom of work and commerce

Along with the right of security and possession of personal property, the freedom of work and commerce was emphasized in Nāṣir al-Dīn Shāh's Royal Proclamation of May 1888 (Ramadan 1305), many years before the Constitutional Decree was issued, and some political freedoms were legitimized by the first majlis. This proclamation stipulates that

> all our subjects are free and independent as regards their persons and property; it is our will and pleasure that they should, without fear or doubt, employ their capital in whatever manner they please, and engage in any enterprises, such as combination of funds, formation of companies for construction of factories and roads, or in any measures for the promotion of civilization and security.[83]

However, there is no evidence to show that this proclamation helped to develop freedom of work and commerce. The government could still confiscate personal properties with no reason or legal permission.[84] Also, the taxation system and policy, particularly custom tax, remained unfair and disordered. The authorization of major cities' customs was annually given to men of power and wealth in return for a small sum, and they arbitrarily asked people to pay custom duties. The powerful merchants were exempt from paying customs while small businesses and ordinary merchants had to bear their burden.[85]

Hoping to find a secure source of income to repay the loans borrowed from Russia and England, the government had to reform the customs into a European style. This reform created a new order, but was not able to remove the corruption in the system; as a result, the increasing dissatisfaction with the operation of the customs apparatus (which stemmed from the imposition of heavy custom tariffs, the contract made between the Iranian customs and Russia as well as the discovery of a fancy-dress party photograph which showed Joseph Naus, the Belgian director of customs, in clerical attire) became one of the primary driving forces behind the Constitutional Revolution.[86] Another excuse for merchants and guilds to join the Constitutional Movement was the protest that formed when a few sugar merchants had the soles of their feet beaten at the order of ʿAlāʾ al-Dawlah, the governor of Teheran, for allegedly having raised the price of sugar.

Both events indicated that an objective of the Constitutional Revolution was to ensure the freedom of work and commerce. During the first and second constitutional periods, legislators attempted to correct the taxation system and guarantee the possession of personal property. However, two groups criticized these attempts: the first group, namely the *pro-mashrūʿah* clerics, regarded the imposition of common restrictions on the right of possession, such as governmentally determined prices or custom taxes, as a violation of the religious principle which stipulates that 'people have command of their properties and their lives'.[87] The other group, from the perspective of social justice, criticized the legislators' efforts and demanded more revolutionary legislation, such as the transfer of the possession of agricultural lands to farmers.[88] Repeatedly insisting upon the dignity of work and workers and the proletariat's significance in the country's development, this group warned against the unjust consequences of the new laws that would cause wealth concentration and economic inequality. For instance, the author of an editorial in *Ṣūr-i Isrāfīl* wrote:

> As much as civilization is developed through political freedoms and spiritual tolerance, the enacted law increases the number of capitalists and major landlords and paves the way for the dominance of the plutocrat and the privation of the poor.
>
> In periods of absolute tyranny, although arbitrary rule (*khvud'sarī*) often causes oppression and misery for most people, sometimes wars, internal struggles, and the ever changeable will and desire of autocrats and governors lead to a distribution of wealth. However the law, despite all its undoubtable public benefits, conserves the dominance of the rich and the obedience of the

> poor, and maintains wealth concentration in certain centres; it eternizes the supremacy of one part of society and perpetuates the slavery of the other.[89]

Criticizing political freedoms and modern laws and their roles in wealth concentration from the perspective of social justice, the author goes on to recommend socialism:

> If Iran's children want to postpone reforming their social affairs until their political and spiritual issues have been resolved, they will not only lose their national balance . . . for a while, but they will also make the future generations' task a million times harder.

The author believes that there are no obstacles in this path, because

> [Firstly] holy Islam is the religion most compatible with the principles of socialism and [secondly] as there are few capitalists in Iran, there is good opportunity for the pursuit of any kind of social reform . . . now, employing the pro-poor principles of the holy Islam would be sufficient to eliminate any existing economic dominances and to prevent any prospective authorities of wealth (*iqtidār'hā-yi muknatī-i mustaqbal*).[90]

Some other aspects of work as an aim of freedom were also examined by the intellectuals of the time; these included issues of forced labor, freedom of career choice, meritocracy in governmental jobs, and illegal business. Overall, it can be said that freedom of work was among the widely discussed questions in both legal and sociopolitical literatures.

4.3.4 Freedom of thought and lifestyle

Freedom of thought or freedom of conscience, which should not be mistaken for freedom of religion and freedom of speech, is the freedom to hold or examine an idea, opinion, or thought, independent of the opinions of others.

In late Qajar Persian literature, this freedom was addressed by terms such as *ikhtiyār-i khiyāl* (liberty of imagination), *āzādī-i ʿaqāyid* (freedom of opinions), and *ḥurrīyat dar afkār* (liberty of thought). Here, I consider this freedom in its wider sense, including the freedom of religion and even the freedom of lifestyle, as most intellectuals of the time used the word *ʿaqīdah/ʿaqāyid*, in its broader sense, to include both religious and non-religious opinions. Furthermore, they believed that the changes in cultural behaviors and lifestyles went hand in hand with changes in thoughts and viewpoints. Yet demanding freedom of religion as a pillar of constitutionalism was not tolerated; accordingly, proponents of this freedom often preferred to discuss it under the more general title of the freedom of opinion. By contrast, opponents of freedom often rejected any new ideas or new behaviors as *Westophilia* (*farangī'màābī*) and heresy.

Many years before the Constitutional Revolution (approximately 1858–1860 / 1276–1277), Malkam Khān Nāẓim al-Dawlah wrote in his *Daftar-i tanẕīmāt* that 'the opinions of the Iranian people will be free'.[91] It seems that by 'opinions' (*ʿaqāyid*) he also meant the freedom of religion. It has been said that there were some attempts to incorporate freedom of religion in the constitution and the Supplementary Fundamental Laws, but those attempts failed and the Twelver Jaʿfarī school of Shia Islam was stipulated as the official religion of Iran.[92] Muḥammad ʿAlī Shāh and some other opponents of *mashrūṭah* claimed that most constitutionalists were corrupt, Zandiq, Babi, materialist, and Westophile, and that by 'freedom of religion' they meant nothing but 'freedom from religion'. The representatives of the first majlis responded to these accusations several times. For instance, in a speech explaining the constitutionalists' intentions, Sayyid Naṣr Allāh Taqavī stated that

> We would like our religion, namely Twelver Shia Islam, to be widespread, common and accepted among ourselves. However, we intend neither to disturb other nations' religions and beliefs nor to force anyone to convert to our path, 'There is no compulsion in religion';[93] if they find our beliefs rational and defensible, they can accept them, otherwise, they shall have their religion and we shall have ours.[94]

A more conservative position held by some constitutionalists was to basically deny support for freedom of religion rather than trying to separate 'freedom of religion' from 'atheism'. As one of the clerics of Tabriz wrote (in October 1908) in response to the *pro-mashrūʿah* '*Islāmīyah* Association',

> A rumour has been maliciously circulated by proponents of arbitrary rule that some [constitutionalists] want to have freedom of religion and to conduct some irreligious affairs. Yes, atheists have always existed and they intend to utter and conduct whatever they have in mind, but the constitution has limited them.[95]

The fact is that the opponents of *mashrūṭah* and other new ideas spread negative propaganda which limited people's freedom in doing many things that, in principle, are religiously neutral affairs – such as wearing glasses or non-traditional clothes – because they were afraid of being branded as Westophile, Babis, or irreligious. Malik′zādah, who in his youth had witnessed such accusations being made against his father, Malik al-Mutakallimīn, narrates that sitting on wooden benches in schools; wearing short dresses or high-heeled shoes; listening to music; shaving beards and having long hair; sitting on chairs; learning foreign languages, natural sciences, and geography; and any other acts that reeked of imitation of European manners were considered to be Westophilia, impiousness, and atheism. Painting and sculpting were not permitted. Reciting *ruẓah* for Imām Ḥusayn and his family was a necessary part of weddings. Socializing with non-Shia was forbidden, and pious people avoided eating not only European food but also potatoes and tomatoes, which had been introduced from Europe.[96] There is no reason to doubt Malik′zādah's report. What he says about ordinary people's hesitations in accepting new opinions and phenomena had been repeated in various other sources. Such superficiality was thus illustrated in a note published in the *Rūḥ al-Qudus* newspaper:

> The *dāshmashtī* calls the *fukulī* (trendy person) *Babi*; and the *kulāh'namadī* (rustic fellow) calls someone who wears clean clothes and washes himself of dirt . . . *dahrī* and *lā'maẕhab* (materialist and irreligious) . . . and someone who puts a turban on his head for the sake of charlatanry and mendicancy and knows nothing but eating and sleeping, calls other clerics polytheists and infidels as they have just chosen the path of learning contemporary knowledge in order to add the livelihood sciences (*ʿilm al-maʿāsh*) to their religious sciences (*ʿilm al-maʿād*). . . . Unfortunately, this nation still regards newspapers as misleading books, journalists as Babis, teachers and students of foreign languages as infidels, and learning new sciences (which are impossible without knowing French) as causes of loss of faith. . . . Two years after the *mashrūṭah*, this nation has yet learned nothing but the label '*Babi*'. . . . For a long time now, anyone who understands something or has a little conscience has been called Babi.[97]

It may seem that both reports are the constitutionalists' exaggerations; however, the same purport can be found in anti-constitutionalist literature. For instance, in Rajab 1325/August 1907, a *pro-mashrūʿah* cleric named Shaykh ʿAlī Lāhījī blamed constitutionalists in his address to the people:

> Due to excessive intimacy with newspapers, your perception and consciousness have been changed and you tend to socialize with Europeans, westernized people, materialists and atheists as well as Jews, Christians, Zoroastrians and Babis. . . . You have been deceived by the vain words and fruitless promises of a few crafty atheists and materialists creating expectations of the county's prosperity and wealth as well as subjects' freedom. And you have disobeyed the *ʿulamā* and righteous people . . . whereas they had been your lifetime leaders.[98]

Lāhījī believed that the *mashrūṭah's* majlis consisted of a number of materialists, Babis, Westernized people, and ignorant Shias. For him, the supporters and providers of such a majlis were

> the people who had cultivated Iran's lands through establishing new schools and taking their immature children to those schools in order to make materialists out of them and let them become like the Europeans in using glasses, sticks, top hats, trousers, and high-heeled shoes, and in destroying Islam by urinating while standing up.[99]

To this writer and his like-minded fellows, those who believed in new modes of thought and who advocated such ideas in new schools were no more than

Westophiles and materialists. Therefore, it is clear that from this viewpoint, freedom of thought would not be tolerated. Another representative of this attitude castigates the emerging schools and their teachers when he writes that

> These schools are built upon misrepresentation and are the workings of the devil. Their teachers are beasts by nature and angels by appearance. . . . Not only are their teachings built upon misrepresentation, but they also pursue the path to Vienna and Paris. Alas, they are companions of materialist Westerners. . . . [Their teachings consist of] smirking at the rules of the holy sharia, bathing in Western fragrances, breaking their fasts during the day in the holy month of Ramadan, calling the *ʿulamā* savages and regarding the ritual purity (*ṭahārat*) as obsession, while wiping their own behinds with paper.[100]

Another description that reveals the clash between the traditional and Westophile ways of thought and life can be seen in Mīrzā Ḥasan Khān Anṣārī's novel *Shaykh va Shūkh* (published in Muharram 1331/December 1912), which also displays the mutual suspicion between the two sides and the negation of freedom of thought by extremist traditionalists. The author places the two characters, one a seasoned man of the *Bāb al-Qaṣr* seminary (Shaykh) and the other a young student at the *Julfā* teachers' school (Shūkh), against one another as representatives of the two opposing sides. The Shaykh first accuses shūkh of being a Westophile, and castigates the Westophile as occupying a step even inferior to that of the Westerner himself:

> While the Westerner only lacks faith in the last prophet, the Westophile lacks faith in all prophets, from Adam to Muḥammad, and even in the creator himself. The Westerner imbibes a few sips of wine for the sake of digestion, while the Westophile consumes an endless flow of wine and spirits, and saunters drunkenly on the streets. While the Westerner stands upright when urinating, the Westophile urinates against the wall, thus contaminating his garments with the spillage.[101]

Shūkh then starts humiliating Shaykh and calls him a pedicular lousy person whose thought is nonsense and worthless. The Shaykh gives a pungent reply, emphasizing that the new behaviors of Westophiles do not lead to edification:

> Standing upright when urinating, eating soup with a fork, going to the toilet bareheaded, entering the room in shoes, addressing each other as Monsieur, sitting around a table, sleeping on a sofa, . . . wrapping cigarettes, forming moustaches, cutting hair with a clipper, . . . none of these things have edified or purified anyone. Edification needs austerity . . . we, the indigents, have lucubrated fifty years and have burnt the candle at both ends . . . yet we are not purified.[102]

Such superficiality did not leave room for deeper thinking about freedom of thought and reduced an intellectual contestation into a derogatory and pejorative conflict. Both sides of the conflict between the traditional mode of thought and the modern one accused each other of ineffectiveness and futility. However, their arguments consisted of nothing but ridiculing each other's habits and attitudes.

4.4 Concluding remarks

It can be inferred from what was discussed above that in most of their interpretations of the aim of freedom, constitutionalists considered an action permissible only if it was compatible with the public interest as well as the material and spiritual progress of individuals and society. Theoretically, the aim of freedom could not have been the doing of an action that harmed another person or violated his/her freedom. Furthermore, 'the right to be wrong', even if it harmed no one, was never defended. Such a right would include the right to assemble for fruitless affairs, the right to utter blasphemous or void words, the right to conduct harmless 'haram' jobs or trades, and the right to hold wrong beliefs. Nonetheless, in practice, freedom turned into chaos and license in both the first and in the second constitutional periods. This fact has been acknowledged not only by opponents of *mashrūṭah*, but also by constitutionalists; the point of difference is that, for the latter group, chaos and violations of boundaries, especially in the first constitutional period, originated from anti-constitutionalist conspiracies and incitements which aimed to defame *mashrūṭah.*[103] This is in spite of their admittance of the fact that the majority had not accurately understood freedom and interpreted it as a lack of obstacles in doing whatever they desired. After the conquest of Tehran and the establishment of the second constitutional era began a period of plunder, chaos, and disorder in which the constitutionalists themselves were involved. Some causes of this crisis were the weakness of the central government, disputes between the leader of the first *mashrūṭah* and the commanders and leaders of the second *mashrūṭah* over the leadership of the movement,[104] and the confusions and uncertainties of the troop of *Bakhtiyārī* and the troop of *mujāhidīn,*[105] who lacked regular stipends and obeyed no one. And last but not least were the arbitrary interferences of foreign governments, such as the Russian ultimatum.[106]

The unfortunate consequence of such a situation was metaphorically portrayed by Mīrzā Ḥasan Khan Anṣārī in the form of a dialogue between a young man and an elder man, who represent modern Iran and old Iran respectively:

> Oh brother! To what degree do you find freedom and *ḥurrīyat*?
>
> [Asked the young]
>
> Listening to the young man whole-heartedly, the old man bitterly wept and replied: 'Yes, this situation is a dot on *ḥurrīyat* (*yik nuqṭah bālā-yi ḥurrīyat ast*), yet I had thought freedom meant that human-beings would not be servants of Satan'.[107]

The author finely emphasizes that if one transgresses the boundaries of freedom even so much as a dot, *ḥurrīyat* (حریت) or liberty will turn into *kharrīyat* (خریت) or foolishness. Transgression of the boundaries of freedom and its misuse, whether caused by the incitement of tyrants or rooted in people's ignorance, revived a fundamental question: has such a nation become entitled to be free? This question belongs to the set of questions regarding the first variable of the triadic relation of freedom, namely the agent of freedom. In addition to examining the interpretations of the agent of freedom, the following chapter will address this question.

Notes

1 Isaiah Berlin, *Four Essays on Liberty* (London, New York [etc.]: Oxford University Press, 1969), p. xliii.
2 Ian Carter, 'From a Measure of Freedom (1999)', in *Freedom: A Philosophical Anthology*, ed. by Ian Carter, Matthew H. Kramer, and Hillel Steiner (Malden, MA: Blackwell Pub., 2007), pp. 434–9 (p. 434).
3 See, for instance, 'Difāʿ [1]', *Ṣūr-i Isrāfīl* (Tehran, 22 Jumada I 1325 / [3 July 1907]), no. 6, pp. 2–5 (p. 4).; 'Tashakkur', *Ṣūr-i Isrāfīl* (Tehran, 29 Ramadan 1325 / [5 November 1907]), no. 15, p. 1.; and 'Ḥaq'shenāsī', *Ṣūr-i Isrāfīl* (Tehran, 28 Shawwal 1325 / [4 December 1907]), no. 19, pp. 5–6 (p. 5).
4 Nāʾīnī, vol. 2, pp. 446–7.
5 S̱iqat al-Islām Tabrīzī, vol. 2, pp. 393–4. and Najafī Iṣfahānī, vol. 2, p. 327.
6 For the text of the speech, see Mahdī Malik'zādah, *Tārīkh-i inqilāb-i mashrūṭīyat-i Īrān* (Tehran: Intishārāt-i ʿIlmī, 1373), pp. 385–6.
7 Nāʾīnī, vol. 2, p. 482.
8 See S̱iqat al-Islām Tabrīzī, vol. 2, p. 395. 'Difāʿ [2]', *Ṣūr-i Isrāfīl* (Tehran, 21 Jumada II 1325 / [1 July 1907]), no. 7–8, pp. 5–10 (p. 8).
9 '[Āyā barāy-i kamāl va taraqqī basharī sar'ḥaddī hast?]', *Ṣūr-i Isrāfīl* (Tehran, 26 Rajab 1325 / [5 September 1907]), no. 12, pp. 1–3 (p. 2).
10 Ibid., p. 2.
11 'Al-yawm akmalt-u lakum dīnakum wa atmamt-u ʿalaykum niʿmatī', *Ṣūr-i Isrāfīl* (Tehran, 3 Shaʿban 1325 / [12 September 1907]), no. 13, pp. 1–3.
12 'Tawẕīḥ-i vāẕīāḥātī kih tākunūn dar Īrān bih khiyāl-i ān nīstānd', *Ṣūr-i Isrāfīl* (Tehran, 11 Dhu'l Hijja 1325 / [15 January 1908]), no. 20, pp. 3–5 (p. 3).
13 Nāʾīnī, vol. 2, p. 448.
14 For the text of Sayyid ʿAbd al-Ḥusayn Yazdī's letter, see Malik'zādah, pp. 513–14. For two other examples, see Sayyid Aḥmad Ṭabāṭabāʾī's letter to his son-in-law, Āqā Ẕiyāʾ al-Dīn, Shaykh Faẕl Allah's son, as well as Shaykh Faẕl Allah's letter to his son, both cited in Kasravī, pp. 363, 366–7.
15 Sharīf Kāshānī, pp. 239–40.
16 For the text of Muḥammad ʿAlī Shāh's telegram to the clerics of Holy Shrines, see Sharīf Kāshānī, pp. 221–2.
17 The response text of Shaykh Muḥammad Ḥusayn Māzandarānī, quoted by Malik'zādah, p. 885. See also the response text of Shaykh Salmān Sayf al-Īslam Māzandarānī, Malik'zādah, p. 883.
18 Ākhund'zādah, *Maktūbāt-i Kamāl al-Dawlah*, pp. 55–6.
19 Ibid., p. 55.
20 Maḥmūd Katīrāʾī, ed., 'Juzvah-ʾi rāpūrt-i shakhṣī kih dū darajah az farāmūsh'khānah rā ṭiy kardah ast', in *Farāmāsūnrī dar Īrān: az āghāz tā tashkīl-i luzh-i bīdārī-i Īrān*, ed. by Maḥmūd Katīrāʾī (Tehran: Iqbāl, 1347), pp. 176–93 (p. 193).
21 Mīrzā Malkam Khān, 'Sirāṭ al-mustaqīm', pp. 482–5.
22 *ikhtiyār-i badan.*
23 *āzādī-i shakhsīyah: iṭmīnān dar jān va māl va ʿirẕ va nāmūs va kasb va tijārat.*

24 *āzādī-i huvīyat.*
25 *ḥurrīyat dar a'māl.*
26 *ikhtiyār-i nafs.*
27 *ikhtiyār-i māl.*
28 *ikhtiyār-i manzil.*
29 *āzādī dar sāyir-i lavāzim-i ta'ayyush.*
30 *ikhtiyār-i kasb.*
31 *ikhtiyār-i kār va pīshah.*
32 *āzādī dar ṣan'at va kasb.*
33 *ikhtiyār-i khiyāl.*
34 *āzādī-i 'aqāyid.*
35 *ḥurrīyat dar afkār.*
36 *ikhtiyār-i 'aqāyid.*
37 *ikhtiyār-i qalam.*
38 *āzādī-i maṭba'ah.*
39 *āzādī-i maṭbū'āt.*
40 *ikhtiyār-i ṭab' va iẓhār-i afkār.*
41 *āzādī-i qalam va ṭab'.*
42 *ikhtiyār-i jamā'at.*
43 *ikhtiyār-i ijtimā' va tashkīl-i anjuman.*
44 *āzādī-i majāmi'.*
45 *ikhtiyār-i ta'līm va ta'allum.*
46 *ikhtiyār-i 'arẓ.*
47 *āzādī-i siyāsīyah.*
48 *āzādī-i intikhāb.*
49 *ikhtiyār-i zaban.*
50 *āzādī-i bayān.*
51 *ḥurrīyat dar guftār.*
52 See Mīrzā Malkam Khān, 'Sirāṭ al-mustaqīm', p. 193.
53 Ākhund'zādah, *Maktūbāt-i Kamāl al-Dawlah*, pp. 55–6.
54 For a list of some well-known members of these associations and their activities in Kerman, Isfahan, Azerbaijan, Tehran, as well as the Holy Shrines and Istanbul, see Malik'zādah, pp. 202–11.
55 'Mutamim-i qānūn-i asāsī', Article 21. English translation is cited from Browne, p. 90. It is published on DVD and the English translation is cited from Edward Granville Browne, *A Brief Narrative of Recent Events in Persia: Followed by a Translation of 'the Four Pillars of the Persian Constitution'* (London: Luzac and Co., 1909), p. 90.
56 'Afsānah-'i khvāb'rubā ya dāstān-i bi'aṣl', *Ṣūr-i Isrāfīl* (Tehran, 15 Jumada I 1325 / [27 June 1907]), no. 5, pp. 1–4 (p. 4).
57 For some examples of such mistreatments and even persecutions that occurred in Mākū, Niyshābūr, and Zanjān, see Kasravī, pp. 444, 446.
58 'Maktūb-i buq'ah-'i ḥaẓrat-i 'Abd al-'Aẓīm', *Rūḥ al-Qudus* (Tehran, 4 Rajab 1325 [13 August 1907]), no. 2, pp. 3–4 (p. 3).
59 Nā'īnī, vol. 2, pp. 487–8.
60 'Khiṭāb bih anjumanān ya jamā'at-i khuftigān', *Rūḥ al-Qudus* (Tehran, 25 Dhu'l Ḥijja 1325 / [29 January 1908]), no. 16, pp. 1–3.
61 Mustashār al-Dawlah Tabrīzī, *Yik Kalamah va Yik Nāmah*, pp. 54–5.
62 Mīrzā Malkam Khān, 'Nidā-yi *'Adālat'*, in *Risālah'hā-yi Mīrzā Malkam Khān Nāẓim al-Dawlah* (Tehran: Nashr-i Nay, 1381), pp. 136–52 (p. 145).
63 Navvāb 'Alī Bakhsh Mīrzā, 'Mīzān Al-Millal', in *Rasā'il-i mashrūṭīyat: 18 risālah va lāyīḥah darbārah-i mashrūṭīyat*, ed. by Ghulām Ḥusayn Zargarī'nizhād (Tehran: Kavīr, 1374, p. 470.
64 Nā'īnī, vol. 2, p. 482.

65 For instance, see a night-letter cited by Sharīf Kāshānī (pp. 91–3) that, 20 days after issuing the Constitutional Decree, accused the constitutionalist cleric leaders of receiving bribes from the court to step down from the movement's demands and to remain silent on the postponement of the establishment of the majlis. Also, for an example of contemptuous criticism of the majlis for approving of Amīn al-Sulṭānh's Prime Ministry, see 'Alī Akbar Dihkhudā, 'Charand-u-parand', *Ṣūr-i Isrāfīl* (Tehran, 30 Dhu'l Ḥijja 1325 / [3 February 1908]), no. 22, pp. 6–8.
66 'Ẓuhūr-i jadīd', *Ṣūr-i Isrāfīl* (Tehran, 8 Jumada I 1325 / [20 June 1907]), no. 4, pp. 6–7 (p. 6).
67 See 'Difā' [2]', pp. 5–10.
68 Sayyid Jamāl al-Dīn Vā'iẓ Iṣfahānī, 'Ṣūrat-i maqālah-'i jināb-i mustaṭāb Āqā Sayyid Jamāl al-Dīn "dāmat barakātuh"', *Ṣūr-i Isrāfīl* (Tehran, 21 Jumada II 1325 / [1 July 1907]), no. 7–8, pp. 10–13 (p. 11).
69 Nāṣir al-Dīn Parvīn, *Tārīkh-i rūznāmah'nigārī-i īrāniyān va dīgar pārsī'nivīsān* (Tehran: Markaz-i Nashr-i Dānishgāhī, 1377), pp. 492–3.
70 See '[Āyā barāy-i kamāl va taraqqī basharī sar'ḥaddī hast?]', *Ṣūr-i Isrāfīl* (Tehran, 26 Rajab 1325 / [5 September 1907]), no. 12, pp. 1–3 (p. 2).
71 '1st Majlis', Session 2 (Shawwal 1325 / [8 November 1907]).
72 Parvīn, p. 499.
73 For the text of Ṣanī' al-Dawlah's letter, see *Asnād-i maṭbū'āt-i Īrān, 1320–1332 H.Sh*, ed. by Ghulām Riẕā Salāmī and Muḥsin Rūstāyī (Tehran: Intishārāt-i Sāzmān-i Asnād-i Millī-i Īrān, 1371), vol. 2, p. 517.
74 Muḥammad Riẕā Shīrāzī, '[Shāh dar chih ḥāl ast?]', *Musāvāt* (Tehran, 24 Rabi I 1326 / [26 April 1908]), no. 21, pp. 1–5.
75 Kasravī, pp. 716, 693.
76 Parvīn, vol. 2, p. 484.
77 Nūrī, 'Risālah-'i Ḥurmat-i mashrūṭah', vol. 1, p. 262.
78 Kasravī, p. 716.
79 '[Ṣūrat-i maqāṣid-i 'ulamā'-i a'lām va ḥujjaj-i Islām-i muhājirīn]', in *Lavāyiḥ-i Āqā Shaykh Faẕl Allāh Nūrī* (Tehran: Nashr-i Tārīkh-i Īrān, 1362), p. 48.
80 Rustam'ābādī, p. 37.
81 Ibid.
82 Shaykh 'Alī Lāhījī, 'Lāyiḥah dar Sarzanish-i Rūznāmah'hā va Mashrūṭah'khvāhān (Munṭaba'ah dar Zāvīyah-'i Muqaddasah-'i Ḥaẕrat-i 'Abd Al-'Aẓīm, Rajab 1325)', in *Rasā'il-i mashrūṭīyat: mashrūṭah bih ravāyat-i muvāfiqān va mukhālifān*, ed. by Ghulām Ḥusayn Zargarī'nizhād, 2 vols. (Tehran: Intishārāt-i Mu'assisah-'i Taḥqīqāt va Tawsi'ah-'i 'Ulūm-i Insānī, 1378), vol. 1, 241–52 (pp. 248–9).
83 See Nāṣir al-Dīn Shāh. The English translation is quoted in Curzon, *Persia and the Persian Question*, pp. 460–1.
84 See Khusraw Shākirī, *Pīshīnah'hā-yi iqtiṣādī-ijtimā'ī-i junbish-i mashrūṭīyat va inkishāf-i sūsiyāl dimūkrāsī dar Aān 'ahd* (Tehran: Nashr-i Akhtarān, 1384), pp. 66–8, 94–7, 106–7.
85 Katouzian distinguished three phases for the Iranian economy in the nineteenth century: 1800–50, 1850–70, and 1870–1900. The period 1850–70, according to him, was the most flourishing phase, while in the last phase (1870–1900), foreign debts and decline in the value of Iranian currency (following the fall in silver price on which the currency was based) brought about inflationary pressures. Despite such noticeable deterioration, as Katouzian argued, the increase in the trade with Europe indirectly played a significant role in weakening the arbitrary system. In an intensive and in-depth analysis, he outlined such indirect role as follows: 'first, the growing role of imperial powers exposed the weakness of the Iranian state and robbed it of the traditional public belief in its omnipotence, thus prompting Naser al-Din Shah to tell E'temad al-Saltaneh that "the people's eyes and ears had not yet been opened" under Fath'ali Shah. Second, their payments for various concessions and privileges to

the shah and state officials helped weaken the structure of arbitrary rule from within. Third, the greater specialization in the production and export of raw materials, the relative decline of manufacturing, the use of the telegraph as a modern means of communication, the endemically rising inflation, the crippling deficit in foreign payments and the resulting accumulation of foreign debt led to a structural disequilibrium in the economy which the traditional state apparatus could not comprehend, let alone cope with. The turmoil that followed the death of Naser al-Din Shah led to further deterioration of the economy' (Katouzian, *The Persians*, pp. 166–9).

86 Malik'zādah, pp. 227–8; also see Vanessa Martin, 'Constitutional Revolution, ii. Events', in *Encyclopaedia Iranica* (Costa Mesa: Mazda Publishers, 1993), vol. 6, pp. 176–87.

87 For further discussion about this issue, see section 3.2.

88 For instance, see '[Tawsiʿah-ʾi filāḥat], baqīyah az numrah-ʾi qabl', *Ṣūr-i Isrāfīl* (Tehran, 28 Shawwal 1325 / [8 November 1907]), no. 19, pp. 1–3 (pp. 1–2).

89 '[Āyā iṣlāḥāt-i siyāsī muqaddam bar iṣlāḥāt-i ijtimāʿī ast?], baqīyah az shumārah-ʾi 27', *Ṣūr-i Isrāfīl* (Tehran, 12 Rabi II 1326 / [14 May 1908]), no. 29, pp. 1–3 (pp. 1–2).

90 Ibid., p. 2.

91 Mīrzā Malkam Khān, 'Daftar-i tanẓīmāt', p. 39.

92 See Muḥammad ʿAlī Shāh's telegram to the ʿulamā of Najaf cited in Sharīf Kāshānī, pp. 221–2.

93 *Qurʾān*, vol. 2, p. 256.

94 Sayyid Naṣr Allāh Taqavī, '[Maʿnā-yi pulitīk va ẓarūrat-i taghyīr-i ān]', in *Rasāʾil-i mashrūṭīyat: mashrūṭah bih ravāyat-i muvāfiqān va mukhālifān*, ed. by Ghulām Ḥusayn Zargarī'nizhād, 2 vols. (Tehran: Intishārāt-i Muʿassisah-ʾi Taḥqīqāt va Tawsiʿah-ʾi ʿUlūm-i Insānī, 1387), vol. 1, pp. 607–17 (pp. 611–12).

95 Kalima-tu ḥaqq, yurād-u bihā al-bāṭil' (Ramadan 1326 / October 1908), in *Rasāʾil-i mashrūṭīyat: mashrūṭah bih ravāyat-i muvāfiqān va mukhālifān*, ed. by Ghulām Ḥusayn Zargarī'nizhād, 2 vols. (Tehran: Intishārāt-i Muʿassisah-ʾi Taḥqīqāt va Tawsiʿah-i ʿUlūm-i Insānī, 1387), vol. 2, pp. 113–27 (p. 126). See also section 5.3.1.

96 Malik'zādah, p. 70.

97 'Maknūnāt-i Khāṭir', *Rūḥ al-Qudus* (Tehran, 26 Safar 1326 / [30 March 1908]), no. 21, pp. 1–2.

98 Lāhījī, vol. 1, p. 247.

99 Ibid., pp. 247–8.

100 Zargarī'nizhād, Ghulām Ḥusayn, ed., '[Taqaddus-i salṭanat va maʿāyib-i mashrūṭīyat]', in *Rasāʾil-i mashrūṭīyat: mashrūṭah bih ravāyat-i muvāfiqān va mukhālifān*, 2 vols. (Tehran: Intishārāt-i Muʿassisah-ʾi Taḥqīqāt va Tawsiʿah-ʾi ʿUlūm-i Insānī, 1387), vol. 1, 305–51 (p. 331).

101 Mīrzā Ḥasan Khān Anṣārī, 'Ganjīnah-ʾi anṣār yā rumān-i shaykh va shūkh', in *Bunyād-i falsafah-ʾi siyāsī dar Īrān (ʿaṣr-i mashrūṭīyat): talāqī-ʾi andīshah-ʾi siyāsī-ʾi Islām va Īrān bā gharb, bih inẓimām-i davazdaah risālah-ʾi muhim-i siyāsī*, ed. by Mūsá Najafī (Tehran: Markaz-i Nashr-i Dānishgāhī, 1376), pp. 410–46 (p. 412).

102 Anṣārī, 'Rumān-i Shaykh va Shūkh', pp. 414–15.

103 See Malik'zādah, pp. 713–15, 723–6.

104 See Ibid., pp. 1324–7.

105 See Sharīf Kāshānī, pp. 420–1 and Malik'zādah, pp. 1285, 1345–54.

106 Malik'zādah, pp. 1509–10.

107 Mīrzā Ḥasan Khān Anṣārī, 'Nūshdārū yā davā-yi dard-i īrāniyān', in *Bunyād-i falsafah-ʾi siyāsī dar Īrān (ʿaṣr-i mashrūṭīyat): talāqī-ʾi andīshah-ʾi siyāsī-ʾi Islām va Īrān bā gharb, bih inẓimām-i davazdaah risālah-ʾi muhim-i siyāsī*, ed. by Mūsá Najafī (Tehran: Markaz-i Nashr-i Dānishgāhī, 1376), pp. 447–98 (p. 451).

5 Freedom *of*

The question of eligibility and equality

What *person* is entitled to be free? This question is more vital for freedom-seeking pioneers than it is for their descendants, because they, implicitly or explicitly, maintain that they are the first generation to realize their right to freedom, and therefore must have an answer to the question of what distinguishes them from their ancestors. The Iranian pioneers of the freedom-seeking movement asked themselves the similar question of whether the right to freedom is inherent or acquired. If inherent, why were our fathers deprived of this right? And if acquired, what should we do to deserve it? An equally important question was whether all Iranian people must *equally* benefit from freedom. These questions refer to two significant aspects of the first variable of the triadic relation of freedom: the eligibility of the agent of freedom, and the equality of agents in having freedom. Besides addressing these two issues, this chapter will also discuss the actual effects of religion and gender upon the agents' freedom in late Qajar Iran.

5.1 The question of eligibility of the agent of freedom

Late Qajar writings on the eligibility of the agent of freedom can be regarded as an answer to one of the questions formulated below. Some of these formulations have been explicitly stated, while others can be reconstructed from the texts. The formulations can be grouped as follows:

> Group (A): What is the right time for giving freedom to an individual/nation? Who can identify this time? Who gives them this freedom?
> Group (B): When an individual or a nation has not yet reached its rightful time of freedom, does it mean that it is not eligible to have freedom, or does it rather mean that it is incapable of using its freedom? Does giving freedom mean admitting an inherent right, or granting/privileging a right?

These formulations partially overlap, because all are involved with conceptions such as the 'eligibility of freedom'. Accordingly, it might not be possible to regard a given text as an answer to only one of these questions. However, it can be said that the question of eligibility first emerged in the formulations of group (A), with deeper reflections leading to the questions in group (B). Accordingly, I shall begin with the first group of questions.

5.1.1 Immaturity or incapability, that is the question

'Do you think that it is possible to give freedom to this people?' This is a question asked of Malik al-Mutakallimīn by a Russian orientalist, called Nicola Manoski, when he observed the protesters migrating from Tehran to Qum.[1] The questioner's utterance reveals his belief that this was not the right time to grant freedom to Iranians. He reminded Malik al-Mutakallimīn that most of the Iranian people were illiterate and ignorant about the new world conditions. Moreover, not one national party had existed to prepare them for the sociopolitical changes. Malik al-Mutakallimīn, however, had a different approach to the issue. According to him, freedom was an unconditional divine gift. Human beings could achieve freedom since God gave them freedom and wisdom. God had not denied primitive man his freedom, nor had he postponed his freedom on grounds of his having to first be civilized and literate.[2] Accepting that most Iranians were still ignorant, Malik al-Mutakallimīn pointed out that such a weakness could not justify withholding freedom; rather, he believed that freedom would be an essential requisite on the path to civilization.[3]

This was what Malkam Khān had been promoting many years before Malik al-Mutakallimīn. Considering freedom as a requirement for obtaining civilization and knowledge, Malkam Khān attempted to introduce to the Iranians a new sense of humanity compatible with the era of modernity and progress (*tajaddud* and *taraqqī*). Naming this civic human being '*ādam*' (Adam), he identified *ādamīyat* (to become *ādam*) and the union of *ādams* (*ittifāq-i ādamiyān*) as the only way to remedy Iran's decline and establish the rule of law.[4] When Malkam Khān had not yet publicized his invitation to *ādamīyat*, the world of the *farāmūsh'khānah* was to him a small sample of the civilized world of '*ādamiyān*'. And the criterion for admission into this world – which was called 'the city of knowledge' (*madīnah-ʾi ʿilm*) by its members – was deemed to be loyalty to the triadic pillars of the *farāmūsh'khānah*, namely equality, liberty, and fraternity (*musāvāt, ikhtiyār*, and *jamāʿat*), an account of the masonic universal motto. This is evident in the report written by an anonymous member of the *farāmūsh'khānah* to Nāṣir al-Dīn Shāh after the dissolution of the association around 1861.[5]

Supporting the same position, most constitutionalists maintained that 'the development of knowledge' (*tawsiʿah-ʾi maʿārif*) was conditional upon replacing arbitrary rule with the rule of law. Proponents of constitutionalism indicated that they preferred the 'first freedom, then public awareness' strategy to that of 'first public awareness, then freedom'. However, this idea was challenged by some thinkers. For instance, Shaykh Muḥammad Shīrāzī, known as the Philosopher, a member of the *anjuman-i makhfī-i bīdārī* (the Awakening Secret Association), declared the following at the eighth meeting of the *anjuman* in Muharram 1323/ March 1905:

> Do not mention anything about freedom. Ignorant people must remain like obedient slaves. Even if our country becomes law-abiding or consti-

> tutional, or better yet, a republic, will there not be again the same despots and the same tyrants? Yet they would appear in the guise of lawgivers and would ruin our fate (*bih libās-i qānūn'khvāhī dar mī'āyand va pidar-i mā rā mī'sūzānand*).[6]

The most well-known representative of this view is Nāṣir al-Mulk who, at the threshold of the constitutional period, believed that the Iranian nation was not yet eligible for freedom and the constitutional state.[7] It has been said that ʿAyn al-Dawlah made Nāṣir al-Mulk (a political expert educated in England who had gained the respect of clerics) wrote a letter to Ṭabāṭabāʾī confirming that it was still too early to provide constitutionalism in Iran, after Ṭabāṭabāʾī's insistence on pursuing the establishment of the *ʿadālat'khānah*, which had been promised by Muẓaffar al-Dīn Shāh in response to the *ʿulamā's* first migration to the ʿAbd al-ʿAẓīm Shrine (The Lesser Migration).[8] Admiring Ṭabāṭabāʾī as a patriotic man who was deeply concerned about Iran's suffering, Nāṣir al-Mulk states that the cure chosen by him is not effective for the patient:

> Yet, in Iran, advocating an assembly of representatives and insisting on the establishment of the law of equality and talking about freedom and complete justice (as it exists in all blissful civilized nations) are nothing but flogging [the patient who is unable to move] and forcing him to gorge half-cooked camel meat. . . . Not all places across the vast land of Iran are like the streets of Tehran. . . . There are also predators and wildlife, there are Lurs, Kurds, Shahsavans, as well as Qashqais. . . . These ideas that throughout the world are the substance of prosperity, dignity and honour, would be in today's Iran, in my opinion, the source of anarchy, destruction, humiliation, insecurity and thousands of other immoralities. Because we do not yet have the knowledge and capability for the establishment of the new regulations, spreading these ideas would publically weaken the awe and authority of [absolute] power. . . . Suppose that today, His Majesty the Shah would, willingly and of with his complete satisfaction, issue a rescript bestowing complete freedom on the country and pronounce that your Excellency should set up a majlis of representatives, then what would you do? To form this one majlis, you would need at least a thousand cultivated men conversant with the new world conditions and aware of the rights of nations and international law. . . . I swear that if you were to intend to select them diligently, you would not be able to find even one hundred such men throughout Iran. Then why are you shouting? For whom are you struggling?[9]

His decisive solution 'to change the situation into a new order and regulation' is that

> we need *ādam* (I mean learned man (*ʿālim*) in the modern knowledge); I swear to God that we need *ʿālim*! By the Qur'an, we need *ʿālim*! By the Prophet, we

> need *ʿālim*! By Murtaẓá ʿAlī, we need *ʿālim*! By Islam, by the Kaʿba, by the religion, by the faith, we need *ʿālim*! We need *ʿālim*! We need *ʿālim*![10]

Addressing Ṭabāṭabā'ī, Nāṣir al-Mulk goes on to add that the Iranian people would criticize Ṭabāṭabā'ī in the Day of Judgment, asking why he had not done what he could have for the sake of their virtue and happiness. He adds that, if Ṭabāṭabā'ī were to tell them about affairs such as migrating to the ʿAbd al-ʿAẓīm Shrine and writing letters to the government, the people would respond by saying that he should have familiarized them with new world conditions, since the means to spreading knowledge had been in the hands of the clergy alone. This, the people would say, should have come before attending to other affairs. Nāṣir al-Mulk, at the end of his letter, puts forward the idea that the religious schools should not be the 'house-of-the-lazy' (*tanbal'khānah*); rather, they should be equipped with order and properly programmed to teach students not only religious knowledge, but also modern sciences. Under such conditions, he adds, two cohorts of such students would graduate within 12 years, and Iran would have a sufficient number of well-educated men (*ādam-i ʿālim*).[11]

In addition to revealing the writer's opinion on the Iranians' immaturity to have freedom, this letter implicitly indicates two further points: firstly, the writer metaphorically considers himself a pathologist who argues with another pathologist over diagnosing the roots of Iran's weakness as well as its cure, and disagrees with him particularly on identifying the right time to give freedom to the nation. This means that the élite and the intellectual leaders of the society are the referees of the eligibility of the agent of freedom. Secondly, the writer implies that it is the shah who can give freedom to the nation. This may refer to the idea of 'freedom as a royal gift' and can be regarded as an answer to the last aforementioned question in group (A): who gives freedom to a nation? After the issuing of the Constitutional Decree, this question received more attention,[12] when a number of writers admired Muẓaffar al-Dīn Shāh for giving freedom to the people. There were also two rival opinions – the first considered freedom as a divine gift while the second regarded it as a natural right.

5.1.2 Who gives freedom to a nation?

As discussed in the previous chapter, the Constitutional Decree does not make any reference to the freedom of the nation. The shah only briefly hints at the freedom of expression for the representatives of the majlis, and then claims that this freedom and security are given by his royal will. The idea of the shah as the source of freedom was maintained by a number of traditional proponents of monarchy as well as some constitutionalists. For instance, in Ramadan 1324, an anonymous writer wrote:

> Happiness and fortune have assisted the auspicious shah in accepting the advice of men of wisdom, reform and progress, and in sympathizing with the nation and the ruined country, for he has granted them the majlis, freedom of

expression, and the freedom to establish laws in order to promote justice and security and to protect lives and property as well as rights and duties.[13]

At the same time, Mīrzā Abū Ṭālib Mujtahid Zanjānī, a *pro-mashrū ʿah* cleric, maintained that he had been a proponent of constitutionalism and freedom since the time of the *ʿulamā*'s migration to Qum, so he wrote a letter to the shah asking him to give freedom to his subjects and to constitutionalize the monarchy. Zanjānī warned the people that 'the priceless gift of freedom' granted by the kind shah should not be misused or sordidly employed in achieving immoral personal aims.[14] Zanjānī's opinion is shared by Sayyid Naṣr Allāh Taqavī, a constitutionalist cleric and a representative of the first majlis. He also believed that freedom was a magnificent gift that, due to Muẓaffar al-Dīn Shāh's generosity and kindness, had been given to the people without their having demanded it or suffered for it. For him, subjects are the liberated slaves of the shah though they are not eligible for such mercy. Therefore, they must always be grateful to him and pray for his health and success. Contrary to Taqavī, most constitutionalists tend to believe the source of freedom is not the shah, but that it rather stems from God or is inherent in human nature.

Contrary to its two rival ideas, the idea of 'freedom as a royal gift' has not been well explained in late Qajar writings. Although it is not clear why the shah should be supposed as the source of freedom, this belief can reveal much about the benefits that the enemies of freedom hoped to gain from this idea. It is worth mentioning that when Muẓaffar al-Dīn Shāh, who was often known as a just and benevolent king,[15] passed away and his successor, Muḥammad ʿAlī Shāh, who had a desire for arbitrary rule from the first day and finally put an end to the majlis and constitutionalism, sat on the throne, the idea of freedom as a royal gift began to wane.[16] Not being the giver of the Constitutional Decree, the new shah could only claim that he had not neglected to support the *mashrūṭah* and had assisted in its establishment, which was considered by him as the freedom of the nation. However, he could, and he did, claim that the nation was not eligible to gain the gift of freedom and that he accordingly had the right to take their freedom back at his discretion. Inventing this pretext, in his telegram to the *ʿulamā* of Najaf, he wrote that to remedy the country's chaos and disorder, he considered it 'his right and personal duty' 'to dispossess and prevent freedom' (*ṭard va man ʿ-i āzādī*).[17]

In such conditions, even if the constitutionalists could theoretically accept the idea of freedom as a royal gift, in practice they preferred not to award the custody of freedom to its enemy, Muḥammad ʿAlī Shāh. Finding no value in freedom, the monarchists and the proponents of *mashrū ʿah*, on the other hand, were loath to defile the honor of the shah with this imperfection. Likewise, they refused to consider freedom as a divine gift or natural right. Absolving the shah, God, and nature, they had to place the responsibility of being the source of freedom on someone else. In *Tazkirah al-ghāfil wa irshād al-jāhil*, which is attributed to Shaykh Faẓl Allāh Nūrī, *mashrūṭah* is identified as the unpleasant foundation which leads to the aberrance of the granting of absolute freedom.[18] Shaykh Abū al-Ḥasan Najafī Marandī, another clerical opponent of constitutionalism, sarcastically says that the *mashrūṭah* assumes itself to be promoting justice and equality while it has given freedom to dissolute people (*ahl-i fujūr*). From this viewpoint, 'delusive freedom' (*āzādī-i mawhūmah*) is not a right to be pursued, but a false assumption that has emerged with constitutionalism.[19]

It was previously discussed that, in a gathering taking place during the Greater Migration, Sayyid Muḥammad Ṭabāṭabā'ī addressed Nūrī, saying that the people would taste liberty and freedom in the *mashrūṭah*. Unlike Nūrī, however, Ṭabāṭabā'ī does not believe that this freedom is delusive. For him, constitutionalism is a medium for giving the God-given gift of freedom to the people: 'constitutionalism is a thing in which God's servants who have been created free will be released from the yoke of bondage and will be rescued from long-lasting constraint'.[20] The notion of 'God-given freedom' (*āzādī-i khudā'dādī*) was also employed by *S*iqat a-Islām Tabrīzī and Mīrzā Ḥūsayn Nā'īnī. Interpreting several Qur'anic verses, they attempted to support the idea of 'freedom as a divine gift'. For them, one of the main aims of the holy prophets was to liberate the people from bondage. Nā'īnī, who in his *Tanbīh al-umma* employed the notion of 'the God-given gift of freedom' eight times,[21] apparently addressed Nūrī when he wrote:

> It is due to ignorance that wretched man neglects his God-given gift of freedom, his equality with oppressors and usurpers of freedom, and his national rights. He fastens their yoke over his neck with his own hands, and ever more he regards this greatest divine gift and most significant purpose of the prophets and saints as delusive.[22]

If freedom is a divine gift given to everybody at birth, then the nation's subjects are deprived of this privilege due to their ignorance, not because they are ineligible for having freedom but rather because they are merely unable to use their freedom. This is an answer to the questions categorized above in group (B). Drawing another line of argument, Ṭālibuf Tabrīzī arrives at the same conclusion about the source of freedom. Defining freedom as 'public wealth', he regretfully writes that

> Iranians have been deprived of the divine gift of freedom, although as humans they are equal to other nations and their ability is not less than others. They certainly deserve freedom; if it has been denied to them, they must obtain it; if it has been usurped, they must reclaim it; and if this wealth of glory has been kept in the treasury, they must bring it out and use it.[23]

Iran's disorder and lack of law, in his discourse, is interpreted as a sign of the people's immaturity and inability to preserve the public's common wealth that is freedom, and their predecessors are certainly guilty of this immaturity. Ṭālibuf believed that treacherous statesmen had not paved the way for the nation's maturity; thus, he wrote a couple of months before the issuing of the Constitutional Decree, asking the Shah to give the nation custody of their freedom:

> This freedom was confiscated by a sovereign guardian at a time of chaos when the Iranian people were not capable of protecting it due to their earlier

> negligence. He maintained the custody of this freedom under the title of his independence until a time when Iranians would become capable of protecting it and once they requested this freedom, it would be returned to them. At present, the people are not demanding this freedom, which is their wealth. In the past hundred years, out of thirty thousand people, not even ten mature men have dealt with this issue. And even if a couple of people expressed their concern, they were defeated by the majority of usurpers and were trampled under the feet of oppressors. Unless the present pious and virtuous guardian, who is unrivalled in the history of Iran, bestows his grace upon them and opens the gates of happiness unto Iranians and shed the lights of eternal blessings on his people, freedom is not going to be achieved.[24]

Using the metaphor 'public wealth', Ṭālibūf associates freedom with both the legal notion of 'possession' and the moral notion of 'keeping the trust'. He asserts that whoever commits treason against the custody of freedom will be found guilty by posterity. Referencing the philosophers, he defines freedom as a 'common right' and an 'equal ration of all members of the nation'. That is why nobody is allowed to sell his freedom, mortgage it, or present it to anyone else. One may not forsake his own right due to the fact that preserving rights is a sacred responsibility of all humankind.[25]

After the Constitutional Decree was issued, Ṭālibuf again wrote about 'the public wealth of freedom', this time recognizing the eligibility of Iranians to have freedom:

> Now all the people of Iran know that this wealth of glory has been bequeathed to us from our forefathers and has been in the custody of a pious and religious person in a secure treasury such that whenever we reach the age of maturity we could claim it. Since the coming of age of the people is manifested by their desire to sacrifice their lives, property and children for the sake of freedom, the religious excellencies [*ḥujaj-i Islām*] in general and his Excellency [*ḥujat al-Islām*] Ḥājī Mīrzā Muḥammad Āqā [Ṭabāṭabāʾī] in particular, informed Muẓaffar al-Dīn Shāh (God bless his soul, who was naturally willing to implement this sacred wish of the nation) that this maturity had been received. It was then placed under the supervision of 162 representatives in the treasury of the nation.[26]

To sum up, the common conclusion is that for most constitutionalist thinkers, freedom is a divine gift and an unconditional right that all individuals can equally have. However, eligibility does not equate with the ability to use freedom. Oppressors usurp the freedom of others, and those who neglect this usurped divine right or who make no endeavour or sacrifice for it would not be able to utilize freedom due to their ignorance or inaction. This is the very distinction between the right of freedom and the conditions of its exercise that Isiah Berlin highlights: 'if a man is too poor or too ignorant or too feeble to make use of his legal rights, the liberty that these rights confer upon him is nothing to him, but it is not thereby annihilated'.[27]

Likewise, the Iranian freedom-seekers of the late Qajar period made a distinction between the potential right of freedom and the actual one. For most freedom-seekers, Iranians, like the people of other nations, can potentially enjoy this right, but in order to actualize it they must acquire inner eligibilities and remove external obstacles. Nobody can achieve freedom alone; the agent of freedom is the whole nation that collectively reaches a civilized standing through qualities such as reasonableness, selflessness, fairness, law-seeking, and patriotism.

5.2 How did the agents of freedom understand freedom?

Listing the representatives of the first majlis, Kasravī, with deep regret, put most of the representatives into two groups: the first group (such as Vus̱ūq al-Dawlah and Mukhbir al-Mulk) were experienced and resourceful but tended towards arbitrary rule rather than constitutionalist ideals; the second group (such as Mashhadī Bāqir Baqqāl and Ḥājī ʿAlī Akbar Pulaw'paz) represented ordinary people and were pro-constitutionalism but unaware and inexperienced in politics. Kasravī went on to make the following assessment:

> I am not saying, like Nāṣir al-Mulk, that it was too early for Iran to have constitutionalism. If Iran had remained under arbitrary rule, it would always have been too early for constitutionalism. What I am saying is that the movement was immature.[28]

In his opinion, it was the responsibility of the leaders of the movement to awaken the people and to illustrate the true meaning of constitutionalism. However, Ṭabāṭabāʾī and Bihbahānī were not able to do so, and those who were more or less able neglected to fulfil this task.[29] The other side of the coin, according to him, was the people themselves who 'instead of learning, finding out what the meaning of constitutionalism is, and what to do and how to improve it now that it has been achieved, took the opportunity to show off'.[30]

It is hard to estimate how many Iranians would have been familiar with new political ideas such as nation-state, citizen, democracy, constitution, and freedom at the threshold of the constitutional period.[31] According to one estimation, Iran's population at that time was fewer than 12 million, less than 15 percent of which made up the urban population,[32] with only a small number living in the main centers of the Constitutional Movement such as Tehran, Tabriz, and Isfahan. In 1902/1320, Tehran's population reached almost 244,400.[33] According to Malik al-Mutakallimīn's son, Mahdī Malik'zādah, the number of those who were regarded as freedom-seekers and nationalists (*millīyūn*) did not exceed 2,000–3,000, and among them they possessed not even one gun.[34] Yet the extent to which this group was familiar with the new thought is not clear. From Malikzādah's report as well as the reports of others, we know that the number of protestors between 1905 and 1907 gradually increased. Most of them were probably impatient with injustice and followed the clerical leaders of constitutionalism without knowing much about it. In the first significant uprising, namely the migration to the ʿAbd al-ʿAẓīm Shrine in December 1905 (Shawwal 1323), the number of those who accompanied Ṭabāṭabāʾī and Bihbahānī reached about 2,000[35] or even 3,000[36] within a couple of days. One year later, a demonstration took place in Masjid Jāmiʿ in July 1906 (Jumada I, 1324) in protest at the murder of a young cleric called Sayyid ʿAbd al-Ḥamīd. Protestors were violently held back by government agents, and the number of protestors noticeably increased to somewhere between 20,000 and 30,000 persons, as Malik'zādah reports.[37] Most of them had no knowledge of the rule of law and constitutionalism, and were probably ordinary patrons of the mosque's prayers and sermons or were merely protesting at the murder of a young Sayyid. Five days later, on July 15 (23 Jumada I), a group of *ʿulamā* migrated from Tehran to Qum, and a crowd of merchants and guilds simultaneously took *bast* in the British legation compound in north Tehran.[38]

Soon after, the number of migrants reached 2,000,[39] and the population of *bastis* increased to 13,000[40] (some have claimed this number to be as high as 20,000).[41] It was in this phase that request for the *mashrūṭah* and the consultative majlis found their way onto the public demands list; in Kasravī's words, 'the word *mashrūṭah* gained currency and in those few days to some extent the meaning of freedom, constitutionalism, and parliament was taught to the people'.[42] Yet how can one make people fully aware in the space of just a few days? Moreover, the government prevented protesters from spreading awareness by banning telegraphs, so that even Tabriz did not receive news of the events happening in Tehran for a couple of weeks. It is worth noting that, due to its proximity to the Caucasus and Ottoman Empire, and as the Prince Regent's residence, Tabriz was more familiar with new thoughts than other cities of Iran were.[43] To get an idea of the number of proponents of the *mashrūṭah* in the city of Tabriz (whose population in 1881/1298 was approximately 170,000),[44] one can refer to the group of 20,000 people who took *bast* in the Telegraph House in May 1907 (Rabi II), protesting against the majlis's and the shah's delay in the enactment of the constitution. Nonetheless, this large number (almost ten percent of the total population of Tabrīz) does not necessarily mean that the protesters had a clear understanding of their own demand. Kasravī, who was a youth aged 17 years at the time of this mass protest, reported that despite all their fervent and revolutionary behavior, they rarely knew the meaning of the *mashrūṭah* and the law, and that only the leaders understood the distinctions between the constitution and religious law. Happy for having gained new social status and prestige, the preachers merely reiterated the leaders' words.[45]

Similarly simplistic was their understanding of freedom. This ignorance was well expressed by Ṭālibuf Tabrīzī in the very treatise in which he endorsed the Iranian people's maturity and readiness for 'repossession of the inheritance of freedom'. Pained to see the happy people childishly celebrating the newly emerged freedom, he thus wrote:

> If we were as aware of the meaning of the abstract word [freedom] at least as much as we are of gladness, pleasure, and bragging about it, we would

> cry, like a mother who has lost a son, for the heaviness of the duty and the lack of proper knowledge and capability for such a great boon, as well as the embarrassment of entering the realm of civilized nations empty-handed and unprepared; we would also condole each other, we would wake up, and we would communally attempt to become eligible for the great honour of freedom and its holy duties.[46]

The people's ignorance of the meaning of freedom is frequently reported in the constitutionalists' writings. The extent of this ignorance was described by an anonymous writer in March 1907 (Safar 1325) as follows: 'ninety-nine percent of the people are completely ignorant about the meaning of the *mashrūṭah* and the usage of freedom as they suppose that freedom requires public acts of immorality'.[47] It may seem that this is an overstatement; however, even the revolutionary activists held more or less the same opinion. The most famous and best-selling newspaper of the time, the *Ṣūr-i Isrāfīl*,[48] wrote in its first issue that 'Iran has changed' and that 'the people are not last year's people'. Blaming traitorous ministers for denying the nation political awareness and for placing an obstacle on the path of freedom, it went on to say that 'this nation does not deserve such words'.[49] Soon after, however, the writers of the *Ṣūr-i Isrāfīl* modified their opinion so that in the next leading article, they admitted that the people were not yet aware of their rights.[50] After four months, contrary to their initial hope, they challenged the readers' misinterpretations of the newspaper's contents and thus wrote:

> The best lesson learned by publishing 12 issues of the *Ṣūr-i Isrāfīl* was that we understood the enthusiasm and braveness of one person, ten persons, hundred persons or even thousand persons would not be sufficient to resist most of the population of a country for whom deception, thievery, dishonesty, hypocrisy, and flattery had become inherent.[51]

5.3 The question of equality

Although it was hard for many people to understand freedom properly and to distinguish between liberty and license, the meaning of equality was intelligible to almost all people, for equality can be easily understood through both common sense and moral intuition.[52] Understanding equality, however, does not amount to the acceptance of the legal equality of all society members. Any Iranian who lived in the cultural tradition of that time and who was conversant with the sharia knew that man and woman, Muslim and non-Muslim, did not have equal rights. However, this inequality was acceptable for most people and was perceived as compatible with justice. This being said, although the concept of equality has existed in the Iranian intellectual and religious heritage, the question of legal equality was a newly emerged idea. Using the concept of freedom, the question can be formulated as follows: must all Iranian citizens enjoy equal freedom?

This question, which may not seem difficult for us, was one of the most controversial issues of the time. The contestation began when in the 8th article of the

Supplementary Fundamental Laws of October 1907, it was stipulated that 'the people of Iran are to enjoy equal rights before the governmental laws'.

From the viewpoint of Shaykh Fazl Allāh Nūrī and some other opponents of the article, the contestation can be stated as follows:

> If governmental laws are in accordance with Islam, it will be impossible to grant equal rights, and if they are against Islam, according to the aforementioned [article 2] what is against Islam will be illegitimate and invalid.[53]

To support his identification of this dilemma, Nūrī highlighted the distinctions that existed between subjects of the Islamic commandments, namely

> mature and immature, recognizer and non-recognizer, wise and mad, healthy and sick, free and forced and constrained, pleased, and grudger, original and deputy, master and servant, father and son, husband and wife, rich and poor, learned and unlearned, skeptic and accepter, follower and *mujtahid*, *Sayyid* and non-*Sayyid*, Muslim and different types of infidel (*kāfir-i zimmī* and *ḥarbī* and *aṣlī*), and different types of apostates (*murtad-i millī* and *fiṭrī*) and so on and so forth.[54]

Nūrī went on, providing some examples of the unequal religious commandments; for instance, a Muslim man is free to contract a temporary marriage with a *zimmī* infidel woman, while an infidel is not allowed to marry a Muslim woman. Likewise, a Muslim can receive inheritance from an infidel, while no infidel can inherit from a Muslim. Also, if an infidel buys land from a Muslim, the buyer must pay *khums* but a Muslim in the same case would not be under such an obligation.[55] All of Nūrī's examples refer to the inequality between Muslim and non-Muslim and between man and woman. This being said, he pessimistically claims that the *mashrūṭah* is the plot of the misled cult (*ṭāyifah-ʾi ẓāllah*) who wish to defy the Islamic commandments about apostates and who want to gain rights equal to those of Muslims. Addressing Muslim constitutionalists, he adds that 'Islam has granted Muslims privilege and honour, while thou revokest thy privilege, saying that I must be brother of and equal to Zoroastrian, Christian, and Jew. May God curse the one who does not acknowledge his privilege!'[56]

From the viewpoint of constitutionalists, the issue can be stated differently. Overall, they held two positions on the question of equal rights of freedom: a group of them demanded the enactment of laws granting all members of society equal rights, while the other group interpreted equality as equality in the implementation, rather than the enactment, of laws.

Believing in the equality of all humans, the first group maintain that all the agents of freedom, whether woman or man, whether Muslim or non-Muslim, should enjoy equal rights. Fatḥ ʿAlī Ākhūnd'zādah was a pioneer in the idea of the complete equality of the agents of freedom. In his letter to Yūsuf Khān Mustashār al-Dawlah on 8 November 1875, which criticizes the treatise *Yik kalamah*, he argued that 'would the sharia be the origin of justice, it should have enforced the first foundation of the constitution,[57] namely equality in rights and equality before the judicial court'. He went on to address a number of legal inequalities in Islam. Here are two of his examples: an instance of the violation of the equality in rights is the sharia's discrimination between men and women, 'particularly the commandment of the *hijab* that sentences women to life imprisonment and makes them unfortunate and deprived of the boon of life'. A counterexample for judicial equality is that in an Islamic court, non-Muslims are incompetent to testify as witnesses. Ākhūnd'zādah then criticized the sharia's granting permission for the buying and selling of infidel slaves (even if they convert to Islam). To support this criticism, he referred to the British who, despite having religious permission, recognized the immorality of slavery and understood that 'infidels and atheists are our human brothers too. No one should be deprived of freedom rights under the pretext of having different beliefs'.[58]

Undoubtedly, at that time and even later during the constitutional period, such sharp criticism of the sharia could not be expressed in the public sphere. Thus, at the end of his letter, Ākhūnd'zādah himself sarcastically addressed the author of *Yik kalamah* saying that

> by God, I regret that my pen wrote these words. What can I do? When I saw *Yik Kalamah*, I got madly angry and went into a delirium. I shall repent: I am asking my God to forgive me and I am coming back to Him (*astaghfir-u Allāh-a rabbī wa atūb-u ilayh*).[59]

It was probably for similar reasons that those constitutionalists who believed in complete equality tended to express their opinions in purely philosophical or legal discourses and avoided religious discourse. As they developed the idea of equality on a meta-religious level, its incompatibility with the *pro-mashrūʿah* interpretation of the sharia often remained unspoken. A notable instance is Ṭālibūf's clear explanation of the equal rights of the agents of freedom. Assuming freedom and equality to be correlated, he believes that one is meaningless without the other since equality is the limitation of freedom, which otherwise would be absolutism and a violation of the others' rights.[60] According to him, equality of the agents of freedom, or in his words 'equality of freedom rights' (*musāvāt-i ḥuqūq-i āzādī*), serves to prevent people from infringing on the rights of others. Since freedom is the 'common right and public wealth' that must be equally rationed between all members of the nation, 'nobody is allowed to sell, loan, or give his freedom to anyone else'.[61]

Along similar lines, an instance of a secular legal explanation of complete equality was offered by Muḥammad ʿAlī Furūghī. Although he clearly wrote that 'equality before laws means that all laws with regards to all people are to be enacted and implemented equally', he did not make any reference to the two well-known legal discriminations in Islam, namely inequality between man and woman and inequality between Muslim and non-Muslim. He merely added that

> lineage, class and wealth should not determine the law; legal judgment should be similar for all people – whether poor or wealthy, whether common or

> noble – when they face similar situations including ordinary life matters such as transactions, contracts, and inheritance, or even crimes and punishments.[62]

Likewise, on the issue of judicial equality, it sufficed to say that men of wealth and clerics should not have a separate court of their own; rather, all should be judged in the same judicial court. However, he did not present the question of whether or not witnesses should be treated equally, regardless of their gender or religion.[63]

The second group of proponents of equality explicitly emphasized that they did not mean that all people are equal in religious duties; rather, they believed that each religious commandment which has been enacted as a law should be enforced equally for all cases. Among this group, some thinkers remained within the traditional framework of Shia *fiqh*, while some others attempted innovatively to set the meta-religious values in the Islamic legal system. An example of the first subgroup is Mullā ʿAbd al-Rasūl Kāshānī, who emphasized the distinctions between man and woman, the slave and the free man, as well as Muslim and infidel, declaring that this inequality refers to the imperfectness inherent in both freedom and humanity. According to him, women and slaves cannot reach complete freedom, the former being too weak in their abilities and the latter being inherently impious and accordingly falling beneath the reign of law.[64] He reduced equality in rights to equality in bodies, and ranks souls on grounds of differing levels of knowledge. He thus warned the common people not to assume equality with a learned man upon merely hearing the word 'equality'.[65] Such an interpretation of equality is closer to the *pro-mashrūʿahs'* opinion than it is to that of the constitutionalists.

One of the innovative thinkers was Ḥāj Mīrzā Muḥammad Ḥusayn Nāʿīnī, who called Nūrī's objections to 'the pure principle of equality' the second fallacy of religious despotism.[66] In his opinion, Nūrī and his followers falsely claimed that equality as the constitutionalists believed it meant denying different duties for different types of duty-bound people (*aṣnāf-i mukhtalifa-tul-aḥkām*). This difference, Nūrī believed, was an obvious principle of all religions and even non-religious people, since they all discriminated between able and unable, free and forced, wealthy and poor, wise and mad, in their rational commandments. The constitutionalists' definition of equality, Nāʾīnī points out, is equality between all members of the nation and with the rulers in general matters (*nawʿīyāt*), namely the matters that are shared between all humankind.[67] He distinguishes between the two kinds of social rights: (a) fundamental rights or primary subjects, which generally belong to all the people of the country (*ʿanāvīn-i avvalīyah-ʾi mushtarak biyn-i ʿumūm-i ahālī*); and (b) specific rights or specific subjects (*ʿanāvīn-i khāṣah*), which exclusively belong to a certain sect or group of people. All humans are equal in terms of the first type of rights, while only the members in each group are entitled to the second type of rights. Nāʾīnī puts the following items on a list of fundamental rights:

> security of the person's soul, reputation, and property, sanctity of the home, inviolability of the person, protection of privacy, immunity from unlawful

> imprisonment and banishment, freedom of legal assembly and other common matters belonging to all rather than a specific group.[68]

These rights and freedoms, according to him, belong to all Iranian people without presumption or cost of privilege and all are equal in enjoying them.

The agent of freedom, however, may claim a freedom which cannot be included on this list. Should this happen, the agent's eligibility to enjoy that freedom depends on the specific group to which the agent belongs, because in such cases different groups have to obey different commandments, and they therefore enjoy different freedoms. Here, Nāʾīnī reduces 'equality' to 'equality in the enforcement of religious commandments'. Accepting the sharia as the source of judgment and the *faqīh* as the legitimate judge, he believes that the legal discriminations between men and women and between Muslims and non-Muslims do not contradict the principle of equality. That is to say that, to him, even men and women are two groups with different commandments (*aṣnāf-i mukhtalifat al-aḥkām*), and equality between different types of duty-bound people is against both 'the necessary principles of all religions' and 'independent reason'. He continues his argument by responding to Nūrī's objection to the 8th article of the Supplementary Fundamental Laws. His response indicates that Nāʾīnī's understanding of the role of law in constitutionalism does not correspond with the reality. The main claims of his complicated statements can be restated as follows:

(1) The constitution serves only to determine the duties and responsibilities of government and the limits of its dominance, and to make distinctions between common duties (*vaẓāyif-i nawʿīyah*) and non-common duties.
(2) Parliamentary laws also address either political non-religious matters (enacted to establish order in society) or religious matters shared between all the people of the country.
(3) None of the governmental and parliamentary laws and regulations are related to matters of religious duty, contracts, marriage, other agreements and one-sided dispositions (*ʿuqūd va īqāʿāt*), inheritance, and retaliation. The authoritative source for such commandments are the *ʿulamā's jurisprudential practical treaties* (*risālah-ʾi ʿamalīyah*). The government and the parliament have no right to interfere in these affairs.
(4) In religious judicial courts,[69] only a legitimate *mujtahid* has the authority to issue decrees of religious retaliation, recompense (*diyah*), and prescribed punishment (*ḥadd*) to be enforced on Muslim, infidel, and apostate. Judicial equality thus means nothing but the fact that all suits and actions must be referred to an authorized *mujtahid* and that his decree, whatever and whoever it be about, must be equally imposed.[70]

The fact is that, contrary to what Nāʾīnī supposed, the constitutionalist majlis intended to make decisions about all issues related to the interests of the nation and the country, including commercial and judicial affairs.[71] The only condition was that the enactment of such laws should not go against the sharia.[72] Governmental laws were thus applicable to different types of duty-bound people, and if the religious legal discriminations between woman and man or Muslim and non-Muslim were echoed in the laws, how could one say that 'the people of Iran are to enjoy equal rights before governmental laws'?

5.3.1 Article 8 as an answer to the question of equality of Muslim and non-Muslim

Nā'īnī, through his minimalistic interpretation of equality as equality in the implementation rather than the enactment of laws, could not resolve the difficult problem of equality. During the days when the opponents of equality were attempting to refuse Article 8 in the first majlis, a writer in *Ḥabl al-matīn* newspaper wrote:

> If we do not accept equal rights to be implemented, we will face serious difficulties. One difficulty would be that a Zoroastrian, a Jew, or an Armenian who would see that according to law, his blood price is equal to almost 25 *Tūmāns*, would not remain under this nationality or obey its monarchy and laws, and would complain to representatives of other governments asking, 'What have I done wrong to merit my blood being less valuable than that of an animal?' . . . Another concern would be whether a law containing such discriminations will be acceptable in the human rights community. What will foreign nations say about the members of such a nation?[73]

The opponents and proponents of the principle of equality struggled together over introducing equal rights into the constitution. As Mukhbir al-Salṭanah, Mahdī Qulī Hidāyat pointed out in his notes, the necessity of this principle to some degree stemmed from capitulation:

> Iran has been forced to accept capitulation. Therefore, laws should be enacted in such a way that will make it possible for them to be discarded in the future. The prerequisite for this is equality of rights between non-Muslims and Muslims.[74]

Another significant factor behind the enactment of Article 8 was the Zoroastrians' and other religious minorities' demand for it. The Zoroastrians had financially sponsored the Constitutional Movement and were the only religious minority that could send a non-Muslim representative to the majlis. Again, Hidāyat informs us that

> Over the article regarding the equality of non-Muslims with Muslims in prescribed punishments, some people brought their mattresses to the building of the majlis and stayed there for six months [i.e. took bast in the majlis]. Finally, they found a solution for the implementation of prescribed punishments and wrote that 'the people of Iran are to enjoy equal rights before governmental laws' (Article 8). Yet it is not clear what 'governmental laws' means.[75]

An instance of the Zoroastrians' insistence was an appeal submitted to the majlis four months before the enactment of the Supplementary Fundamental Laws. It was indeed the fourth letter to the majlis written by them. Repeating their request for equality in human rights (*ḥuqūq-i insānīyah*), they wrote that 'we do not expect to get a share in the religious laws of others; our demand is equality in governmental rights and punishments'. They asked the legislators to employ the exact phrase of 'governmental rights and equality in the punishments of all people', which sought to protect religious minorities from the harm of cruel men.[76]

After reading the appeal in the majlis, one of the representatives, Āqā Muḥammad Malik al-Tujjār, said that 'they do not demand "equality in Islamic rights" but rather "equality in punishment laws" and, as it was stipulated in the law yesterday, they have already met their demand'. Another representative, Ḥāj Sayyid Muḥammad Imām Jumʿah, said that 'they have lived with us for 1300 years and enjoyed certain rights. We are currently doing our best to grant them more rights. We don't know who has provoked them to insist so much'. Implicitly arguing that this inequality originates from the sharia, Taqī'zādah then said, 'we know that religious rights cannot be altered. We too want to preserve and increase their rights, but we must understand the reason behind this complain. Provocation is not necessary; injustice alone is provocation'.[77]

To precisely understand the notion of equality in Article 8 of the Supplementary Fundamental Laws, the question to which this article was written as an answer should be reconstructed. As mentioned, the Zoroastrians' demand was a part of this question. They demanded equality in rights, including equality with Muslims in punishment regulations. As far as many people of the time understood, such equality had been guaranteed under Article 8. For instance, in the 171th session of the majlis, which took place a few days after the enactment of the Supplementary Fundamental Law (enacted on 29 Sha'ban 1325/7 October 1907), several letters and telegrams from Zoroastrians and Armenians were read, in which they thanked the majlis for endorsing the equality of rights.[78] Opponents of equality also understood the article in the same way in the early days. When a group of people gathered in Yazd on 13 October 1907 (6 Ramadan 1325) to elect the second representative of the city, Āqā Sayyid Yaḥyá Mujtahid said that he had asked the first representative to go to Tehran in order to prevent the majlis from accepting the Zoroastrians' demand for equality. He went on to add:

> Zoroastrians must feel slighted in Yazd. I asked him to go to Tehran and explain to the representatives that Yazd is not like other cities in Iran. For instance, we have heard that in other cities Zoroastrians ride horses, mules and asses. They wear fine clothes and hats. These are against the sharia. A Zoroastrian must wear a burlap cassock.[79]

A group of constitutionalists had a similar understanding of Article 8. Mukhbir al-Salṭanah Hidāyat, who played a role in drafting the Supplementary Fundamental Laws, described this article as 'the equality of different believers in punishments' which he interpreted as 'to avenge a Muslim for the sake of a non-Muslim'.[80]

Explaining Shaykh Fazl Allāh Nūrī's objection to the Supplementary Fundamental Laws, Yaḥyá Dawlat'ābādī wrote:

> The religious fanaticism of different classes of people sharpens [Nūrī's] sword [against constitutionalism], particularly considering the fact that equal rights are being discussed. Majlis representatives are debating over the discriminations between Muslims and infidels imposed by the sharia and over some other important controversial punitive issues.[81]

This 'religious fanaticism', along with a political trap, resulted in a tragic incident: on the night of 7 January 1908, a group of hoodlums who were provoked and supported by the royal court killed a constitutionalist Zoroastrian merchant, named Farīdūn Pārsī, at his home before the eyes of his wife.[82] According to Kasravī, after the interrogation of the accused hoodlums, it was revealed that he was killed under the pretext of his financial support of constitutionalism and 'in the name of hostility towards the majlis and the constitution that grants Zoroastrians equality'.[83] The incident led to public horror; outraged, a large number of people, particularly Zoroastrians, demanded that the majlis punish the murderers.

The constitutionalist clerical leaders were faced with a difficult dilemma: to sentence several persons to death for the murder of only one victim, especially a Zoroastrian, was considered against the sharia. There is contradictory information about the punishment of the murderers in historical sources. Undoubtedly, no death sentence was passed. It has been said that several persons[84] were sentenced to heavy lashing and 15 years of imprisonment in Kalāt, a remote city in Khorasan. A report claims that each of them was given 1,500 lashes.[85] Whatever the truth, word spread that some of the murderers had died under the lash, and this led to serious objections voiced by pro-*mashrūʿah* leaders.[86] One of them wrote, 'if equality did not exist, those heterodox people would not have cruelly executed several Muslims for the sake of one Zoroastrian while [spectators] were shouting "long live Islam". Such punishment has never been prescribed in our divine laws'.[87] He further asks, 'why did they take bribes and humiliate Islam for the sake of a Zoroastrian woman [Farīdūn's wife]?'[88] Even some constitutionalists criticized the punishments as unfair and violent. Majd al-Islām Kirmānī, a cleric constitutionalist and the editor of the *Nidā-yi vaṭan* newspaper, stated that to lash a human being in such a cruel way is not tolerable even under the most barbaric law. He further said that killing seven Muslims in retaliation for a Zoroastrian would be considered a violation of the sharia and as a consequence of *mashrūṭah.* This, he believed, would result in the hatred of religious and civilized people toward the majlis.[89]

There is sufficient evidence to prove that even some of the enlightened elite of the time were not prepared to accept equality and to acknowledge the fundamental rights of non-Muslims. A clear instance would be what Mīrzā Ḥasan Rushdīyah, one of the pioneers of modern elementary education in Iran, wrote about the murder of Farīdūn Pārsī. He explained that Sālār al-Dawlah, who was house-bound and unable to leave his home, had assigned him the responsibility of selling his village. Although 'Farīdūn-i Gabr' offered the highest price among all the buyers,

Rushdīyah was reluctant to sell the lands to an infidel. 'Having anxiety and not being able to sleep', he wrote:

> I invocated the holy soul of the Prophet . . . and told him [in my imagination] that if at the day of judgment you were to ask 'why did you sell such vast lands to Zoroastrians after I had sacrificed many Muslim lives in order to take the land of Iran from the Zoroastrians and give it to you?', then please rid me of this person! Thank God! At the morning, news spread across the city that Farīdūn had been murdered in such and such way. 'You did not smite when you smote [the enemy], but it was Allāh who smote' [Qur'an: 8:17]. It is indeed a strange [incident].[90]

In such an unprepared society, granting equal rights of freedom for non-Muslims seemed almost impossible. Therefore, the fact that the religious leaders accepted a set of equal fundamental rights for all Iranians should be considered a great achievement for the Constitutional Movement. If what Nā'īnī put forward had met with public acceptance, a list of liberties would be granted equally and to all agents of freedom. This would accordingly result in the expansion of common liberties through increasing the number of common fundamental rights.

The emergence of the new concept of citizenship with its completely new socio-political indications could lead to the establishment of a new legal system. During the Qajar period, however, the differences between a citizen of the nation and a subject of the shah or a member of the *ummah* did not receive enough attention. Although the word 'subject/s' (*ra'īyat/ru'āyā*) was gradually replaced by different words such as 'nationals' (*taba'ah*) or 'residents' (*ahālī*) of Iran, these terms belonged to the old political system and did not refer to a new identity with different sociopolitical rights.[91] The words *ahālī*, *mardum*, and *millat* were often used interchangeably, and the rights guaranteed for them were understood as limitations on rights of the shah (*ḥuqūq-i salṭanat*). In contrast with the word *shahrvand*, these words had no proper connotation that emphasized the individual's natural rights and which preserved these rights from legal limitations easily imposed in the name of public interests or the majority vote. Nonetheless, all *ahālī* of Iran were no longer the very *ru'āyā* kept in bondage of the shah; and for the first time being Iranian, and not necessarily being Muslim, was introduced as the only condition of enjoying some equal rights. This legal achievement was the fruit of the semantic transformation of the notion of '*millat*' from its traditional sense (religion and faith) into its modern sense (nation or residents of a country). However, Iranian society was taking its first steps in experiencing the rule of law and had a long way to go to rectify its discriminatory culture and to establish equal rights.

5.3.2 Women's freedom in a patriarchal culture

The problem of equality was not limited to the issue of non-Muslim minority rights. Women made up half of the society's population, but they did not enjoy even a fraction of the rights and liberties of men.[92] Women's right to political participation, namely the right to vote and stand for election, will not be the focus of this section since women's suffrage at this time was still a mere dream, even in most of the developed European countries. Furthermore, most Iranian men did not have the right to vote as doing so was conditional upon having a certain amount of wealth. It was in the second majlis that the question of women's right to vote was posed for the first time. However, it received a very negative response; Sayyid Ḥasan Mudarris, a leading *mujtahid* of the majlis, put forward the 'argument' that God did not give women enough capabilities, and that they, like the impoverished, were not eligible for such rights due to the weakness of their mental abilities. Furthermore, since women in Islam are under the guardianship of men, Mudarris maintained that they would never have the right to vote and that men must preserve their rights.[93]

It was not the sharia or laws but rather widespread insecurity that caused the violation of many fundamental rights for women. The government had no effective remedy for the social circumstances in which a woman could not go out safely in the public unless accompanied by a man. Both in the pre- and post-revolutionary era, the lack of security and the government's inability to protect public order and to punish molesters was among the leading causes which limited women's liberties. Although this may seem like an obvious point, it has been neglected in historical research on women's rights and liberties, which have often reductively considered discriminatory governmental and religious laws or patriarchal culture as the obstacles to women's freedom at the time. For instance, it is true that there were many disagreements over women's rights to education and that some religious authorities strongly rejected the establishments of girls' schools. However, from a discussion between Nāẓim al-Islām Kirmānī and Sayyid Muḥammad Ṭabāṭabā'ī in February 1905, it is evident that the objections stemmed to some extent from concerns about security. In this meeting, Ṭabāṭabā'ī first explained the vital role of educational reforms and the significance of the development of libraries and schools for the country's progress and public awareness. He then emphasized the importance of educating girls who would become the prospective mothers and educators of the nation's sons. When Nāẓim al-Islām asked Ṭabāṭabā'ī for his opinion on the establishment of girls' schools, Sayyid Ṣādiq, Ṭabāṭabā'ī's son, answered on behalf of his father. He explained that there were three obstacles in the path of the establishment of girls' schools: the lack of security for pupils to come and go between home and school without being harassed, the objections of opponents and those who would invent pretexts, and the lack of educated and virtuous female teachers as well as proper course books. He went on to conclude that

> Supposing that his Excellency Ḥujjat al-Islām [Ṭabāṭabā'ī] dismisses the opponents' objections, what would we do with rioting youths and unmarried irrepressible persons? If one of them were to molest a girl, who would prevent him and who would punish him? If a girl were to go to her friend's home instead of going to school, how would her parents know? How would they find their daughter in the home of a stranger?[94]

In addition to the issue of security, another noticeable obstacle in the way of equal liberties between the two genders was patriarchal culture and 'patriarchal readings' of Islam. My emphasis on 'patriarchal readings' does not intend to overlook the legal inequality and discrimination between women and men explicitly imposed by the sharia, such as discriminations in inheritance and recompense (*diyah*). Rather, I wish to highlight the opportunities where there are no religious commandments to justify discrimination, but where opponents of gender equality, under the pretext of avoiding wickedness and sin, deny women's liberties. An illustrative example of such a barrier created in the name of religion was the rejection of women's right of assembly. In a parliamentary discussion on 13 March 1908 (9 Safar 1326), a representative who had recently seen a membership card from 'the Association of Tehran's Women' (*anjuman-i nisvān-i Ṭihrān*) addressed the majlis representatives after an introductory speech on the necessity of Islamization of all country's affairs, and asked them whether such an association was legal according to the sharia. The initial reactions were not only opposed to the association but also against the proposal of such questions in the majlis. When Vakīl al-Ruʿāyā asked whether the gathering of women in a place had ever been prohibited in Islam, Āqā Sayyid ʿAlī Naqī compared this association with the newspapers, since both are scourges of the faith and both must be resisted. The only person who strongly defended women's right of assembly was Sayyid Ḥasan Taqī'zādah, who argued that there are no legal or religious prohibitions against such an association, as Muslim women have always had gatherings. He added that 'in the constitution, the word "Iranian" includes both men and women. As long as the association does not disturb religious or worldly matters, it poses no harm and is not prohibited'.[95] In support of this argument, another representative asked what harm there was in a group of women gathering to say, 'let us not wear foreign clothes or let us learn crafts and dressmaking'.[96] However, Mīrzā Faẕl ʿAlī Āqā, a cleric representative from Tabriz, responded by saying that

> The association itself is not injurious to religion, but we know our country's women; I do not think that virtuous and chaste women will join these assemblies; rather, the corrupt and the disbelieving will gather in such assemblies with the intent to commit acts of immorality. Therefore such assemblies must be banned in order to prevent possible future corruptions.[97]

Several representatives raised further serious objections to such a question and asked for a change of subject. Finally, Ḥāj Sayyid Muḥammad Imām Jumʿah put an end to the discussion by saying that:

> Although there were no religious prohibitions against a woman going outside of the home for a gathering with her husband's permission, there were some conversations and discussions taking place in these assemblies that I do not want to repeat. This brief remark was more than enough.[98]

The proceedings of that session did not provide further information. Imām Jumʿah's comments show that the content of discussions of the members of *anjuman-i nisvān-i Ṭihrān* was mentioned and discussed in the majlis, but the representatives probably decided not to publicize this part of the proceedings.

Here, the question of what was discussed in the assemblies of women is an important one. According to a report published in the *anjuman-i Tabrīz* newspaper, it was in Tabriz that in early 1907 (a couple of months after the Constitutional Decree was issued), the first Iranian women's association, called '*anjuman-i nisvān-i Tabrīz*', was established. It is evident from the report that in the association, 'respected ladies' (*khavatīn mukarramah*) talked about their dresses and other common issues, and looked for ways to reduce the consumption of foreign goods and clothes and to save money. The members of the association hoped to achieve the country's independence from foreign productions through 'women's contentment with their old clothes' and 'the endeavours of men working hard in Iran's companies'.[99]

The Association of Tehran's Women, also called 'the Association of Ladies' Endeavor (*anjuman-i himmat-i khavātīn*)', was set up in early 1908 in the neighbourhood of the *Sangilaj* district of Tehran. This association seems to have been more organized than the Association of Tabriz's Women. Every member had a membership card with her complete name and address;[100] this was a new phenomenon, particularly for women. As ʿAyn al-Salṭanah reported, Taqī'zādah, on behalf of the Association of Āzarbāyjān, paid for the monthly expenses of the association. Malik al-Mutakallimīn and Sayyid Jamāl Vāʿiẓ preached to the women; as ʿAyn al-Salṭanah claimed, 'they interpreted the Qur'anic verses on the *hijab* and expressed sorrow for the suffering that women have undergone because of being veiled (*mastūrī*)'.[101] This report does not provide further information.

It is hard to accept that Malik al-Mutakallimīn and Sayyid Jamāl Vāʿiẓ would have opposed the *hijab*; they may have attempted to exempt the face and two hands from having to be covered, as most of the *ʿulamā* in the *Imāmī Shīʿa* maintain that it is permissible for a woman to uncover her face and hands as long as there is no infatuation. This interpretation of *hijab* was promoted in the constitutional period when the social participation and education of women was receiving increasing attention. *Pro-mashrūʿah* clerics regarded such an interpretation as a heretical consequence of the *mashrūṭah*. Mullā Muḥammad ʿAlī Rustam'ābādī, for instance, wrote in August 1907 that 'the constitutionalists interpreted the holy verse of hijab in a suggestive and lascivious way'.[102]

Whatever the content of discussions in the Association of Tehran's Women may have been, it led to widespread denunciation, voiced even by a group of constitutionalists. Rumours circulated that Sayyid Muḥammad Ṭabāṭabāʾī had endorsed the association. In a letter written in March 1908, a preacher who was severely against the association asked for Ṭabāṭabāʾī's fatwa. The question the preacher posed – similar to most cases of such *istiftāʾs* – had been tendentiously formulated as it had hinted at a favourable answer by claiming that the association had been set up at the provocation of a group of corrupt and malevolent persons. Ṭabāṭabāʾī's answer was so unexpected that had it not been published in the *Kawkab-i durrī* newspaper – whose editor was his follower and friend, Nāẓim al-Islām Kirmānī – it would be hard to confirm its authenticity. In his answer, issued on 27 March 1908/23 Safar 1326, he wrote:

> I was the first to object to the Association of [Tehran's] Women. I expressed my indignation; I voiced my disapproval; I argued its disadvantages. Everyone who has accused me of being a supporter of that inauspicious Association, has done so out of spite. May God punish him! I do say, one more time, that the Association of Women is against the sharia and will result in many unpleasant consequences; a man will no longer be able to control his wife. It is necessary for all zealous Muslims to endeavour to disturb that Association.[103]

It should be noted that Iranian constitutionalism never intended to free women from the dominance of men. Emphasizing that such accusations were made by their opponents, the constitutionalists, from leading clerics to ordinary people, attempted to refute it.[104]

Another 'unpleasant' consequence often regarded as a result of the women's associations was their imitation of European women. On this topic, an anonymous writer warned about the threat that would loom if women were to be given freedom:

> I seek refuge in God from the contemporary women of both the present and the future! It can be seen from their signs and gestures that many seditions are looming and that an absolute hell is upon us. They will put the word of freedom – which is a part of the forbidden tree [of the *mashrūṭah*] – at the center of their circle of corruption. And it is as if I see, as all will see very soon, that womenfolk and the armies of the devil, especially in Tehran, will be forming associations and schools for learning French and English . . ., all in imitation of European women. Then they will write articles and newspapers [criticizing] the government and the nation; they will make speeches in public forums and [the audiences] will say 'what a good speech made by such and such lady!'[105]

Such are the aforementioned 'patriarchal readings' of Islam, which limited and condemned women's freedoms and which did not even grant them the right to write in newspapers or to make public speeches and be applauded by audiences. The patriarchal culture that defines woman as *ẕaʿīfah* and *kamīnah* (literally: weak and inferior) was so dominant in society that it sometimes met with the serious objections of women. In a letter to the *Ḥabl al-matīn* newspaper, one woman complained about the fact that they had not published her article: 'Do you believe that a woman does not deserve [to publish her works] or did you think that I was wrong . . . or that we, women, have no right to speak in our homeland?'[106] Complaining about the fact that her abilities and freedoms are less than those of a man, another woman wrote: 'Alas, I wish I was a man to say what I know, and to do what I want'.[107] Desiring to have more freedom, she was undoubtedly not the only woman of her time to express such a wish.

Notes

1 He reports that he observed a massive group of migrating people and met with some of the leading figures of this movement, such as Sayyid Jamāl Vāʿiẓ and Malik al-Mutakallimīn, as he had already heard about them through a socialist party (*kumītah-ʾi ijtimāʿīyūn-i ʿāmīyūn*) in Caucuses (Malik'zādah, pp. 364–5).

2 Mīrzā Naṣr Allāh Malik al-Mutakallimīn, cited in Malik'zādah, pp. 364–5.

3 For his view on the significance of promoting education and literacy, see also his sermon in Association of the Clerics Union (Mīrzā Naṣr Allāh Malik al-Mutakallimīn, 'Khulāṣah-ʾi Nuṭq-i Jināb-i Ḥāj Mīrzā Naṣr Allāh Malik al-Mutakallimīn dar anjuman-i muqaddas-i ittiḥādīyah-ʾi ṭullāb-i muḥtaram-i ʿulūm-i dīnīyah (shayyad Allāh arkānah)', *Ṣūr-i Isrāfīl* (Tehran, 17 Rabi II 1325 / [30 May 1907]), no. 1, pp. 5–6.

4 Although the idea of '*ādamīyat*' can be traced back to *farāmūsh'khānah's* teachings, his organized efforts for developing it began later with the publication of his newspaper, *Qānūn*. In *Qānūn* (established February 1890), he attempted to identify his readers with a new identity in order to lead a social movement toward the establishment of the law. He called them '*ādam*', a common name which is the 'title of the lord of all creatures' (*laqab-i ashraf-i makhlūqāt*) and 'the requirement of Islam', so that anyone with any belief can enter this group and no tyrant can hurt someone on the grounds of his being *ādam* (see *Qānūn*, no. 26, p. 4). Addressing the readers of the *Qānūn* newspaper, Malkam Khān warned them that 'if, God forbids, you are not *ādam* . . . immediately stop reading this paper and do not touch it again' (*Qānūn*, no. 13, p. 1.). 'Become *ādam*, and demand the law! (*ādam bishuv va Qānūn bikkvāh*!)'(*Qānūn*, no. 10, p. 3) was the motto of the newspaper.

5 See 'Rāpūrt-i farāmūsh'khānah', pp. 178, 188.

6 Shaykh Muḥammad Shīrāzī, quoted in Nāẓim al-Islām Kirmānī, vol. 1, p. 282.

7 For a criticism of this conservative idea, see 'Alī Akbar Dihkhudā, 'Du kalamah khiyānat', *Ṣūr-i Isrāfīl* (Tehran, 17 Rabi II 1325 / [30 May 1907]), no. 1, pp. 2–3.

8 The letter is quoted by Nāẓim al-Islām Kirmānī, *Tārīkh-i bīdārī-i īrāniyān*, ed. by Saʿīdī Sirjānī (Tehran: Piykān, 1376), vol. 2, pp. 454–62, and Kasravī, pp. 126–32. Referring to Ṭabāṭabāʾī's son, however, Malik'zādah cast doubt on the authenticity of this letter (Malik'zādah, p. 177). Nonetheless, the view expressed was fairly widespread at the time.

9 Nāṣir al-Mulk, 'Nāmah-ʾi Nāṣir al-Mulk bih Ṭabāṭabāʾī' [Jumada I 1324 / July 1906]', in Aḥmad Kasravī, *Tārīkh-i mashrūṭih-ʾi Īrān* (Tehran: Hermes Publishers, 2010), pp. 126–32 (pp. 128–9) and Nāẓim al-Islām Kirmānī, vol. 2, pp. 454–62.

10 Nāṣir al-Mulk, pp. 126–32.

11 Ibid., pp. 131–2.

12 This question and answer, as Herodotus reports, can be traced in the ancient Persian. Explaining the priority of monarchy over oligarchy and democracy, the Achaemenid king Darius the Great (c. 550–486 BCE) spoke thus: 'Whence, I ask, was it that we got the freedom which we enjoy? Did democracy give it to us, or oligarchy, or a monarch? As a single man recovered our freedom for us, my sentence is that we keep to the rule of one. Even apart from this, we ought not to change the laws of our forefathers when they work fairly; for to do so is not well' (Herodotus, *The History of Herodotus*, trans. by George Rawlinson (London: John Murray, 1862), vol. 2, p. 396). It should be noted that in this report, the word freedom probably means nothing more than being released from jail and slavery; therefore, this elementary conception of freedom should not be anachronistically compared with modern sociopolitical freedoms.

13 'Maktūb-i Shahrī: [Ahammīyat-i sarvat dar istiqlāl-i mamlakat va rāh'hā-yi taḥṣīl-i ān]', in *Rasāʾil-i mashrūṭīyat: mashrūṭah bih ravāyat-i muvāfiqān va mukhālifān*, ed. by Ghulām Ḥusayn Zargarī'nizhād, 2 vols. (Tehran: Intishārāt-i Muʿassisah-ʾi Taḥqīqāt va Tawsiʿah-ʾi ʿUlūm-i Insānī, 1387), vol. 1, pp. 585–93 (p. 589).

14 Mīrzā Abū Ṭālib Mujtahid Zanjānī, '[Maraẕ rā qabl az istīlā ʿalāj kunīm]', in *Rasāʾil-i mashrūṭīyat: mashrūṭah bih ravāyat-i muvāfiqān va mukhālifān*, ed. by Ghulām Ḥusayn Zargarī'nizhād, 2 vols. (Tehran: Intishārāt-i Muʿassisah-ʾi Taḥqīqāt va Tawsiʿah-ʾi ʿUlūm-i Insānī, 1387), vol. 1, pp. 169–71.

15 The epigraph identifying and dating the majlis building on *Bahāristān* Street was the phrase '*ʿadl-i Muẓaffar* (Muẓaffar's Justice)', a famous chronogram that stands for the date of Iranian Constitutionalism (1324).

16 For instance, on 15 Jumada I 1326 (15 June 1908), in their letter to Muḥammad ʿAlī Shāh, the majlis's representatives complained about the interference of the court entourage and reminded him that their demand for reform in the monarchy (*taghyīr-i maslak-i salṭanat*) relied on two principles: first, that the political powers derive from the people, and second, 'the sovereignty is a trust confided (as a Divine gift) by the people to the person of the king'. That is to say that according to them, freedom is not a royal gift; rather, the monarchy itself is bestowed on the shah by the people. In reply to their concern, Muḥammad ʿAlī Shāh, unprecedentedly, opens his letter by introducing himself as *Sulṭān ibn Sulṭān ibn Sulṭān ibn Sulṭān* in order to remind them that his dynastic antecedents reached back to Fatḥ ʿAlī Shāh. Rejecting popular sovereignty, he then states that his concession to constitutionalism and to the peoples' role in public affairs was out of his paternal kindness (for the text of majlis's letter and the shah's reply, see Malik'zādah, pp. 713–15, 723–6).

17 See Muḥammad ʿAlī Shāh's telegram to the ʿulamā of the Holy Thresholds (*ʿatbat-i ʿālīāt*) quoted in Sharīf Kāshānī, pp. 221–2.

18 Nūrī, 'Tazkirah al-Ghāfil', vol. 1, p. 288.

19 Shaykh Abū al-Ḥasan Najafī Marandī, 'Dalāyil barāhīn al-furqān fī buṭlān qavanīn navāsikh muḥkamāt al-Qurʾān', in *Rasāʾil-i mashrūṭīyat: mashrūṭah bih ravāyat-i muvāfiqān va mukhālifān*, ed. by Ghulām Ḥusayn Zargarī'nizhād, 2 vols. (Tehran: Intishārāt-i Muʿassisah-ʾi Taḥqīqāt va Tawsiʿah-i ʿUlūm-i Insānī, 1387), vol. 1, pp. 353–514 (p. 406).

20 Ibn Mīrzā Naṣr Allāh Mustawfī Tafrishī, *Tārīkh-i inqilāb-i mashrūṭah-ʾi Īrān* (Malik Library, MS 3819, Sha'ban 1325 / September 1907), pp. 27–8.

21 He used the phrase '*āzādī-i khudā'dādī*' (five times) and '*ḥurrīyat-i mawhūbah-ʾi ilāhīyah*' (three times). The latter was also employed by Shaykh ʿAbd Allāh Māzandarānī and Mullā Kāẓim Khurāsānī (see Muḥammad Kāẓim Khurāsānī, *Siyāsat'nāmah-ʾi Khurāsānī: qiṭaʿāt-i siyāsī dar ās̱ār-i Ākhūnd Mullā Muḥammad Kāẓim Khurāsānī ṣāḥib-i Kifāyah (1255–1329 Hijrī Qamarī)*, ed. by Muḥsin Kadīvar (Tehran: Kavīr, 1385), pp. 240–1. The word '*mawhūbah* (موهوبه)' (gifted) is a near homonym of the word '*mawhūmah* (موهومه)' (delusive) to respond to Nūrī's understanding of freedom.

22 Nāʾīnī, vol. 2, p. 471.

23 ʿAbd al-Raḥīm Ṭālibūf Tabrīzī, *Masāʾil al-ḥayāt* (Tiflīs: Maṭbaʿah-ʾi Ghiyrat, 1906), p. 99.

24 Ṭālibūf Tabrīzī, *Masāʾil al-ḥayāt*, pp. 100–1.

25 Ibid., p. 93.

26 Ṭālibūf Tabrīzī, 'Īẓāḥāt dar khuṣūṣ-i āzādī', p. 110.

27 Berlin, *Four Essays on Liberty*, p. liii.

28 Kasravī, p. 218.

29 Ibid., pp. 218–19.

30 Ibid., p. 163.

31 For a study about an emerging class of intelligentsia (*ʿuqalāʾ or munavvar al-fikrān*) and their self-imposed missions in this era, see Mongol Bayat, 'The Rushanfekr in the Constitutional Period: An Overview', in *Iran's Constitutional Revolution: Popular Politics, Cultural Transformations and Transnational Connections*, ed. by H. E. Chehabi and Vanessa Martin (London; New York, NY: I.B. Tauris : In Association with

Iran Heritage Foundation; Distributed in the U.S. and Canada Exclusively by Palgrave Macmillan, 2010), pp. 165–91.

32 The nomadic population was about 25–30 percent and the villagers were 60 percent of the total population. Abrahamian accepts this estimation (see Ervand Abrahamian, *A History of Modern Iran* (Cambridge, UK; New York: Cambridge University Press, 2008), p. 6). The primary sources often counted the total population between 10 and 15 million. For instance, in a letter to Muẓaffar al-Dīn Shah, Ṭabāṭabāʾī wrote: 'Please do not forget your 15 million children only for the sake of one tyrant' (for the text of the letter, see Kasravī, pp. 118–20).

33 Tehran's population was estimated to be 155,736 persons in 1852/1268 (ʿAbd al-Ghaffār Munajjim'bāshī Iṣfahānī, 'Jughrāfiyā dar nufūs-i ahālī-i dār al-khilāfah-ʾi nāṣirah', in *Āmār-i dār al-khialāfah-ʾi Ṭihrān*, ed. by Sīrūs Saʿdvandiyān and Manṣūrah Ittiḥādīyah (Tehran: Nashr-i Tārīkh-i Īrān, 1368), pp. 341–50 (p. 346)) and 210,000 persons in 1922 / 1301 H.Sh.

34 Malik'zādah, p. 349.

35 Ibid., p. 272.

36 Sharīf Kāshānī, p. 33.

37 Malik'zādah, p. 358.

38 For more information about popular politics such as mass strikes, demonstrations, and *basts* in constitutionalist Iran, see Stephanie Cronin, 'The Constitutional Revolution, Popular Politics, and State-Building in Iran', in *Iran's Constitutional Revolution: Popular Politics, Cultural Transformations and Transnational Connections*, ed. by H. E. Chehabi and Vanessa Martin (London; New York, NY: I.B. Tauris: In Association with Iran Heritage Foundation; Distributed in the U.S. and Canada Exclusively by Palgrave Macmillan, 2010), pp. 81–97 (pp. 87–90).

39 Malik'zādah, p. 365.

40 Kasravī, p. 148.

41 Malik'zādah, p. 374.

42 Kasravī, p. 149.

43 See Kasravī, pp. 167–9; Malik'zādah, p. 158. For more information about sociopolitical conditions of Tabriz before and after the Constitutional Revolution, see Vanessa Martin, *Iran between Islamic Nationalism and Secularism: The Constitutional Revolution of 1906* (London: I.B. Tauris, 2013), pp. 44–61, 122–46.

44 See Muṣṭafá Muʾminī 'Tabrīz', *Dānish'nāmah-i jahān-i Islām* (*Encyclopaedia of the World of Islam*) (Tehran: Kitāb-i Marjaʿ, 1381).

45 Kasravī, pp. 384–5.

46 Ṭālibūf Tabrīzī, 'Īẓāḥāt dar khuṣūṣ-i āzādī', pp. 87–8.

47 'Maʿāyib-i kār natāyij-i biʿamalī ast', in *Rasāʾil-i mashrūṭīyat: mashrūṭah bih ravāyat-i muvāfiqān va mukhālifān*, 2 vols. (Tehran: Intishārāt-i Muʿassisah-ʾi Taḥqīqāt va Tawsiʿah-i ʿUlūm-i Insānī, 1387), vol. 1, pp. 701–6 (pp. 703–4). See also Āqā Mīrzā Yūsuf Fazil Khurāsānī Tarshīzī, 'Kalamah-ʾi jāmiʿah-ʾi Shams Kāshgharī', in *Rasāʾil-i mashrūṭīyat: mashrūṭah bih ravāyat-i muvāfiqān va mukhālifān*, 2 vols. (Tehran: Intishārāt-i Muʿassisah-ʾi Taḥqīqāt va Tawsiʿah-ʾi ʿUlūm-i Insānī, 1387), vol. 2, pp. 591–655 (p. 632).

48 Parvīn, vol. 2, p. 520. ʿAbd Allāh Mustawfī reported that *Ṣūr-i Isrāfīl* had a circulation of 24,000 copies ('Abd Allāh Mustawfī, *Sharḥ-i zindagānī-i man, yā, tārīkh-i ijtimāʿī va idārī-i dawrah-ʾi Qājārīyah* (Tehran: Kitābfurūshī-i Zavvār, 1345), vol. 2, p. 249).

49 'Īrān taghyīr kardah', *Ṣūr-i Isrāfīl* (Tehran, 17 Rabi II 1325 / [30 May 1907]), no. 1, pp. 2–3; Dihkhudā, 'Du kalamah khiyānat'.

50 'Alī Akbar Dihkhudā, '[Istīfā-ʾi ḥuqūq-i ādamīyat]', *Ṣūr-i Isrāfīl* (Tehran, 24 Rabi II 1325 / [6 June 1907]), no. 2, pp. 1–2.

51 '[ʿillat-i mukhālifat bā *Ṣūr-i Isrāfīl*]', *Ṣūr-i Isrāfīl* (Tehran, 10 Shåbān 1325 / [19 September 1907]), no. 14, pp. 1–5 (p. 1).

52 Since equality was a well-known concept in the Muslim thought, one of the great figures of the Arab enlightenment movement (*al-Nahḍa*), Rafāʿa al-Ṭahṭāwī (1801–73), presented the notion of freedom as justice and fairness in the Muslim tradition while discussing the changes in the rights of the people after the reform of 1831 in the account of his journey to Paris: 'And what in France is named liberty (*al-ḥurrīya*) and desired by the people is the very thing we call justice (*al-ʿadl*) and fairness (*al-inṣāf*)' (Rifā'ah Rāfi' Ṭahṭāwī, *al-Dīwān al-nafīs fī īwān Bārīs aw takhlīṣ al-ibrīz fī talkhīṣ Bārīz*, ed. by ʿAlī Aḥmad Kanʿān (Beirut: al-Muʾassasah al-ʿArabīyah Lil-Dirāsāt wa al-Nashr, 2002), p. 124.
53 Nūrī, 'Risālah-ʾi Ḥurmat-i Mashrūṭah', vol. 1, p. 266.
54 Ibid., p. 265.
55 Ibid., p. 266.
56 Ibid., pp. 266–7.
57 He employed the French pronunciation of the term: 'كونستتيوسيون'.
58 See letter to Mīrzā Yūsuf Khān (8 Number 1875), in Fatḥ ʿAlī Ākhund'zādah, *Maqālāt*, ed. by Bāqir Mu'minī (Tehran: Intishārāt-i Āvā, 1972).
59 Ibid.
60 Ṭālibūf Tabrīzī, *Masāʾil al-ḥayāt*, pp. 92–3.
61 Ibid., p. 93.
62 Furūghī, vol. 1, p. 841
63 Ibid.
64 Mullā ʿAbd al-Rasūl Kāshānī, 'Risālah-ʾi inṣāfīyah', in *Rasāʾil-i mashrūṭīyat: mashrūṭah bih ravāyat-i muvāfiqān va mukhālifān*, 2 vols. (Tehran: Intishārāt-i Muʿassisah-ʾi Taḥqīqāt va Tawsiʿah-ʾi ʿUlūm-i Insānī, 1387), vol. 2, 529–90 (p. 568).
65 Ibid., pp. 568–9.
66 The first fallacy of religious despotism, according to Nāʾīnī, is to show divine freedom to be nothing but a delusive matter, resulting in the committing of immoralities and sins.
67 See Nāʾīnī, vol. 2, p. 448.
68 Ibid., p. 449.
69 The Supplementary Fundamental Laws recognized two types of courts: religious judicial courts (*maḥākim-i sharʿīyah*) for religious matters, and common judicial courts (*maḥākim-i ʿadlīyah*) for non-religious and political matters (see 'Mutamim-i qānūn-i asāsī', Articles 27, 71, and 72).
70 Nāʾīnī, vol. 2, pp. 450–1.
71 See 'Mutamim-i qānūn-i asāsī', Article 15.
72 Ibid., Article 2.
73 *Ḥabl al-matīn*, cited in Kasravī, p. 393.
74 Mahdī Qulī Hidāyat, *Guzārish-i Īrān* (Tehran: Nashr-i Nuqrah, n.d.), vol. 2. p. 185.
75 Ibid., pp. 188–9.
76 For the text of the appeal, see '1st Majlis', Session 4 (Jumada I 1325 / [15 June 1907]).
77 Ibid.
78 See '1st Majlis', session 171 (11 Ramadan 1325 / [18 October 1907]).
79 See 'Ṣūrat-i majlis va nuṭq-i ahalī-i Yazd barāy-i intikhāb-i vakīl', *Ṣūr-i Isrāfīl* (Tehran, 14 Shawwal 1325 / [20 November 1907]), no. 17, pp. 3–5 (p. 4).
80 Mahdī Qulī Hidāyat, *Khāṭirāt va khaṭarāt* (Tehran: Kitābfurūshī-i Zavvār, 1385), p. 151.
81 Sayyid Yaḥyá Dawlat'ābādī, *Ḥayāt-i Yaḥyá* (Tehran: ʿAṭṭār, 1371), vol. 2, p. 108.
82 Sharīf Kāshānī, p. 157 and Kasravī, pp. 641–2.
83 Kasravī, p. 644. See also Hidāyat, *Khāṭirāt va khaṭarāt*, p. 166.
84 See Sharīf Kāshānī, p. 160: (5 persons); Aḥmad Majd al-Islām Kirmānī, *Tārīkh-i inḥiṭāṭ-i majlis, faṣlī az tārīkh-i inqilāb-i mashrūṭīyat-i Īrān*, ed. by Maḥmūd Khalīlpūr (Isfahan: Nashr-i Dānishgāh-i Iṣfahān, 1351), pp. 291–2: (7 persons); Dawlat'ābādī, vol. 2, p. 243; and Kasravī, p. 680: (9 persons).

85 Majd al-Islām Kirmānī, pp. 291–2.

86 Nobody had died under the lash, but rather soon after the Lesser Arbitrary Rule, they returned to Tehran and were awarded by Muḥammad ʿAlī Shāh (Dawlat'ābādī, vol. 2, p. 375).

87 Nūrī, 'Tazkirah al-ghāfil', vol. 1, p. 289.

88 Ibid., p. 290. The rumor about taking bribes by the majlis and ʿulamā to impose a heavy sentence was frequently reported in sources. In his letter to Sharīf Kāshānī, for instance, Iḥtishām al-Salṭanah, the chairman of the majlis, mentioned that at that time, a Zoroastrian merchant named Shāh'jahān Khān sent him money and gifts and asked for a speedier investigation into the case of Farīdūn Pārsī. He considered the gifts as a bribe and rejected them, but later on learned that Sayyid ʿAbd Allāh Bihbahānī had accepted them (for the text of the letter, see Sharīf Kāshānī, p. 159). Referring to such a scandal several times, Yaḥyá Dawlat'ābādī also implicitly admitted that it was true to some extent (see Dawlat'ābādī, vol. 2, pp. 244, 272, 311).

89 Majd al-Islām Kirmānī, vol. 1, pp. 291–2. See also Dawlat'ābādī, vol. 2, pp. 244, 272.

90 See Rushdīyah's letter to Sharīf Kāshānī in Sharīf Kāshānī, p. 160.

91 In his Royal Proclamation of May 1888 (Ramadan 1305), Nāṣir al-Dīn Shāh addressed Iranians four times with the word *ruʿāyā*, twice with the word *mardum* (people), and once with the word *ahālī-i Īrān*. In the Constitutional Decree of August 1906, Muẓaffar al-Dīn Shāh used the term *qāṭibah-ʾi ahālī* (all residents) three times, the term *millat-i Īrān* (the nation of Iran) twice, and the expression *ruʿāyā-yi ṣiddīq-i mā* (our loyal subjects) a single time. Finally, in the constitution and its supplement, *ruʿāyā* was replaced by *ahālī-i Īrān*; and after a couple of decades, the Persian word *sharvand* became prevalent as the equivalent of 'citizen'.

92 For a summary account of the position of women in Qajar Iran, see Vanessa Martin, *The Qajar Pact: Bargaining, Protest and the State in Nineteenth-Century Persia* (London; New York: I. B. Tauris, 2005), pp. 96–8.

93 See '2nd Majlis', Session 8 (Sha'ban 1329 / [4 August 1911]). For further information about the debates on women's suffrage, see Rasūl Jaʿfariyān, 'Pīshīnih-yi ḥaqq-i rảy-i zanān dar majlis-i shūrā-yi millī (1390–1341)', *Khabar Online* <www.khabaronline.ir/detail/126461/weblog/jafarian> [accessed 24 March 2014].

94 Nāẓim al-Islām Kirmānī, vol. 1, p. 244.

95 '1st Majlis', Session 9 (Safar 1326 / [13 March 1908]).

96 Ibid.

97 Ibid.

98 Ibid.

99 'Anjuman-i nisvān-i Tabrīz', *rūznāmah-ʾi anjuman-i Tabrīz* (Tabriz, 25 Dhu'l Hijja 1324 / [2 February 1907]), no. 41.

100 See 'Anjuman-i nisvān-i Ṭihrān', *Kawkab-i durrī* (Tehran, 23 Rabi I 1325 / [25 April 1908]) yr. 4, no. 7.

101 ʿAyn al-Salṭanah, *Yāddāsht'hā-yi ʿAyn al-Salṭanah*, ed. by Masʿūd Sālūr and Īraj Afshār (Tehran: Asāṭīr, 1377), vol. 3, p. 2009.

102 Rustam'ābādī, p. 37.

103 Sayyid Muḥammad Ṭabāṭabāʾī, '[Fatvā-yi Āqā Sayyid Muḥammad Ṭabāṭabāʾī darbāb-ʾi anjuman-i nisvān-i Ṭihrān]', *Kawkab-i durrī* (Tehran, 23 Rabi I 1325 / [25 April 1908]) yr. 4, no. 7.

104 For instance, in a letter written in the Lesser Arbitrary Rule era, Mullā ʿAbd Allāh Māzandarānī, who was one of the three leading *marjaʿs* of the Holy Shrines in Iraq and who strongly supported the *mashrūṭah*, referred to deceptions of 'the men of turban' (*ʿammāmah'dār'hā*) in their opposition against the *mashrūṭah*. He wrote: 'May God put fire on the mouth of that deceptive preacher who told the ignorant people that "the *mashrūṭah* means that if a man's wife wants to be with another man, the husband has no authority to prevent her from doing so" ' (see Mullā ʿAbd Allāh

Māzandarānī, '[Dast'khaṭ-i Mullā ʿAbd Allāh Māzandarānī bih Āqā Sayyid Kāẓim Khalkhālī]', *Ṣūr-i Isrāfīl* (Yverdon-Suisse, 15 Muharram 1327 / [18 February 1908]), Suisse series, no. 2, pp. 6–7). For an example of an ordinary writer's reaction to such an accusation, see '*Kitābchah-i majmaʿ-i inṣāf*', cited in Sharīf Kāshānī, pp. 712–13.

105 Zargarī'nizhād, '[Taqaddus-i salṭanat va maʿāyib-i mashrūṭīyat]', pp. 305–51 (p. 351).

106 'Taghayyur', *Ḥabl al-matīn* (Tehran, 28 Jumada I 1325/ [9 July 1907]), no. 64.

107 'Maqālah-ʾi yikī az mukhaddarāt-i vaṭn'dūst', *Ṣūr-i Isrāfīl* (Tehran, 21 Jumada II 1325 / [1 July 1907]), no. 7–8, pp. 4–5 (p. 5).

Epilogue

Since the early nineteenth century, a very challenging question has been repeatedly posed by many educated and worldly wise Iranians. The question has two simple formulations: What is the cause of Iran's decline (weakness or backwardness)? What is the cause of Muslims' decline (weakness or backwardness)? Iran's/Muslims' backwardness or weakness was understood in comparisons with Europe or with Iran's glorious past before Islam or its golden age after Islam. As time went by, the frequency of this question and the variety of its answers increased. Therefore, it can be said that the awareness of the decline is the range of vision and horizon of meaning within which most of the sociopolitical texts of the time were formed.[1] It was gradually revealed that we need freedom of speech and freedom of the press in order to pose the question of decline and to diagnose its causes. To consult and collectively think about a remedy for the crisis, we need to set up societies and associations, which would be impossible without freedom of assembly. Likewise, freedom of work and commerce was required for the development of industry and the progress of national wealth. And all these freedoms were violated by arbitrary rule and lawlessness. On the other hand, in order to legislate and supervise the implementation of the law, people needed the right of popular sovereignty, as well as freedom to be elected and to elect. Arbitrary rule is nothing but the absolute freedom of the rulers to interfere in the people's freedom. The monarchy would have to become limited and 'conditioned' (*mashrūṭ*). Even Muḥammad ʿAlī Shāh found that 'the constitutionalism of the government would be the freedom of the nation'.[2]

Freedom was suggested as an answer to the question of Iran's decline. The expansion of the meaning of freedom, however, led to new questions. I classified these questions under three groups regarding three variables of the concept of freedom, namely the agent, the constraint, and the purpose of freedom. What is worth recapitulating here is some of the significant questions posed in this period in order to illustrate how the Qajar thinkers could open new possibilities for questioning and expand the space of the thinkable. These questions were 'real questions' as long as they had more than one possible answer and the questioners were able to choose one of the possible answers on the basis of the questioner's own reasoning or free will.[3]

Some questions on the agent of freedom could be formulated as follows: Is it the right time for giving freedom to Iranians? Is it required to first make people aware and then give them freedom, or is public awareness impossible without freedom? Who can identify people's maturity to have freedom?[4] Who gives freedom to an individual/a nation? When an individual or a nation has not yet reached its rightful time of freedom, does it mean that it is not eligible to have freedom, or does it rather mean that it is incapable of using its freedom? Does giving freedom mean admitting an inherent right, or granting/privileging a right?[5] Must all the people of Iran enjoy equal freedom?[6]

The second group of questions were about the constraint of freedom: What are the limits of freedom? What are the differences between legal constraints and illegal constraints? How can one prevent freedom from turning into license and chaos?[7] To what extent and wherefore is the majlis considered a legitimate authority to make the laws which impose limitations on the freedoms of individuals? What does parliamentary legislation mean? And what is the source of legitimacy for parliamentary law which allows it to determine the king's and the nation's rights and duties? What is the relationship between parliamentary laws and the sharia? Are they religiously legislated (*qānūn-i tashrīʿī*)? Or are they meant for 'determining subjects' (*taʿyīn-i mawẓūʿ*) or for 'legislating rules for the implementation of Islamic laws'?[8] Is the majority vote legitimate to put a limit on freedoms guaranteed by the sharia or to permit what has been forbidden by religious law?[9] Does the state have authority to enact laws that restrain the public rights held naturally and inherently by all the people? Is the government allowed to temporarily limit people's freedoms to eliminate terrorism and provide national security?[10]

The third group of questions were on the aim of freedom: Who is eligible to define the aim of a person's freedom? Is human perfection the aim of freedom? And if so, who can determine the requirements of this perfection? Is it the person himself or herself? The shah and statesmen? The *ʿulamā* as the interpreters of Islam? Or the majlis as the representative of the majority?[11] Is freedom an aim by itself or an instrument to reach aims?[12]

These questions address normative matters and inquire about the value of arbitrary human actions. There is also another set of questions which address the objective reality of freedom. Some of the descriptive questions posed in this period can be formulated as follows: Why do many people understand freedom as chaos, license, and absolute negation of government? Why do 'unaccountability, unlawfulness, and disorder become one hundred degrees worse than the era of arbitrary rule' while it is said that 'our country has turned constitutionalist'?[13] Why, when we previously had only one shah, are we now 'under the oppression and cruelty of thousands of shahs with the hat or the turban'?[14] What do people want freedom for? Do they want it in order to shirk obedience to God?

In the previous chapters, I discussed several formulations of both of two aforementioned groups of questions as well as some suggested answers. Questioning these aspects of freedom, however, does not necessarily mean that they were thought about freely and critically. As it was discussed in the introduction, free thinking begins with a 'real question'[15] and with an intention and ability to freely consider the possible answers. Suppose that a questioner asks: is it permissible to limit a freedom guaranteed by religion on the basis of the majority vote? For instance, despite the fact that slavery has been permitted in Islam, are we allowed to abolish it because of the majority's opposition?

Now imagine that although the questioner rationally tends to respond that 'some religiously tolerated freedoms, including slavery, must be abolished when the majority believe that these freedoms are violating the rights of others', the questioner is not actually able to choose this answer as a result of some causes, like the questioner's faith in the sharia as eternal law, or a fear of Muslims' reactions, or personal benefits that the questioner may find in slavery. In such a case, the questioner's real question would not lead to free thinking.

In the same line of analysis, many normative questions listed above were real questions; however, only a few questioners dared to be wise and think autonomously, by means of reason and free from the dictates of external authority, and without relying on religious or traditional *unthoughts*.

Regardless of its possibility, how useful was it to think independently from the sharia? The dispute over the concept of freedom in the Iranian constitutional period was not merely a philosophical and abstract contestation, but rather pursued a practical and objective aim, namely the establishment of a set of sociopolitical rights. Freedom-seekers endeavoured to convince the majlis to give more and more freedoms to the nation. However, according to the second article of the Supplementary Fundamental Laws, 'no legal enactment of the sacred national majlis . . . must be at variance with the sacred rules of Islam'. In such a situation, thinking independently from the sharia was useful only if it could prove that its result was in accordance with the sharia.

It is true that many freedoms, such as freedom of life, freedom of property, freedom of settlement, and freedom of commerce and trade, had a long history in traditional regulations. The emergence of the notion of the nation-state in the modern era, however, had brought about two radical changes: the agent of these freedoms had been transformed from subject into citizen, and the law's and government's interferences to regulate people's freedom had been fundamentally changed. Such a transformed situation could provide the opportunity for Iranian thinkers to approach social freedoms as newly emerged phenomena about which the religious text is silent. Some thinkers were able to ingeniously take advantage of the possibilities of thinking within the existing tradition of thought. For instance, Shaykh Isma'īl Gharavī Maḥallātī employed the principle of cohesion between rational precept and religious precept (*mulāzimah-ʿi bayn-i ḥukm-i ʿaqlī va ḥukm-i sharʿī*) to infer from the rational obligation of 'freedom from arbitrary rule' (*wujūb-i ʿaqlī*) that this freedom is also religiously obligatory (*wujūb-i sharʿī*).[16] Also, it was suggested that 'changes in circumstances require the interpretation, contraction and expansion of laws'.[17] Based on this principle, those new freedoms that seemed to be incompatible with the sharia could be permissible for the sake of the public interest of the Muslim society.

Likewise, in spite of the fact that sociopolitical indications of the new concept of citizenship did not receive enough attention, it was acknowledged that 'all residents' (*ahālī*) of Iran were no longer the very 'subjects' (*ruʿāyā*) of the shah; and the notion of '*millat*' was semantically transformed from its traditional sense (religion and faith) into its modern sense (nation or residents of a country). In light of this change, the constitution stipulated that 'the people of Iran [and not necessarily Muslims] are to enjoy equal rights before governmental laws'. Furthermore, Nā'īnī, as a leading mujtahid, wrote about a set of fundamental freedoms that generally and equally belongs to all the people of the country. To illustrate such fundamental rights, he named some of them, including

> security of the person's soul, reputation, and property, sanctity of the home, inviolability of the person, protection of privacy, immunity from unlawful imprisonment and banishment, freedom of legal assembly and other common matters belonging to all rather than a specific group.

He ended his list with 'and so on' (*va nahv zālik*) to show that more rights can be added.[18]

In the end, I would like to emphasize what Nā'īnī pointed out about the close collaboration between religious despotism and political despotism as the two main obstacles to the establishment of freedom in Iran. From the viewpoint of an *uṣūlī* faqīh, he made the most serious and effective criticism of a group of clerics' anti-freedom efforts and warned that freedom from obedience of kings is much easier than freedom from duplicity and falsification of religious despotism. This branch of despotism (*shu'bah-'i istibdād*), according to Nā'īnī, is the 'arbitrary dominative precepts posed by leaders of sects and faiths under the name of religion'[19] and is a fallacious misuse of religion by 'ill-natured clerics and brigands of true religion (*'ulamā'-i sū' va rāh'zanān-i dīn-i mubīn*)' who seek to preserve 'the pernicious tree of despotism' (*shajarah-'i khabīs-i istibdād*).[20] Nā'īnī attempted to demonstrate that religion, rather than being connected with despotism, is correlated to justice, freedom, and equality. His criticism, however, indicates that religion has the potentiality of despotic interpretations and unjust readings. Nā'īnī teaches the Iranian freedom-seekers that it is impossible to remove arbitrary rule and to achieve freedom without revealing 'religious despotism's fallacies'.[21] In the last hundred years, his *Tanhīh al-ummah* has provided inspiration for Iranian reformists in two various political situations. The first instance occurred when, several decades later, Sayyid Maḥmūd Ṭāliqānī (1911–79), the leading clerical commentator of the Qur'an, republished *Tanhīh al-ummah* with his introduction and comments in 1955, when Muḥammad Riẓā Shāh Pahlavī's despotism was going to put an end to many achievements of constitutionalism. The second instance was when Muḥammad Khātamī, a former president of Iran, employed Nā'īnī's ideas in developing post-revolutionary reformist discourse, implying that although the Islamic Revolution of 1979 was able to overthrow the monarchic despotism, it failed to defeat religious despotism. A research project that applies the questions of the present study to these two eras is a suitable subject for a future study. Such a study would explore the intellectual endeavors that expanded the constitutionalist thinkers' legacy in opposition to anti-freedom readings of Islam and which believed in the possibility of reconciling Islam with human rights and democracy.

Notes

1 See section 1.1.
2 See Muḥammad ʿAlī Shāh's telegram to the clerics of the Holy Shrines, cited in Sharīf Kāshānī, pp. 221–2.
3 See introduction, section II.i.
4 There were two main trends in answering these questions. Most constitutionalists, including Malkam Khān and Malik al-Mutakallimīn, believed that freedom was an unconditional divine gift that could be achieved despite the fact that most Iranians were still ignorant. They argued that such a weakness could not justify withholding freedom; rather, liberty would be an essential requisite on the path to civilization. The other trend supported a different strategy: 'first public awareness, then freedom'. Reminding of 'Iranians' immaturity', a famous representative of this view, Nāṣir al-Mulk, argued that it was still too early to talk about freedom. He believed that the intellectual leaders of the society were the referees of the eligibility of the agent of freedom (for more discussion, see section 5.1).
5 An answer tended to think of freedom as a royal gift. When Muḥammad ʿAlī Shāh sat on the throne, this idea began to wane. Because if he was the one who could give the gift of freedom to the nation, then he could claim that he had the right to take their freedom back at his discretion since they were not eligible to gain such gift. In such conditions, the constitutionalists preferred not to award the custody of freedom to its enemy, Muḥammad ʿAlī Shāh. Another answer regarded freedom as a divine gift. Some leading clerics, such as Sayyid Muḥammad Ṭabāṭabāʾī, Ṣiqat a-Islām Tabrīzī, and Mīrzā Ḥūsayn Nāʾīnī, shared this idea. They argued that this divine gift was given to everybody at birth. A nation might be deprived of this privilege due to their ignorance and inability to use their liberties, not because they are ineligible for having freedom (for further discussion, see section 5.2).
6 For some answers to this question, see section 5.3.
7 These three questions were about the criterion based on which freedoms of the people can be legitimately limited in order to keep rights and duties in balance. It was accepted that a person's freedom should be limited by the freedom of others or by the public interests. However, in practice, most of the legal limitations on a person's freedom were legislated by virtue of the priority of public interests over personal interests. In some cases, public interest and the exigencies of production and business in the modern world forced constitutionalist legislators to put a limit on freedoms guaranteed by the sharia in the old order (for more details, see section 3.4.2).
8 These questions addressed the problem of the legitimacy of non-religious legislation in a Muslim society. Distinguishing parliamentary law from religious law, constitutionalist *ʿulamā* argued that parliamentary laws were not religiously legislated, but were either 'legislating rules for the implementation of Islamic laws' or legislating general political matters and worldly and supervisory affairs that are 'consultable, adaptable and changeable' (for a few *pro-mashrūʿah* criticisms of this argument, see section 3.2).
9 An answer to this question was what Shaykh Faẕl Allāh Nūrī wrote: 'in religious matters one should refer to the guardianship rather the deputation; and in the Major Occultation, the guardianship must be held by the *faqīhs* and *mujtahids* not by such and such grocer and draper' (Shaykh Faẕl Allāh Nūrī, 'Risālah-ʾi ḥurmat-i mashrūṭah, p. 260. See sections 3.2 and 3.4.2).
10 Some more detailed legal questions on the constraint of freedom were: When is it justifiable to trespass on a person's life, property, home, and honor? When is it permitted to arrest a person, to issue a verdict, to execute punishment, or to banish the person? When is it allowed to enter a person's house without the person's permission? When is it allowed to occupy a property, to confiscate assets and properties, or to dispossess properties and lands possessed by owners or occupiers? When is it permissible to seize and disclose postal correspondence or telegrams without permission of their

sender? When is it permissible to refer an individual from a court, in which the person is expected to be judged, to another court? When is it justifiable to prevent the teaching and learning of science, knowledge, and industry? When is it permissible to pose prior censorship (*mumayyizī*) on the press and books? When is it allowed to ban communities and associations? When is it permitted to ban a newspaper? (For some answers to these questions, see chapter 3).

11 Likewise, there were different answers to these correlative questions on the aim of freedom. Some thinkers bravely invite people to release from the tutelage of any shah or religious leader, and to dare to find their own way of progress. The right to be wrong, however, was never defended. Yet the permissible aim of freedom must be compatible with the public interest as well as the material and spiritual progress of individuals and society (for more discussion, see section 4.2).

12 Some more detailed questions on the aim of freedom were: What is the aim of freedom of assembly? Can one use this right to set up a harmlessly fruitless association or must it only be employed to achieve an individual/common good? Is one allowed to express profane or useless words under the name of freedom of expression? Is it permissible to have a sinful job or business which does not violate the rights of others? Do I have the right to hold a wrong opinion? (For some answers to these questions, see chapter 4.)

13 Sharīf Kāshānī, p. 573.

14 Taqsīm-i istibdād yā tajziyah-ʾi salṭanat', *Rūḥ al-Qudus* (Tehran, 13 Safar 1326 / [17 March 1908]), no. 20, pp. 1–4 (p. 3).

15 A real question is a question with more than one possible answer that actually engages the questioner and lets the questioner consider and choose one or more possible answers among several undetermined possibilities on the basis of reasoning.

16 See section 3.2.

17 'Al-yawm akmalt-u lakum dīnakum wa atmamt-u ʿalaykum niʿmatī', pp. 1–3. Also see section 4.2.

18 See section 5.3.1.

19 '*taḥakkumāt-i khvudʹsarānah-ʾi rūʾasā-ʾi mazāhib va millal . . . kih bih ʿunvān-i diyānat irāʾah mīʹdahand*' (Nāʾīnī, vol. 2, p.426).

20 Nāʾīnī, vol. 2, p.426.

21 Nāʾīnī, vol. 2, p.426.

Bibliography

Abrahamian, Ervand, *A History of Modern Iran* (Cambridge, UK; New York: Cambridge University Press, 2008).

Abū al-Ḥasan Khān Īlchī, *Ḥayrat'nāmah: safar'nāmah-'i Mīrzā abū al-Ḥasan Khān Īlchī bih Landan* (Tehran: Mu'assasah-i Khadamāt-i Farhangī-i Rasā, 1364).

Ādamīyat, Farīdūn, *Andīshah-i taraqqī va ḥukūmat-i qānūn: 'aṣr-i Sipahsālār* (Tehran: Shirkat-i Sihāmī-i Intishārāt-i Khvarazmī, 1351).

———, *Fikr – i āzādī va muqaddamah – i nihẕat – i mashrūṭīyat* (Tehran: Sukhan, 1961).

ʿAdl (Manṣūr al – Salṭanah), Sayyid Muṣṭafá, *Huqūq-i asāsī yā uṣūl-i mashrūṭīyat* (Tehran: Nashr-i Chashmah, 1389).

'Afsānah-ʾi khvāb'rubā ya dāstān-i bi'aṣl', *Ṣūr-i Isrāfīl* (Tehran, 15 Jumada I 1325 / [27 June 1907]), no. 5, pp. 1–4.

Afshār, Īraj, 'Book Translations as a Cultural Activity in Iran 1806–1896', *Iran*, 41 (2003), 279–89 <http://dx.doi.org/10.2307/4300649>.

———, ed., *Āzādī va siyāsat* (Tehran: Saḥar, 1366).

Afshār, Muṣṭafá, *Safar'nāmah-ʾi Khusraw Mīrzā bih Piṭirzbūrgh*, ed. by M. Gulbun (Tehran: Kitābkhānah-'i Mustawfī, 1349).

Ākhund'zādah, Fatḥ 'Alī, '[Autobiography]', in *Alifbā-yi jadīd va maktūbāt*, ed. by Ḥamīd Mūhammad'zādah (Tabriz: Nashr-i Iḥyāʾ, 1357), pp. 349–55.

———, '[Letter to Mīrzā Yūsuf Khān Mustashār al-Dawlah Tabrīzī (1872)]', in *Alifbā-yi jadīd va maktūbāt*, ed. by Ḥamīd Mūhammad'zādah (Tabriz: Nashr-i Iḥyāʾ, 1357), pp. 270–7.

———, '[Letter to Yūsuf Khān Mustashār Al-Dawlah Tabrīzī (Mars 1871)]', in *Alifbā-yi jadīd va maktūbāt* (Tabriz: Nashr-i Iḥyāʾ, 1357), pp. 199–202.

———, *Maktūbāt-i Kamāl al-Dawlah* ([n.p.]: Intishārāt-i Mard-i Imrūz, 1364).

———, *Maqālāt*, ed. by Bāqir Mu'minī (Tehran: Intishārāt-i Āvā, 1972).

'Al-yawm akmalt-u lakum dīnakum wa atmamt-u ʿalaykum niʿmatī', *Ṣūr-i Isrāfīl* (Tehran, 3 Shaʿban 1325 / [12 September 1907]), no. 13, pp. 1–3.

Amanat, Abbas, 'The Downfall of Mirza Taqi Khan Amir Kabir and the Problem of Ministerial Authority in Qajar Iran', *International Journal of Middle East Studies*, 23 (1991), 577–99.

'Anjuman-i nisvān-i Tabrīz', *rūznāmah-ʾi anjuman-i Tabrīz* (Tabriz, 25 Dhu'l Hijja 1324 / [2 February 1907]), no. 41.

'Anjuman-i nisvān-i Ṭihrān', *Kawkab-i durrī* (Tehran, 23 Rabi I 1325 / [25 April 1908]), yr. 4, no. 7.

Anṣārī, Mīrzā Ḥasan Khān, 'Ganjīnah-ʾi anṣār yā rumān-i shaykh va shūkh', in *Bunyād-i falsafah-ʾi siyāsī dar Īrān (ʿaṣr-i mashrūṭīyat): talāqī-ʾi andīshah-ʾi siyāsī-ʾi Islām va*

Īrān bā gharb, bih inẓimām-i davazdaah risālah-ʾi muhim-i siyāsī, ed. by Mūsá Najafī (Tehran: Markaz-i Nashr-i Dānishgāhī, 1376), pp. 410–46.

———, 'Nūshdārū yā davā-yi dard-i Īrāniyān', in *Bunyād-i falsafah-ʾi siyāsī dar Īrān (ʿaṣr-i mashrūṭīyat): talāqī-ʾi andīshah-ʾi siyāsī-ʾi Islām va Īrān bā gharb, bih inẓimām-i davazdaah risālah-ʾi muhim-i siyāsī*, ed. by Mūsá Najafī (Tehran: Markaz-i Nashr-i Dānishgāhī, 1376), pp. 447–98.

Arkoun, Mohammed, *The Unthought in Contemporary Islamic Thought* (London: Saqi, 2002).

Āṣaf, Muḥammad Hāshim, *Rustam al-tavārīkh* (Tehran: Amīr Kabīr, 1973).

'[Āyā barāy-i kamāl va taraqqī basharī sar'ḥaddī hast?]', *Ṣūr-i Isrāfīl* (Tehran, 26 Rajab 1325/ [5 September 1907]), no. 12, pp. 1–3.

'[Āyā iṣlāḥāt-i siyāsī muqaddam bar iṣlāḥāt-i ijtimāʿī ast?], baqīyah az shumārah-ʾi 27', *Ṣūr-i Isrāfīl* (Tehran, 12 Rabi II 1326 / [14 May 1908]), no. 29, pp. 1–3.

ʿAyn al-Salṭanah, *Yāddāsht'hā-yi ʿAyn al-Salṭanah*, ed. by Masʿūd Sālūr and Īraj Afshār (Tehran: Asāṭīr, 1377).

Bayat, Mongol, 'The Rushanfekr in the Constitutional Period: An Overview', in *Iran's Constitutional Revolution: Popular Politics, Cultural Transformations and Transnational Connections*, ed. by H.E. Chehabi and Vanessa Martin (London; New York, NY: I.B. Tauris: In Association with Iran Heritage Foundation; Distributed in the U.S. and Canada Exclusively by Palgrave Macmillan, 2010), pp. 165–91.

Berlin, Isaiah, *Four Essays on Liberty* (London; New York, etc.: Oxford University Press, 1969).

———, 'Two Concepts of Liberty', in *Four Essays on Liberty* (Oxford: Oxford University Press, 1969), pp. 118–72.

Boozari, Amirhassan, *Shi'i Jurisprudence and Constitution: Revolution in Iran* (New York: Palgrave Macmillan, 2011).

Browne, Edward Granville, *A Brief Narrative of Recent Events in Persia: Followed by a Translation of 'the Four Pillars of the Persian Constitution'* (London: Luzac and Co., 1909).

Burdett, Francis, *Sir Francis Burdett to His Constituents: Denying the Power of the House of Commons to Imprison the People of England* (London: Printed for R. Bagshaw and J. Budd, 1810).

Camel [?], James, trans., 'Tārīkh-i Iskandar' (Tehran, MS Farsi / 1680, The Iranian National Library).

Carter, Ian, 'From a Measure of Freedom (1999)', in *Freedom: A Philosophical Anthology*, ed. by Ian Carter, Matthew H. Kramer, and Hillel Steiner (Malden, MA: Blackwell Pub., 2007), pp. 434–9.

———, *A Measure of Freedom* (New York: Oxford University Press, 1999).

———, 'Positive and Negative Liberty', in *The Stanford Encyclopedia of Philosophy*, ed. by Edward N. Zalta (Spring, 2012) <http://plato.stanford.edu/archives/spr2012/entries/liberty-positive-negative/> [accessed 18 July 2014].

Carter, Ian, Matthew H. Kramer, and Hillel Steiner, eds., *Freedom: A Philosophical Anthology* (Malden, MA: Blackwell Pub., 2007).

Carter, Ian, and Edward N. Zalta, eds., 'Positive and Negative Liberty', in *The Stanford Encyclopedia of Philosophy*, (Spring 2012) <http://plato.stanford.edu/archives/spr2012/entries/liberty-positive-negative/> [accessed 21 June 2014].

Collingwood, Robin George, *An Autobiography* (London; New York, etc.: Oxford University Press, 1939).

———, *An Essay on Metaphysics* (Oxford: Clarendon Press, 1940).

Cranston, Maurice, *Freedom: A New Analysis*, 3rd edn. (London: Longmans, 1976).

Cronin, Stephanie, 'The Constitutional Revolution, Popular Politics, and State-Building in Iran', in *Iran's Constitutional Revolution: Popular Politics, Cultural Transformations and Transnational Connections*, ed. by H. E. Chehabi and Vanessa Martin (London; New York, NY: I.B. Tauris: In Association with Iran Heritage Foundation; Distributed in the U.S. and Canada Exclusively by Palgrave Macmillan, 2010), pp. 81–97.

Curzon, George Nathaniel, *Persia and the Persian Question* (London: Longmans, Green, and Co., 1892).

Dawlat'ābādī, Sayyid Yaḥyá, *Ḥayāt-i Yaḥyá* (Tehran: ʿAṭṭār, 1371).

'Difāʿ [1]', *Ṣūr-i Isrāfīl* (Tehran, 22 Jumada I 1325 / [3 July 1907]), no. 6, pp. 2–5.

'Difāʿ [2]', *Ṣūr-i Isrāfīl* (Tehran, 21 Jumada II 1325/ [1 July 1907]), no. 7–8, pp. 5–10.

Dihkhudā, 'Alī Akbar, 'Charand-u-parand', *Ṣūr-i Isrāfīl* (Tehran, 30 Dhu'l Ḥijja 1325 / [3 February 1908]), no. 22, pp. 6–8.

———, 'Du kalamah khiyānat', *Ṣūr-i Isrāfīl* (Tehran, 17 Rabi II 1325 / [30 May 1907]), no. 1, pp. 2–3.

———, '[Istīfā-ʾi ḥuqūq-i ādamīyat]', *Ṣūr-i Isrāfīl* (Tehran, 24 Rabi II 1325 / [6 June 1907]), no. 2, pp. 1–2.

———, *Lughat'nāmah* (Tehran: Chāpkhānah-'i Majlis, 1325).

Fażil Khurāsānī Tarshīzī, Āqā Mīrzā Yūsuf, 'Kalamah-ʾi jāmiʿah-ʾi Shams Kāshgharī', in *Rasāʾil-i mashrūṭīyat: mashrūṭah bih ravāyat-i muvāfiqān va mukhālifān*, 2 vols. (Tehran: Intishārāt-i Muʿassisah-ʾi Taḥqīqāt va Tawsiʿah-ʾi ʿUlūm-i Insānī, 1387), vol. 2, pp. 591–655.

Firqah-ʾi siyāsī-i dimukrāt-i Īrān, 'Marām'nāmah-ʾi firqah-ʾi siyāsī-i dimukrāt-i Īrān (ʿāmīyūn) [1329/1911]', in *Marām'nāmah'ha va niẓām'nāmah'hā-yi aḥzāb-i siyāsī-i Īrān dar duvumīn majlis-i shūrā-yi millī*, ed. by Manṣūrah Ittiḥādīyah (Tehran: Nashr-i Tārīkh-i Īrān, 1361), pp. 1–8.

Furūghī, Muḥammad, ʿAlī, 'Ḥuqūq-i asāsī yaʿnī ādāb-i mashrūṭīyat-i duval', in *Rasāʾil-i mashrūṭīyat: mashrūṭah bih ravāyat-i muvāfiqān va mukhālifān*, ed. by Ghulām Ḥusayn Zargarī'nizhād, 2 vols. (Tehran: Intishārāt-i Muʿassisah-ʾi Taḥqīqāt va Tawsiʿah-ʾi ʿUlūm-i Insānī, 2008), vol. 1, pp. 773–843.

Gadamer, Hans-Georg, *Truth and Method*, trans. by Joel Weinsheimer and Donald G. Marshall (London: Continuum, 1975).

Gibbon, Edward, 'Tārīkh-i tanazzul va kharabī-i dawlat-i Rūm', trans. by Mīrzā Riẓā Muḥandis (Tehran, Ms Farsi / 66, The Iranian National Library).

Ḥāirī, 'Abd al-Hādī, 'Afghani on the Decline of Islam', *Die Welt des Islams*, 13 (1971), 121–5.

———, 'Afghani on the Decline of Islam: A Postscript', *Die Welt des Islams*, 14 (1973), 116–28 <http://dx.doi.org/10.2307/1570026>.

———, 'Āzādī', in *The Encyclopaedia of Islam*, ed. by P.J. Bearman, T. Bianquis, C.E. Bosworth, E. Van Donzel, and W.P. Heinrichs, vol. 2 (Leiden: Brill, 2004).

———, *Azādīhā-yi siyāsī va ijtimāʿī az dīdgāh-i andīshah'garān: guzarī bar nivishtah'hā-yi pārsī dar dū sadah-'i vāpasīn* (Mashhad: Jihād-i Dānishgāhī-i Mashhad, 1374).

'Ḥaq'shināsī', *Ṣūr-i Isrāfīl* (Tehran, 28 Shawwal 1325 [4 December 1907]), no. 19, pp. 5–6.

Hashemi, S. Ahmad, 'Tarjumah: tarjumah-i Fārsī dar dawrah-i muʿāsir: Qājār, Pahlavī, pas az inqilāb-i Islāmī', in *dānish'nāmah-i jahān-i Islām* (*Encyclopaedia of the World of Islam*) (Tehran: Kitāb-i Marjaʿ, 1381).

Herodotus, *The History of Herodotus*, trans. by George Rawlinson (London: John Murray, 1862).

Hidāyat, Mahdī Qulī, *Guzārish-i Īrān* (Tehran: Nashr-i Nuqrah, n.d.).

———, *Khāṭirāt va khaṭarāt* (Tehran: Kitābfurūshī-i Zavvār, 1385).

Ḥizb-i ijtimāʿīyūn-i ʿitidālīyūn, 'Dastūr-i mashrūḥ-i maslakī yā marām'nāmah-ʾi ḥizb-i ijtimāʿīyūn-i ʿitidālīyūn', in *Marām'nāmah'ha va niẓām'nāmah'hā-yi aḥzāb-i siyāsī-i Īrān dar duvumīn majlis-i shūrā-yi millī*, ed. by Manṣūrah Ittiḥādīyah (Tehran: Nashr-i Tārīkh-i Īrān, 1361).

Horn, Paul, and Heinrich Hübschmann, *Asās-i ishtiqāq-i fārsī*, trans. by Jalāl Khāliqī'muṭlaq (Tehran: Bunyād-i Farhang-i Īrān, 1356).

'[ʿillat-i mukhālifat bā *Ṣūr-i Isrāfīl*]', *Ṣūr-i Isrāfīl* (Tehran, 10 Shàbān 1325 / [19 September 1907]), no. 14, pp. 1–5.

ʿImād al-ʿUlamāʾ Khalkhālī, 'Bayān-i maʿnī-i salṭanat va fawāyid'ihā', in *Rasāʾil-i mashrūṭīyat: mashrūṭah bih ravāyat-i muvāfiqān va mukhālifān*, ed. by Ghulām Ḥusayn Zargarī'nizhād, 2 vols. (Tehran: Intishārāt-i Muʿassisah-ʾi Taḥqīqāt va Tawsiʿah-ʾi ʿUlūm-i Insānī, 1387), vol. 2, pp. 9–57.

'Īrān taghyīr kardah', *Ṣūr-i Isrāfīl* (Tehran, 17 Rabi II 1325 / [30 May 1907]), no. 1, pp. 2–3.

Iʿtimād al-Salṭanah, Muḥammad Ḥasan Khān, *Rūznāmah-ʿi khāṭirāt-i Iʿtimād al-Salṭanah*, ed. by Īraj Afshār (Tehran: Amīr Kabīr, 1343).

Ittiḥādīyah, Manṣūrah, *Majlis va intikhābāt az mashrūṭah ta pāyān – i Qājār* (Tehran: Nashr-i Tārīkh-i Īrān, 1375).

———, ed., *Marām'nāmah'ha va niẓām'nāmah'hā-yi aḥzāb-i siyāsī-i Īrān dar duvumīn majlis-i shūrā-yi millī* (Tehran: Nashr-i Tārīkh-i Īrān, 1361).

Jaʿfarīan, Rasūl, 'Darbārah-ʾi faṣl al-khiṭāb', in *ʿIlal-i bar'uftādan-i Ṣafavīyān: mukāfāt'nāmah*, ed. by Rasūl Ja'faīiyān (Tehran: Sāzmān-i Tabīghāt-i Islāmī, 1993), pp. 257–81.

———, 'Darbārah-ʾI Risālah-ʾi Ṭib al-Mamālik', in *ʿIlal-i bar'uftādan-i Ṣafavīyān: mukāfāt'nāmah*, ed. by Rasūl Ja'farīyān (Tehran: Sāzmān-i Tabīghāt-i Islāmī, 1993), pp. 201–13.

———, 'Pīshīnah-ʾi ḥaqq-i rày-i zanān dar majlis-i shūrā-yi millī (1390–1341)', *Khabar Online* <www.khabaronline.ir/detail/126461/weblog/jafarian> [accessed 24 March 2014].

Jaubert, Pierre Amédée Émilien Probe, *Voyage en Arménie et en Perse, Fait Dans les Années 1805 et 1806* (Paris: Pélicier [etc.], 1821).

Jazāirī, 'Abd al-Laṭīf ibn Abī Ṭālib, *Tuḥfat al-ʿālam va zayl al-tuḥfah* (Tehran: Kitābkhānah-i Ṭahūrī, 1363).

Jefferson, Thomas, *Political Writings: Representative Selections* (New York: Liberal Arts Press, 1955).

Kāshānī, Mullā ʿAbd al-Rasūl, 'Risālah-ʾi inṣāfīyah', in *Rasāʾil-i mashrūṭīyat: mashrūṭah bih ravāyat-i muvāfiqān va mukhālifān*, 2 vols. (Tehran: Intishārāt-i Muʿassisah-ʾi Taḥqīqāt va Tawsiʿah-ʾi ʿUlūm-i Insānī, 1387), vol. 2, pp. 529–90.

Kasravī, Aḥmad, *Tārīkh-i mashrūṭah-ʾi Īrān* (Tehran: Hermes Publishers, 2010).

Katīrā'ī, Maḥmūd, ed., 'Juzvah-ʾi rāpūrt-i shakhṣī kih dū darajah az farāmūsh'khānah rā ṭiy kardah ast', in *Farāmāsūnrī dar Īrān: az āghāz tā tashkīl-i Luzh-i Bīdārī-i Īrān* (Tehran: Iqbāl, 1347), pp. 176–93.

———, ed., 'Taʿāvun-i māsūnī', in *Farāmāsūnrī dar Īrān: az āghāz tā tashkīl-i luzh-i bīdārī-i Īrān* (Tehran: Iqbāl, 1361).

Katouzian, Homa, 'Arbitrary Rule: A Comparative Theory of State, Politics and Society in Iran', *British Journal of Middle Eastern Studies*, 24 (1997), 49–73.

———, *Iranian History and Politics: The Dialectic of State and Society* (London; New York: RoutledgeCurzon, 2003).

———, 'Liberty and Licence in the Constitutional Revolution of Iran', *Journal of the Royal Asiatic Society*, 8: 3 (1998), 159–80.
———, *The Persians: Ancient, Mediaeval, and Modern Iran* (New Haven: Yale University Press, 2009).
———, 'The Revolution for Law: A Chronographic Analysis of the Constitutional Revolution of Iran', *Middle Eastern Studies*, 47 (2011), 757–77.
———, 'The Short-Term Society: A Study in the Problems of Long-Term Political and Economic Development in Iran', *Middle Eastern Studies*, 40 (2004), 1–22.
Keane, John, *The Life and Death of Democracy* (New York: W.W. Norton & Co., 2009).
———, 'More Theses on the Philosophy of History', in *Meaning and context: Quentin Skinner and His Critics*, ed. by James Tully (Cambridge; Oxford: Polity Press & Basil Blackwell, 1988), pp. 204−17.
Keddie, Nikki R., *Religion and Rebellion in Iran: The Tobacco Protest of 1891–1892* (London: Cass, 1966).
'Khiṭāb bih anjumanān ya jamāʿat-i khuftigān', *Rūḥ al-Qudus* (Tehran, 25 Dhu'l Ḥijja 1325 / [29 January 1908]), no. 16, pp. 1–3.
Khurāsānī, Muḥammad Kāẓim, *Siyāsat'nāmah-'i Khurāsānī: qiṭa'āt-i siyāsī dar āsār-i Ākhūnd Mullā Muḥammad Kāẓim Khurāsānī ṣāḥib-i Kifāyah (1255–1329 Hijrī Qamarī)*, ed. by Muḥsin Kadīvar (Tehran: Kavīr, 1385).
Kitābkhānah-i Millī-i Īrān, *Fihrist-i nusakh-i khaṭṭī-i Kitābkhānah-'i Millī-i Īrān*, ed. by 'Abd Allāh Anvār (Tehran: Kitābkhānah-i Millī-i Īrān, 1365).
Kuhan, Gūʾil, *Tārīkh-i sānsūr dar maṭbū'āt-i Īrān* (Tehran: Āgāh, 1360).
Lāhījī, Shaykh ʿAlī, 'Lāyiḥah dar sarzanish-i rūznāmah'hā va mashrūṭah'khvāhān (Munṭabaʿah dar Zāvīyah-ʾi Muqaddasah-ʾi Ḥaẕrat-i ʿAbd Al-ʿAẓīm, Rajab 1325)', in *Rasāʾil-i mashrūṭīyat: mashrūṭah bih ravāyat-i muvāfiqān va mukhālifān*, ed. by Ghulām Ḥusayn Zargarī'nizhād, 2 vols. (Tehran: Intishārāt-i Muʿassisah-ʾi Taḥqīqāt va Tawsiʿah-ʾi ʿUlūm-i Insānī, 1378), vol. 1, pp. 241–52.
Lewis, Bernard, 'Democracy in the Middle East: Its State and Prospect', *Middle Eastern Affairs*, 6 (1955), 101–8.
———, 'Islam and Liberal Democracy: A Historical Overview', *Journal of Democracy*, 7: 2 (1996), 52–63.
———, *The Political Language of Islam* (Chicago: University of Chicago Press, 1988).
———, *Political Words and Ideas in Islam* (Princeton, NJ: Markus Wiener Publishers, 2008).
———, *Race and Slavery in the Middle East: An Historical Enquiry* (New York: Oxford University Press, 1990).
Lukes, Steven, *Marxism and Morality* (Oxford; New York: Clarendon Press; Oxford University Press, 1985).
'Maʿāyib-i kār natāyij-i biʿamalī ast', in *Rasāʾil-i mashrūṭīyat: mashrūṭah bih ravāyat-i muvāfiqān va mukhālifān*, 2 vols. (Tehran: Intishārāt-i Muʿassisah-ʾi Taḥqīqāt va Tawsiʿah-ʾi ʿUlūm-i Insānī, 1387), vol. 1, pp. 701–6.
MacCallum, Gerald C., 'Negative and Positive Freedom', *The Philosophical Review*, 76 (1967), 312 <http://dx.doi.org/10.2307/2183622>.
Maḥallātī Gharavī, Shaykh Muḥammad Ismāʿīl, 'Al-lààlī al-marbūṭah fī wujūb al-mashrūṭah', in *Rasāʾil-i mashrūṭīyat: mashrūṭah bih ravāyat-i muvāfiqān va mukhālifān*, ed. byGhulām Ḥusayn Zargarī'nizhād, 2 vols. (Tehran: Intishārāt-i Muʿassisah-ʾi Taḥqīqāt va Tawsiʿah-ʾi ʿUlūm-i Insānī, 1387), vol. 2, pp. 199–276.
Majd al-Islām Kirmānī, Aḥmad, *Tārīkh-i inḥiṭāṭ-i majlis, faṣlī az tārīkh-i inqilāb-i mashrūṭīyat-i Īrān*, ed. by Maḥmūd Khalīlpūr (Isfahan: Nashr-i Dānishgāh-i Iṣfahān, 1351).

Majlis-i shūrā-yi millī-i Irān, 'Javāb-i ṣādir az majlis-i muqaddas va muḥtaram-i Shūrā-yi Millī-i Irān- 3 Shaʿbān 1325', in *Lavāyiḥ-i Āqā Shaykh Fazl Allah Nūrī* (Tehran: Nashr-i Tārīkh-i Īrān, 1362), p. 68.

'Maknūnāt-i khāṭir', *Rūḥ al-Qudus* (Tehran, 26 Safar 1326 / [30 March 1908]), no. 21, pp. 1–2.

'Maktūb az Kirmānshāhān', *majlis* (Tehran, 23 Rabi I 1325 / [7 May 1907]), no. 86, pp. 1–2.

'Maktūb-i buqʿah-ʾi ḥaẓrat-i ʿAbd al-ʿAẓīm', *Rūḥ al-Qudus* (Tehran, 4 Rajab 1325 [13 August 1907]), no. 2, pp. 3–4.

Malikal-Mutakallimīn, Mīrzā Naṣr Allāh, 'Khulāṣah-ʾi nuṭq-i jināb-i Ḥāj Mīrzā Naṣr Allāh Malik al-Mutakallimīn dar anjuman-i muqaddas-i ittiḥādīyah-ʾi ṭullāb-i muḥtaram-i ʿulūm-i dīnīyah (shayyad Allāh arkānah)', *Ṣūr-i Isrāfīl* (Tehran, 17 Rabi II 1325 / [30 May 1907]), no. 1, pp. 5–6.

Malik'zādah, Mahdī, *Tārīkh-i inqilāb-i mashrūṭīyat-i Īrān* (Tehran: Intishārāt-i ʿIlmī, 1373).

'Maqālah-ʾi yikī az mukhaddarāt-i vaṭn'dūst', *Ṣūr-i Isrāfīl* (Tehran, 21 Jumada II 1325 / [1 July 1907]), no. 7–8, pp. 4–5.

Martin, Vanessa, 'Constitutional Revolution, II. Events', in *Encyclopaedia Iranica* (Costa Mesa: Mazda Publishers, 1993), pp. 176–87.

———, 'An Evaluation of Reform and Development of the State in the Early Qājār Period', *Die Welt des Islams*, 36 (1996), 1–24.

———, *Iran between Islamic Nationalism and Secularism: The Constitutional Revolution of 1906* (London: I.B. Tauris, 2013).

———, *Islam and Modernism: The Iranian Revolution of 1906* (Syracuse, NY: Syracuse University Press, 1989).

———, *The Qajar Pact: Bargaining, Protest and the State in Nineteenth-Century Persia* (London; New York: I. B. Tauris, 2005).

'Mashrūḥ-i muzākirāt-i majlis-i avval (Proceeding of the 1st Majlis)', *Lawḥ-i mashrūḥ-i muzākirāt-i majālis shūrā-yi millī va Islāmī* (Tehran: Kitābkhānah, Mūzih va Markaz-i Asnād-i Majlis-i Shūrā-yi Isāmī, 2015) [on DVD].

'Mashrūḥ-i muzākirāt-i majlis-i duvum (Proceeding of the 2nd Majlis)', *Lawḥ-i mashrūḥ-i muzākirāt-i majālis shūrā-yi millī va Islāmī* (Tehran: Kitābkhānah, Mūzih va Markaz-i Asnād-i Majlis-i Shūrā-yi Isāmī, 2015) [on DVD].

Māzandarānī, Mullā ʿAbd Allāh, '[Dast'khaṭ-i Mullā ʿAbd Allāh Māzandarānī bih Āqā Sayyid Kāẓim Khalkhālī]', *Ṣūr-i Isrāfīl* (Yverdon-Suisse, 15 Muharram 1327 / [18 February 1908]), Suisse series, no. 2, pp. 6–7.

Mīrzā Abū Ṭālib Bihbahānī, 'Minhāj al-ʿulā', in *Rasāʾil-i siyāsī-i ʿaṣr-i Qājār*, ed. by Ghulām Ḥusayn Zargarī'nizhād (Tehran: Kitābkhānah-ʾi Millī-i Jumhūrī-i Islāmī-i Īrān, 2001).

Mīrzā Abū Ṭālib Khān Iṣfahānī, *Masīr-i ṭālibī* (Tehran: Intishāt-i ʿIlmī va Farhangī, 1363).

Mīrzā Malkam Khān, 'Daftar-i tanẓīmāt yā kitābchah-ʾi ghaybī', in *Risālah'hā-yi Mīrzā Malkam Khān Nāẓim al-Dawlah*, ed. by Ḥujjat Allāh Aṣīl (Tehran: Nashr-i Nay, 1381), pp. 23–59.

———, '[Īrān mamluvv ast az naʿamāt-i khudā'dād]', *Qānūn* (London: Rajab, 1307), no. 1, pp. 1–2.

———, 'Nidā-yi ʿAdālat', in *Risālah'hā-yi Mīrzā Malkam Khān Nāẓim al-Dawlah* (Tehran: Nashr-i Nay, 1381), pp. 136–52.

———, 'Sirāṭ al-mustaqīm', in *Risālah'hā-yi Mīrzā Malkam Khān Nāẓim al-Dawlah* (Tehran: Nashr-i Nay, 1381), pp. 433–98.

———, '[Yikī zz ḥarf'hā-yi tāzah-ʾi mā]', *Qānūn* (London: 1 Rajab 1307 / [28 February 1890]), no. 1, pp. 2–4.

Mīrzā Muḥammad Ṣāliḥ Shīrāzī, *Guzārish-i safar*, ed. by H. Shahīdī (Tehran: Rāh-i Naw, 1373).

Muhājirīn-i zāvīyah-ʾi muqaddasah, 'Rāfiʿ al-shubahāt', in *Lavāyiḥ-i Āqā Shaykh Faẓl Allah Nūrī* (Tehran: Nashr-i Tārīkh-i Īrān, 1362), pp. 51–3.

Muḥammad Riẓā Shīrāzī, '[Shāh dar chih ḥāl ast?]', *Musāvāt* (Tehran, 24 Rabi I 1326 / [26 April 1908]), no. 21, pp. 1–5.

Mujtahid Zanjānī, Mīrzā Abū Ṭālib, '[Maraẓ rā qabl az istīlā ʿalāj kunīm]', in *Rasāʾil-i mashrūṭīyat: mashrūṭah bih ravāyat-i muvāfiqān va mukhālifān*, ed. by Ghulām Ḥusayn Zargarī'nizhād, 2 vols. (Tehran: Intishārāt-i Muʿassisah-ʾi Taḥqīqāt va Tawsiʿah-ʾi ʿUlūm-i Insānī, 1387), vol. 1, pp. 169–71.

Mulligan, Lotte, Judith Richards, and John Graham, 'Intentions and Conventions: A Critique Quentin Skinner's Method for the Study of the History of Ideas', *Political Studies*, 27: 1 (1979), 84–98.

Mumtaḥin al-Dawlah Mahdī Khān Shaqāqī, Mīrzā Mahdī Khān, *Khāṭirāt-i Mumtaḥin al-Dawlah* (Tehran: Firdawsī, 1362).

Munajjim'bāshī Iṣfahānī, ʿAbd al-Ghaffār, 'Jughrāfiyā dar nufūs-i Ahālī-i dār al-khilāfah-ʾi nāṣirah', in *Āmār-i dār al-khialāfah-ʾi Ṭihrān*, ed. by Sīrūs Saʿdvandiyān and Manṣūrah Ittiḥādīyah (Tehran: Nashr-i Tārīkh-i Īrān, 1368), pp. 341–50.

Mustashār al-Dawlah Tabrīzī, Mīrzā Yūsuf Khān, *The Essence of Modernity: Mirza Yusof Khan Mustashar Ad-Dowla Tabrizi's Treatise on Codified Law (Yak Kalima)*, trans. by A.A. Seyed-Gohrab (Amsterdam: West Lafayette, Ind; Rozenberg Publishers; Purdue University Press, 2007).

———, *Yik kalamah va yik nāmah* (Tehran: Intishārāt-i Ṣabāḥ, 1382).

Mustawfī, 'Abd Allāh, *Sharḥ-i zindagānī-i man, yā, tārīkh-i ijtimāʿī va idārī-i dawrah-ʾi Qājārīyah* (Tehran: Kitābfurūshī-i Zavvār, 1345).

Mustawfī Tafrishī, Ibn Mīrzā Naṣr Allāh, *Tārīkh-i inqilāb-i mashrūṭah-ʾi Īrān* (Malik Library, MS 3819, Sha'ban 1325 / September 1907).

'Mutamim-i qānūn-i asāsī (The Supplementary Fundamental Laws of October 1907)', *Lawḥ-i qānūn: Majmūʿah-i qavāmīn va muqarrāt-i kishvar* (Tehran: Markaz-i Pazhūhishha-yi Majlis-i Shūrā-yi Islamī, n.d.) [on DVD].

Muẓaffar, Muḥammad Riẓā, *Uṣūl al-fiqh*, trans. by Muḥsin Gharaviyān (Qum: Intishārāt-i Dār al-Fikr, 1385).

Nāʾīnī, Muḥammad Ḥusayn, 'Tanbīh al-ummah va tanzīh al-millah', in *Rasāʾil-i mashrūṭīyat: mashrūṭah bih ravāyat-i muvāfiqān va mukhālifān*, ed. by Ghulām Ḥusayn Zargarī'nizhād (Tehran: Intishārāt-i Muʿassisah-ʾi Taḥqīqāt va Tawsiʿah-ʾi ʿUlūm-i Insānī, 1387), vol. 2, pp. 403–90.

Najafī Iṣfahānī, Nūr Allāh, 'Muklimāt-i Ḥājī-i Musāfir va Muqīm dar bayān-i ḥaqīqat-i maʿnā-yi mashrūṭah va muṭlaqah', in *Rasāʾil-i mashrūṭīyat: mashrūṭah bih ravāyat-i muvāfiqān va mukhālifān*, ed. by Ghulām Ḥusayn Zargarī'nizhād (Tehran: Intishārāt-i Muʿassisah-ʾi Taḥqīqāt va Tawsiʿah-ʾi ʿUlūm-i Insānī, 1387), vol. 2, pp. 297–364.

Najafī Marandī, Shaykh Abū al-Ḥasan, 'Dalāyil barāhīn al-furqān fī buṭlān qavanīn navāsikh muḥkamāt al-Qurʾān', in *Rasāʾil-i mashrūṭīyat: mashrūṭah bih ravāyat-i muvāfiqān va mukhālifān*, ed. by Ghulām Ḥusayn Zargarī'nizhād, 2 vols. (Tehran: Intishārāt-i Muʿassisah-ʾi Taḥqīqāt va Tawsiʿah-ʾi ʿUlūm-i Insānī, 1387), vol. 1, pp. 353–514.

Nāṣir al-Dīn Shāh, 'Iʿlān-i rasmī-i dawlatī', *Īrān* (Tehran, 19 Ramadan 1305 / [30 May 1888]), p. 1.

Nāṣir al-Mulk, 'Nāmah-ʾi Nāṣir al-Mulk bih Ṭabāṭabāʾī [Jumada I 1324 / July 1906]', in *Tārīkh-i mashrūṭih-ʾi Īrān* (Tehran: Hermes Publishers, 2010), pp. 126–32.

Navvāb ʿAlī Bakhsh Mīrzā, 'Mīzān al-Millal', in *Rasāʾil-i mashrūṭīyat: 18 risālah va lāyīḥah darbārah-ʾi mashrūṭīyat*, ed. by Ghulām Ḥusayn Zargarī'nizhād (Tehran: Kavīr, 1374).

Nayrīzī Shīrāzī, Quṭb al-Dīn, 'Ṭib al-mamālik', in *ʿIlal-i bar'uftādan-i Ṣafavīyān: mukāfāt'nāmah*, ed. by Rasūl Jaʿfarīyān (Tehran: Sāzmān-i Tabīghāt-i Islāmī, 1993), pp. 217–34.

Nāẓim al-Islām Kirmānī, *Tārīkh-i bīdārī-i īrāniyān*, ed. by Saʿīdī Sirjānī (Tehran: Piykān, 1376).

Nelson, Eric, 'Liberty: One Concept Too Many?', *Political Theory*, 33: 1 (2005), 58–78.

Nūrī, Shaykh Faẕl Allah, *Lavāyiḥ-i Āqā Shaykh Faẕl Allah Nūrī* (Tehran: Nashr-i Tārīkh-i Īrān, 1362).

———, 'Risālah-ʾi ḥurmat-i mashrūṭah, yā pāsukh bih suʾāl az ʿillat-i muvāfiqat-i avvalīyah bā mashrūṭīyat va mukhālifat-i sānavīyah bā ān', in *Rasāʾil-i mashrūṭīyat: mashrūṭah bih ravāyat-i muvāfiqān va mukhālifān*, 2 vols. (Tehran: Intishārāt-i Muʿassisah-ʾi Taḥqīqāt va Tawsiʿah-ʾi ʿUlūm-i Insānī, 1387), vol. 1, pp. 253–73.

———[?], 'Tazkirah al-ghāfil wa irshād al-jāhil', in *Rasāʾil-i mashrūṭīyat: mashrūṭah bih ravāyat-i muvāfiqān va mukhālifān*, ed. by Ghulām Ḥusayn Zargarī'nizhād, 2 vols. (Tehran: Intishārāt-i Muʿassisah-ʾi Taḥqīqāt va Tawsiʿah-ʾi ʿUlūm-i Insānī, 1387), vol. 1, pp. 275–303.

Nūrī, Shaykh Faẕl Allah, and Muhājirīn, '[Mā munkir-i majlis nīstīm]', in *Lavāyiḥ-i Āqā Shaykh Faẕl Allah Nūrī* (Tehran: Nashr-i Tārīkh-i Īrān, 1362), pp. 44–5.

Parvīn, Nāṣir al-Dīn, *Tārīkh-i rūznāmah'nigārī-i īrāniyān va dīgar pārsī'nivīsān* (Tehran: Markaz-i Nashr-i Dānishgāhī, 1377).

Patterson, Melville Watson, *Sir Francis Burdett and His Times (1770–1844)* (London: Macmillan and Co., Limited, 1931).

Popper, Karl R., *The Myth of the Framework: In Defence of Science and Rationality* (London; New York: Routledge, 1994).

———, *The Open Society and Its Enemies* (London: G. Routledge & Sons, Ltd., 1945).

'Qānūn-i asāsī-i mashrūṭah, (The Fundamental Laws of December 1906)', *Lawḥ-i qānūn: Majmūʿah-i qavāmīn va muqarrāt-i kishvar* (Tehran: Markaz-i Pazhūhishha-yi Majlis-i Shūrā-yi Islamī, n.d.) [on DVD].

Q. Ḥ. T., 'Qābil tavajjuh-i ʿumūm-i aʿẕā-ʾi anjuman'hā-yi ukhuvvat-i īmānīyah va himmat', *majlis* (Tehran, Rabi I 1325), pp. 2–3.

Rawls, John, *A Theory of Justice* (Cambridge, MA: Belknap Press of Harvard University Press, 1971).

Ringer, Monica M., *Education, Religion, and the Discourse of Cultural Reform in Qajar Iran* (Costa Mesa, CA: Mazda Publishers, 2001).

Riẕā Qulī Mīrzā, *Safarnāmah-ʾi Riẕā Qulī Mīrzā navah-ʾi Fatḥ ʿAlī Shāh*, ed. by Aṣghar Farmānfarmāʾī Qājār (Tehran: Dānishgāh-i Tihrān, 1346).

Rosenthal, Franz, *The Muslim Concept of Freedom prior to the Nineteenth Century* (Leiden: Brill, 1960).

Rosenthal, Franz, and Lewis, Bernard, 'Ḥurrīya', in *The Encyclopaedia of Islam*, ed. by B. Lewis, V.L. Ménage, C. Pellat, and J. Schacht, vol. 2 (Leiden: Brill, 1971).

Rustam'ābādī, Mullā Muḥammad ʿAlī Mujtahid, '[Ṣūrat-i javāb-i taqāẕā-yi tashrīḥ-i ḥaq va bāṭil]', in *Lavāyiḥ-i Āqā Shaykh Faẕl Allah Nūrī* (Tehran: Nashr-i Tārīkh-i Īrān, 1362), pp. 35–7.

Salāmī, Ghulām Riẕā, and Muḥsin Rūstāyī, eds., *Asnād-i maṭbūʿāt-i Īrān, 1320–1332 H.Sh* (Tehran: Intishārāt-i Sāzmān-i Asnād-i Millī-i Īrān, 1371).

Sasānī, Khān Malak, *Siyāsatgarān-i dawrah-ʾi Qājār* (Tehran: Kitābkhānah-ʾi Ṭuhūrī, 1338).

Shākirī, Khusraw, *Pīshīnah'hā-yi iqtiṣādī – ijtimā'ī-i junbish-i mashrūṭīyat va inkishāf-i sūsiyāl dimūkrāsī dar ān 'ahd* (Tehran: Nashr-i Akhtarān, 1384).

Sharīf Kāshānī, Muḥammad Mahdī, *Vāqi'āt-i ittifāqīyah dar rūzgār* (Tehran: Nashr-i Tārīkh-i Īrān, 1362).

Shaykh Mahdī Tabrīzī, 'Su'āl'hā'ī dāyir bih mashrūṭīyat', in *Rasā'il-i mashrūṭīyat: mashrūṭah bih ravāyat-i muvāfiqān va mukhālifān*, ed. by Ghulām Ḥusayn Zargarī'nizhād, 2 vols. (Tehran: Intishārāt-i Mu'assisah-'i Taḥqīqāt va Tawsi'ah-'i 'Ulūm-i Insānī, 1387), vol. 2, pp. 59–76.

S̱iqat al-Islām Tabrīzī, Mīrzā 'Alī, 'Risalah-'i lālān', in *Rasā'il-i mashrūṭīyat: mashrūṭah bih ravāyat-i muvāfiqān va mukhālifān* (Tehran: Intishārāt-i Mu'assisah-'i Taḥqīqāt va Tawsi'ah-'i 'Ulūm-i Insānī, 1387), vol. 2, pp. 365–401.

Skinner, Quentin, 'Meaning and Understanding in the History of Ideas', *History and Theory*, 8: 1 (1969), 3–53.

'Ṣūrat-i majlis va nuṭq-i ahalī-i Yazd barāy-i intikhāb-i vakīl', *Ṣūr-i Isrāfīl* (Tehran, 14 Shawwal 1325 / [20 November 1907]), no. 17, pp. 3–5.

'[Ṣūrat-i maqāṣid-i 'ulamā'-i a'lām va ḥujjaj-i Islām-i muhājirīn]', in *Lavāyiḥ-i Āqā Shaykh Faẕl Allah Nūrī* (Tehran: Nashr-i Tārīkh-i Īrān, 1362), p. 48.

Ṭabāṭabā'ī, Sayyid Muḥammad, '[Fatvā-yi Āqā Sayyid Muḥammad Ṭabāṭabā'ī darbāb-i anjuman-i nisvān-i Ṭihrān]', *Kawkab-i durrī* (Tehran, 23 Rabi I 1325 / [25 April 1908]) yr. 4, no. 7.

Muṣṭafá Mu'minī, 'Tabrīz', in *Dānish'nāmah-i jahān-i Islām* (*Encyclopaedia of the World of Islam*) (Tehran: Kitāb-i Marja', 1381).

Tabrīzī, Muḥammad Ḥusayn ibn 'Alī Akbar, 'Kashf al-murād min al-mashrūṭah wa al-istibdād', in *Rasā'il-i mashrūṭīyat: mashrūṭah bih ravāyat-i muvāfiqān va mukhālifān*, ed. byGhulām Ḥusayn Zargarī'nizhād, 2 vols. (Tehran: Intishārāt-i Mu'assisah-'i Taḥqīqāt va Tawsi'ah-'i 'Ulūm-i Insānī, 1387), vol. 1, pp. 173–230.

Tabrīzī, Muḥammad Raẕī, trans., 'Ḥavādis'nāmah' (Tehran, MS Farsi / 80, the Iranian National Library).

'Taghayyur', *Ḥabl al-matīn* (Tehran, 28 Jumada I 1325 / [9 July 1907]), no. 64.

Ṭahṭāwī, Rifā'ah Rāfi', *Al-Dīwān al-nafīs fī īwān Bārīs aw takhlīṣ al-ibrīz fī talkhīṣ Bārīz*, ed. by 'Alī Aḥmad Kan'ān (Beirut: al-Mu'assasah al-'Arabīyah Lil-Dirāsāt wa al-Nashr, 2002).

Ṭālibūf Tabrīzī, 'Abd al-Raḥīm, 'Īẓāḥāt dar khuṣūṣ-i āzādī', in *Āzādī va siyāsat*, ed. by Īraj Afshār (Tehran: Saḥar, 1366).

———, *Masā'il al-ḥayāt* (Tiflīs: Maṭba'ah-'i Ghiyrat, 1906).

Taqavī, Sayyid Naṣr Allāh, '[Ma'nā-yi pulitīk va ẕarūrat-i taghyīr-i ān]', in *Rasā'il-i mashrūṭīyat: mashrūṭah bih ravāyat-i muvāfiqān va mukhālifān*, ed. by Ghulām Ḥusayn Zargarī'nizhād, 2 vols. (Tehran: Intishārāt-i Mu'assisah-'i Taḥqīqāt va Tawsi'ah-'i 'Ulūm-i Insānī, 1387), vol. 1, pp. 607–17.

———, 'Maqālah-'i su'āl va javāb dar favāyid-i majlis', in *Rasā'il-i mashrūṭīyat: mashrūṭah bih ravāyat-i muvāfiqān va mukhālifān*, ed. by Ghulām Ḥusayn Zargarī'nizhād, 2 vols. (Tehran: Intishārāt-i Mu'assisah-'i Taḥqīqāt va Tawsi'ah-'i 'Ulūm-i Insānī, 1387), vol. 1, pp. 547–62.

'Taqsīm-i istibdād yā tajziyah-'i salṭanat', *Rūḥ al-Qudus* (Tehran, 13 Safar 1326 / [17 March 1908]), no. 20, pp. 1–4.

'Tashakkur', *Ṣūr-i Isrāfīl* (Tehran, 29 Ramadan 1325 [5 November 1907]), no. 15, p. 1.

Tavakoli-Targhi, Mohamad, *Refashioning Iran: Orientalism, Occidentalism, and Historiography* (Houndmills, Basingstoke, Hampshire; New York: Palgrave, 2001).

‘[Tawsiʿah-ʾi filāḥat], baqīyah az numrah-ʾi qabl’, *Ṣūr-i Isrāfīl* (Tehran, 28 Shawwal 1325 / [8 November 1907]), no. 19, pp. 1–3.
‘Tawẕīḥ-i vāẕīāḥātī kih tākunūn dar Īrān bih khiyāl-i ān nīstānd’, *Ṣūr-i Isrāfīl* (Tehran, 11 Dhu’l Hijja 1325 / [15 January 1908]), no. 20, pp. 3–5.
Vāʿiẓ Iṣfahānī, Sayyid Jamāl al-Dīn, ‘Dar mȧnī-i āzādī’, *al-Jamāl* (Tehran, 11 Rabi I 1325 / [24 April 1907]), no. 7, pp. 1–3.
———, ‘Ṣūrat-i maqālah-ʾi jināb-i mustaṭāb Āqā Sayyid Jamāl al-Dīn “dāmat barakātuh”’, *Ṣūr-i Isrāfīl* (Tehran, 21 Jumada II 1325/ [1 July 1907]), no. 7–8, pp. 10–13.
Yik Nafar Dimūkrāt, ‘Uṣūl-i dimūkrāsī bih qalam-i yik nafar dimūkrāt’, in *Marām'nāmah'ha va niẓām'nāmah'hā-yi aḥzāb-i siyāsī-i Īrān dar duvumīn majlis-i shūrā-yi millī*, ed. by Manṣūrah Ittiḥādīyah (Tehran: Nashr-i Tārīkh-i Īrān).
Zargarī'nizhād, Ghulām Ḥusayn, ed., ‘Kalima-tu ḥaqq, yurād-u bihā al-bāṭil’, in *Rasāʾil-i mashrūṭīyat: mashrūṭah bih ravāyat-i muvāfiqān va mukhālifān*, 2 vols. (Tehran: Intishārāt-i Muʿassisah-ʾi Taḥqīqāt va Tawsiʿah-ʾi ʿUlūm-i Insānī, 1387), vol. 2, pp. 113–27.
———, ed., ‘Maktūb-i shahrī: [ahammīyat-i sarvat dar istiqlāl-i mamlakat va rāh'hā-yi taḥṣīl-i ān]’, in *Rasāʾil-i mashrūṭīyat: mashrūṭah bih ravāyat-i muvāfiqān va mukhālifān*, 2 vols. (Tehran: Intishārāt-i Muʿassisah-ʾi Taḥqīqāt va Tawsiʿah-ʾi ʿUlūm-i Insānī, 1387), vol. 1, pp. 585–93.
———, ed., *Rasāʾil-i mashrūṭīyat: mashrūṭah bih ravāyat-i muvāfiqān va mukhālifān*, 2 vols. (Tehran: Intishārāt-i Muʿassisah-ʾi Taḥqīqāt va Tawsiʿah-ʾi ʿUlūm-i Insānī, 1387).
———, ‘[Taqaddus-i salṭanat va maʿāyib-i mashrūṭīyat]’, in *Rasāʾil-i mashrūṭīyat: mashrūṭah bih ravāyat-i muvāfiqān va mukhālifān*, 2 vols. (Tehran: Intishārāt-i Muʿassisah-ʾi Taḥqīqāt va Tawsiʿah-ʾi ʿUlūm-i Insānī, 1387), vol. 1, pp. 305–51.
‘Ẓuhūr-i Jadīd’, *Ṣūr-i Isrāfīl* (Tehran, 8 Jumada I 1325 / [20 June 1907]), no. 4, pp. 6–7.

Index

For Product Safety Concerns and Information please contact our EU representative GPSR@taylorandfrancis.com Taylor & Francis Verlag GmbH, Kaufingerstraße 24, 80331 München, Germany